POWER IN
THE BLOOD

POWER IN THE BLOOD

A Christian Response to AIDS

David Chilton

Wolgemuth & Hyatt, Publishers, Inc.
Brentwood, Tennessee

Wolgemuth & Hyatt, Publishers, Inc.
P.O. Box 1941, Brentwood, Tennessee 37027.

Printed in the United States of America.

ISBN 0-943497-05-1

First printing, November, 1987.
Second printing, March, 1988.

To Steve and Sue
Companions in Prayer

CONTENTS

ACKNOWLEDGEMENTS

Many people have contributed in various ways to this book.

Thanks must be given in the first place to my publishers, Robert Wolgemuth and Michael Hyatt, who patiently saw the project through from beginning to end, hoping against hope. It is refreshing to work with men whose commitment to Christian ethics is woven into every aspect of their business.

George Grant, my editor, has been a good friend and a wise adviser. I would never have finished the book without the almost daily encouragement provided by George and his wife, Karen. George helped bring me down to earth with many practical suggestions, and he is responsible for much of the content of Chapters 3 and 11.

I am privileged to minister in the Church of the Redeemer, in Placerville, California, where the people have been most understanding and helpful. Elder Richard Yanick and his wife, Jenny, read through most of the book and suggested improvements. Ray and Susie Bartneck generously assisted me in research; Fritz and Gloria Lienhard and Dennis and Sue Theis supplied me with materials.

Several other friends helped as well. The Rev. David Cole and his wife, Wendy, read most of the manuscript, engaged in lengthy and wide-ranging discussions with us, and became dear friends in the process. Darlene and I have learned much from their shining examples of ministry and service. The Rev. Charles McIlhenny and his wife, Donna, have deepened our understanding of Christian love and the message of the Gospel in both theory and practical application on the front lines. These battle-scarred veterans are engaged every day in a difficult and demanding ministry; intense and articulate about the faith, rigorous and precise in their creed and practice, they are also disarmingly open, generous, and hospitable. Like David and Wendy, they show what it means to *live* the Gospel.

Further materials for this book were provided by Jay and Linette Baggett and Harley David Belew. Steve and Sally Samson read several chapters and, as with other books, helped me to separate the wheat from the chaff. I thank God for their sharp intellects and warm friendship.

The Rev. John Martin graciously took time from his busy schedule to proofread the book under a tight deadline, and covered a multitude of my typographical sins. I am deeply grateful to Typesetter Dave Thoburn for his long labors of love, his close and challenging friendship, and his bracing and vigorous criticism. *Power in the Blood* is definitely richer and more Biblical because of our discussions.

Dad and Mom, in the midst of their busy schedule in a new ministry, managed to find time to read portions of the manuscript. As ever, they were kind, encouraging, and thoughtful, gently forcing me to think deeper and, I hope, clearer. Their life of faithful service was a model for the concept of ministry in this book.

My greatest earthly love, Darlene, always patient and supportive, really had her work cut out for her during the writing of this book. Combining a compassionate heart with a level head, she sustained my spirits, guided me past cliffs and pitfalls, and helped keep my work readable and applicable.

Finally, I must mention Steve and Sue Rutt, of Camp Verde, Arizona, where Steve is Pastor of the Valley Christian Fellowship. They, too, are praiseworthy examples of Christian service toward others, reaching out in special ways to the weak and helpless, seeking to apply the Gospel in its fullness to every area of life. More than being an observer of their ministry, however, I have been a recipient of it: they have blessed me with special kindness and love in moments of crisis. In admiration of their work, in gratitude for their true friendship, and in recognition of their influence on my life and thought as *Power in the Blood* was taking shape, I have dedicated this book to them.

INTRODUCTION

This book is written for the Church. It is not a book for politicians. What little it says about political measures will not be accepted by the politicians or by those who are accustomed to seek political salvation. The AIDS crisis is on a downhill roll now, and much of its destructive force simply will not be stopped by anyone. Sadly, the tragedy is just beginning.

But this book is about solutions. It is about *the* Solution, the Lord Jesus Christ. And it is about how the Church, His Body, can apply the power of His blood to the problem. There is a way for us to halt the disease of AIDS. We can stop it in its tracks right now. But the answer is only in Christ, nothing less. Without Him we will not survive.

Let me give fair warning, therefore: if what I just said seems strange to you, you're in for a real rollercoaster in this book. It is unashamedly Christian. It begins with these central presuppositions: God has revealed Himself in Christ our Savior, and His commands for every area of life, His answers for all our problems, are to be found in the Holy Bible, His infallible Word. Further, He has commissioned the Church to bring Christ and His Word to the world, and through the gift of the Holy Spirit has empowered us to be successful in that task. These convictions dominate every line of the following pages.

Even if you sympathize with my views, you still may need a roadmap to get you through this book. Here's a brief outline.

Chapter 1, "The Plague," explains how AIDS works, and what its social and economic ramifications are likely to be over the next few decades.

Chapter 2, "Deathstyle," shows how homosexuality spawned AIDS (along with many other diseases), and what the Bible says about *why* this is true. This chapter is extremely explicit and should not be read before meals.

Chapter 3, "All the King's Horses," explains that the proposed legal, political, medical, and educational solutions are colossal failures, because they fail to understand how the world works.

Chapter 4, "How the World Works," will be for you an early wake-up call on a cold morning. It should definitely be read before meals. And during thunderstorms.

Chapter 5, "The Failed Priesthood," shows why the Church has the solution to the AIDS problem, in spite of the fact that it caused it in the first place. This will not be the most popular chapter in the book.

Chapter 6, "Gospel Ethics," tells how Christians should act in the present crisis. It confronts the dilemma of dealing with people who are apparently under God's judgment, and points to the Gospel for the answer.

Chapter 7, "Is Change Possible?" explains the Biblical means of counseling converted homosexuals, enabling them to be progressively transformed into the image of Christ.

Chapter 8, "Ministry and Sacraments," shows how the covenantal pattern of Church government and the administration of the central miracles of Baptism and the Lord's Supper restore us to the divine order for life.

Chapter 9, "Healing in the Church," argues that the healing power of Christ is available to us today, and must become a regular part of the Christian ministry.

Chapter 10, "Pure and Undefiled Religion," tells the story of the Christian response to suffering and affliction through the ages. The Church invented health care; it's time for us to get back on the job.

Chapter 11, "The Balm of Gilead," sets forth practical steps that any church can take, and shows how different Christian groups are responding in specific ways to the challenge.

Chapter 12, "The Refuge," is a pep talk on the *eschatology* of AIDS. It explains why God sends problems to us, and what we're supposed to do when He does.

This, therefore, is not the standard AIDS book, or even the standard *Christian* AIDS book. It's not just a collection of horror stories. It's not a book that dodges hard issues with easy answers, the way the politicians and the panic managers are doing. Nor is it a book that tells you to run and hide, the way some survivalists are talking. Instead, it provides some real answers and shows how you can implement them.

The trouble is, some of the answers will take courage and effort. And, once you've read the book, you won't have the excuse of saying you don't know what those answers are. Then it will mainly be an issue of . . . courage and effort.

Now that you know what you've bought, you may want to think twice about reading this book. My publishers will give you a full refund, provided you tell them that this introduction scared you off and you did *not* want to read any further.

On the other hand, I believe a revival is coming. It is possible that AIDS, under the providence of God, will prove to be a means of shaking the Church awake, the way abortion and the crises in education and the family have begun to do, and the way the economic crisis is about to do as well. If so, I hope this book helps to bring about that revival. In the providence of God, may it be so.

Everybody knows that pestilences have a way of recurring in the world; yet somehow we find it hard to believe in ones that crash down on our heads from a blue sky. There have been as many plagues as wars in history; yet always plagues and wars take people equally by surprise. . . .

In this, respect our townsfolk were like everybody else, wrapped up in themselves; in other words they were humanists; they disbelieved in pestilences. A pestilence isn't a thing made to man's measure; therefore we tell ourselves that pestilence is a mere bogey of the mind, a bad dream that will pass away. But it doesn't always pass away and, from one bad dream to another, it is men who pass away, and the humanists first of all, because they haven't taken their precautions.

Albert Camus, *The Plague*
(New York: Penguin Books,
[1948] 1960), p. 34

ONE

THE PLAGUE

For when Your judgments are in the earth,
The inhabitants of the world will learn righteousness.
(Isaiah 26:9)

People are afraid. And well they should be. Even the experts are beginning to shrink back in horror. "In the six years I have been reporting about AIDS, I never imagined it could be so horrible," confesses a hard-bitten journalist from Africa.[1] Dr. Halfdan Mahler, head of the World Health Organization, goes even further: "We stand nakedly in front of a very serious pandemic as mortal as any pandemic there has ever been. I don't know of any greater killer than AIDS. . . ."[2] Dr. Alvin Friedman-Kien, a researcher from the New York University Medical Center and one of the first physicians to diagnose AIDS, said, "If you were the devil, you couldn't conceive of a disease that would be more disruptive and disturbing than this one. It could prove to be the plague of the millennium."[3] And Dr. Ward Cates of the Centers for Disease Control, the government agency responsible for tracking the disease, said, "Anyone who has the least ability to look into the future can already see the potential for this disease being much worse than anything mankind has seen before."[4]

If the experts are speaking in such apocalyptic tones, is it any wonder that the population at large is buffeted by fears that border at times on hysteria?

The Extent of the Problem

As of August 24, 1987, there were more than 40,000 cases of "full-blown" AIDS in the U.S.—more than three times the number in September 1985, when there were 13,800. And the number of cases is now doubling every twenty months.[5] Even more frightening is the fact that, according to Dr. James Curran of the Centers for Disease Control, in many areas the number of people infected with the AIDS virus "is at least one hundred times higher than that of reported cases of AIDS."[6] If so, there may be *four million persons* in the United States alone who have been infected with AIDS.

Worldwide, there were 51,535 reported cases of full-blown AIDS;[7] the actual figure may be twice that, because some nations (in fact, those hardest hit by the epidemic) have refused to report any figures. In Africa, where the disease first struck and where it has been especially severe, more than ten million people had been infected with the AIDS virus by the end of 1985, and governments began restricting the flow of information to the outside world. Twenty-one African nations with known AIDS epidemics do not report any cases to the World Health Organization.[8] The government of Kenya has threatened to jail or banish any reporter who even asks about the disease. Uganda expelled Dr. Wilson Carswell, a highly respected British surgeon who had been practicing in that country for almost twenty years as a physician and teacher, simply because he published his research on the rates of AIDS infection and his projections regarding the menace in the future. Now in London, Carswell believes that AIDS may kill a third of Uganda's citizens. "It is difficult to comprehend a disaster of such magnitude," he says. "It is beyond the scope of one's experience, one's imagination."[9]

C. Everett Koop, the U.S. Surgeon General, estimates that 100 million people will die from AIDS by the end of the century.[10] Some say the number could be 64 million by 1990. More conservatively, *The Economist* of London projected in 1986 that 250,000 Americans would die of AIDS by 1994.[11] Even that figure, observed one commentator, is "five times the casualty rate of eight years of the Vietnam War, which rate stirred the furious protests of the American public."[12]

The Immune System and the AIDS Virus

The immune system is your body's defense against enemy attack. One trillion white blood cells, arising from the bone marrow, work to identify and destroy any substance that does not belong in the body (including the body's own cells that have become cancerous). This army of defenders is divided into three main groups: Phagocytes ("cell eaters"), T cells, and B cells.

Here's how the system works.[13] Viruses—"packages" of foreign genetic information—invade the bloodstream, seeking to take over the machinery of the body's own cells in order to replicate themselves. Some of these invaders are immediately consumed by phagocytes, which then signal "helper" T cells about the danger. The helper T cells identify the enemy and speed to the spleen and lymph nodes to stimulate the production of other T cells, called "killers." Killer T cells begin to search out and destroy the viruses. If a virus has invaded one of the body's own cells, the killer T cell pierces that cell, forcing the virus to spill out before it has completed its deadly work. Meanwhile, helper T cells also stimulate the multiplication of another line of defense: the B cells, which produce an array of powerful chemical weapons known as antibodies. The antibodies bind themselves to the surfaces of the viruses, neutralizing their ability to attack other cells. The presence of antibodies also creates chemical reactions that destroy the infected cells.

Once the infection has been contained, a third type of T cell, called a "suppressor," springs into action to halt the immune response and keep it from going out of control. The defense is called off, most of the T and B cells die, and everything returns to normal—except for "memory" T and B cells left circulating in the blood and lymph for years to come. These memory cells have imprinted on them a code identifying the enemy, so that the immune system can respond even more rapidly should the same virus invade again. If it does, the virus won't have a chance: the body is now immune.

This marvelous system is completely short-circuited by the AIDS virus, whose full name is *human T-cell lymphotropic retrovirus/lymphadenopathy-associated virus,* generally abbreviated to HTLV-III/LAV, and recently shortened further to HIV (the form used in this book), standing for *human immunodeficiency virus.* The virus invades its victim's bloodstream hidden inside a cell from someone else's blood, semen, urine, or other bodily fluid. As soon as it is inside, it is identified as an invader by helper T cells. But as soon as the virus comes into contact with a T cell, it steals inside and disables it. The helper T cell is disarmed before it can signal the troops. The AIDS virus is then free to multiply, at a rate one thousand times faster than other viruses, silently invading and destroying more helper T cells without being detected by the rest of the immune system. Phagocytes and killer cells are never alerted; sufficient antibodies are not produced; eventually the body's first line of protection against infection, the guards and sentinels, are wiped out. HIV has rendered its victim defenseless.

That, at least, is the standard explanation given by most scientists, and the one that will be accepted in the present book. Most of the evidence does, in fact, appear to point to HIV as the disease agent, or at least the major factor involved. But some researchers dispute this claim.

HIV . . . Plus What?

A shocking article was recently published in *The Atlantic Monthly*. The author, who has written extensively on AIDS and has done more digging on the subject than most journalists and official government "experts" have cared to do, points out that several noted researchers are harboring grave doubts about whether HIV is indeed the cause of the disease: "Peter Duesberg, an eminent virologist at the University of California at Berkeley who has twenty years' experience working with retroviruses, is one such skeptic. His objections are disregarded by most of his colleagues. In the March 1 [1987] issue of *Cancer Research,* Duesberg published an article arguing that no one has proved HIV to be the cause of AIDS. In the article he invokes Koch's postulates, the classic basis for establishing a micro-organism as the cause of any disease. Two of these require that the micro-organism be found in all cases of the disease and that the disease be reproduced when a primate is inoculated with the agent. Neither is the case with HIV and AIDS. 'Once they said that HIV alone causes AIDS,' Duesberg says. 'Now they say it is HIV plus co-factors. Well, if you say that AIDS is caused by HIV plus something else, until you know what the something else really is, you are only speculating about both of them as the cause.'

" 'We are told that there is no more HIV activity in people dying of AIDS than in healthy carriers with no symptoms,'

Duesberg says. 'That claim is unprecedented in the study of viral diseases. HIV infects one in ten thousand susceptible cells. We wouldn't be here after three or four billion years if we could die from such a virus. Biologically we are not that fragile. Something has to be done to kill a person; it is not that easy, after all. If you don't use a gun, you have got to do, biochemically, *something*.' Ordinarily, a person is at risk until he forms antibodies to a virus—that is, mounts immunity against it. Yet with AIDS—if one accepts HIV as the cause—disease progresses, paradoxically, once one has formed antibodies. The fact that disease proceeds in the face of persistent immunity, Duesberg believes, strongly suggests that the virus is not the culprit, although he says that blood that is HIV-positive may also contain whatever agent it is that actually causes the disease. He is so certain of his claim that he has offered to be inoculated with HIV."[14]

So the actual biological mechanism involved in contracting AIDS is much more mysterious than most public health officials and experts are willing to admit. At this point in history, no one can be sure about *how* it takes place. What is all too clear, however, is what happens when it does.

Three Stages of AIDS

When the newspaper reports a certain number of AIDS victims, it is only giving us the tip of the iceberg. What is known popularly as AIDS is the third and final, full-blown stage of this deadly disease. But the first two stages are dangerous as well.

The first stage is the *asymptomatic carrier stage*. This means that the victim has been infected but has not yet developed symptoms. It is important to note that this symptomless victim is nevertheless *an AIDS carrier*, able to infect others as easily as a third-stage carrier can. For the rest of his life, whether or not he ever develops the disease, he can transmit the virus to people around him.

Dr. William Haseltine, an AIDS researcher at the Dana-Farber Cancer Institute of Harvard University, puts the case bluntly:

Once infected, a person remains infected for the rest of his life. Once infected a person is infectious.[15]

The second stage of infection, called *AIDS-Related Complex* (ARC) begins when the victim develops any or all of about 50 symptoms. These include sudden weight loss, night sweats, chronic diarrhea, swelling of lymph nodes in the armpits and groin, and chronic fatigue. HIV also invades the brain and the central nervous system, producing chronic memory loss, ataxia (loss of muscle control), seizures, lethargy, personality change, headaches, paranoid psychosis, and dementia — an irreversible degeneration of the brain.[16]

We will return to the greatly neglected subject of AIDS-induced dementia in a few pages. What is important to remember here is that ARC, the second stage of AIDS infection (sometimes called "Pre-AIDS") is extremely serious, and can kill without developing all the way into full-blown AIDS. Cases of ARC never make it into the AIDS statistics, because the Centers for Disease Control and other health agencies record as AIDS only those cases that make it into the third stage.

The third stage of AIDS infection, as already noted, is known as *full-blown AIDS*. There are no survivors of this stage beyond about five years, and the great majority (70 percent) of those who develop stage-three AIDS die within two years — often, not from the AIDS virus itself, but from another disease that has seized the opportunity created by AIDS. When someone's immune system has been sufficiently neutralized by the HIV invasion, he becomes vulnerable against the attack of "opportunistic infections," which ravage the body unopposed. The most common of these diseases among AIDS victims are:

- *Pneumocystis carinii Pneumonia (PCP),* a parasitic infection of the lungs, producing sharp chest pains, shortness of breath, a wheezing cough, and a sensation that one is slowly suffocating to death.

- *Kaposi's sarcoma (KS),* a particularly virulent skin cancer that can grow simultaneously in different parts of the body: the lungs, lymph nodes, liver, stomach, spleen, and intestines.

- *Candidiasis,* a fungal infection in the mouth that creates thrush, signaled by white patches lining the mouth and the tongue. This can spread to the esophagus and the central nervous system.

- *Cytomegalovirus (CMV),* a very destructive virus infecting the lungs and other parts of the body. It has also been implicated in helping to break down the immune system and facilitating the development of KS.

- *Herpes simplex (HSV),* which causes blistering ulcers around the mouth, nostrils, genitals, and anus; colitis, cramps, bleeding, and weight loss can also result from this infection.

- *Herpes zoster,* or "shingles," manifests itself in running blisters and scabs on the mouth, nose, rectum, and other areas, accompanied by severe nerve pain.

- *Toxoplasmosis,* a parasitic infection that is normally mild in its effects on people with healthy immune systems, is harsh on those suffering from AIDS. Exploding throughout the body, it wreaks havoc on the central nervous system, producing headaches, severe lethargy, seizures, vomiting, fever, and psychosis.

- *Cryptosporidiosis,* an intestinal infection, is acquired through contact with infected feces (see Chapter 2). Its symptoms are similar to those of cholera, and can cause up to ten liters of diarrhea per day. This, in turn, leads to dehydration and malnutrition. The disease is extremely resistant to treatment.

- *Cryptococcosis,* a fungal infection, has been linked to meningitis in AIDS patients, resulting in stupor, personality changes, intense headaches, and double vision.

- *Hairy leukoplakia,* a viral infection appearing as thick white lesions on the edge of the tongue, is a new disease (1981) found exclusively in the mouths of male homosexuals. It is often associated with suppression of the immune system and the development of full-blown AIDS.

- *Malignant lymphoma,* an especially intense disease associated with HIV infections, attacks the central nervous system, the rectum, and the anus in AIDS victims. According to the British medical journal *Lancet,* "The prognosis is dismal: response to chemotherapy is poor, relapse rates are high, and mean survival is less than one year."[17]

- *Tuberculosis (TB),* once thought to have been virtually wiped out, is making a comeback in connection with the AIDS epidemic. In AIDS victims the disease attacks not only the lungs but also the kidneys, bones, lymph nodes, and brain. It poses one of the greatest dangers to others because it is highly contagious and *can* be transmitted through "casual contact."

Originally, researchers supposed that only about 10 percent of those infected with HIV would go on to develop full-blown AIDS; evidence now shows that the true figure is at least 50 percent. In fact, the chances of coming down with the disease are greater in the second five years after contracting the virus than in the first five years. Dr. James Curran of the Centers for Disease Control reports:

> As time goes on, only a minority of infected people will remain healthy. I feel less optimistic about a normal life span for *any* infected person.[18]

What this means, in blunt terms, is that the AIDS virus may be 100 percent fatal.

The reasons for this are not rooted so much in the more publicized activity of the disease — its destruction of the body's immune system, making way for opportunistic infections — but in even more basic, little-known characteristics of this unique virus. For, even without attacking the immune system, apparently HIV itself can kill people directly.

HIV: A Lentivirus

One of the most neglected aspects of the AIDS epidemic is the fact that the virus supposed to be its cause, HIV, is a lentivirus (the term comes from the Latin, meaning a "slow virus"). It has an extremely lengthy incubation period, meaning that symptoms take a long time to show up. Until HIV appeared, only three other lentiviruses were known to scientists — viruses that attacked sheep, horses, and goats. The study of these lentiviruses is providing a way to predict both the long-term effects of HIV and the means by which it can be transmitted. And the news is disturbing.

First, lentiviruses are deadly and incurable. Dr. John Seale, writing in the *Journal of the Royal Society of Medicine,* tells how lentiviruses in animals are utterly impervious to therapy. He then makes this startling statement:

Lentivirus infections have proved so lethal and unresponsive to treatment, and vaccines have proved so useless, that slaughter of infected animals has been the universal means of control.[19]

Second, like the lentivirus in sheep, with which it shares several important characteristics, HIV directly attacks the brain, producing a fatal dementia. And it can do this *without* destroying the immune system. The victim slowly goes mad as the virus destroys the cells of the brain and central nervous system.

Dr. James Slaff of the National Institutes of Health reports the case of a medical school teacher who developed dementia without any manifestation of ARC or full-blown AIDS. Viral replication of HTLV-III within the brain and cerebrospinal fluid was cited as the cause of death. Infants have been born without brains or with half brains. On autopsy, the AIDS virus was found in neurological tissue. A strange form of pancreatic cancer has also occurred in young individuals infected with the virus. Cases like these have gone virtually unreported by the media.[20]

When the AIDS virus attacks the body in this manner, the incubation period — the time between the infection and the onset of dementia — can be very long indeed. It can last anywhere from *two to thirty years*, with a mean of fifteen years. It is certainly possible that those who contract HIV but do not develop the classical AIDS immune-suppression syndrome will fall victim instead to AIDS-induced brain disease.[21] In the long run, again, the AIDS virus may be 100 percent fatal.

There is another grim fact: the lentivirus in sheep is spread by *coughing*. There is some evidence that the AIDS virus can be — and has been — spread in the same way.[22] In horses, the lentivirus is spread through copulation, infected needles, and insect bites.

The disease kills half its victims; once infected an animal remains infectious for life; the virus can be found in all tissues, including the brain. Treatment is impossible, so spread of the disease can be prevented only by slaughtering infected animals.[23]

The bottom line here is this: *if AIDS acts like other lentiviruses* — and evidence we've been able to accumulate thus far indicates that it does, over the long haul — we are facing a much greater danger than has been generally realized or admitted.

> The unequivocal facts that are not denied by those doing research on the AIDS virus, or on the disease itself, are that the virus is a lentivirus, that it will be extremely difficult to produce a vaccine or cure, that infection is permanent and can occur by several routes, and that the spectrum of fatal disease is much wider than the CDC [Centers for Disease Control] definition of AIDS. Possibilities which fit the nature of the other lentiviruses but which cannot be assessed yet are that infection in utero may be 100 percent effective and fatal, that the overall fatality rate may approach 100 percent, that it will not be possible to make a vaccine, and, finally, that we are all equally at risk.[24]

No one is absolutely sure how many people in the United States are infected with, and therefore infectious carriers of, the AIDS virus. As we have seen, there is reason to assume that as many as four million persons are carriers. But even on the supposition that the figure should be placed somewhere around 1.5 to 2 million, the fact is that most carriers — over 90 percent — don't know they've got it. They have no symptoms. Their families, friends, associates, and lovers don't know they've got it.[25] Recent studies indicate another frightening statistic: *80 percent* of the wives of bisexual men have no idea that their husbands are engaged in homosexual activity.[26]

As Gene Antonio sums up the problem, AIDS could become a "self-sustaining epidemic":

> AIDS is more dangerous and has far greater capacity for rapid spread than any other of the previous epidemics which have devastated large sections of humanity. With bubonic plague, cholera, smallpox and other epidemics, infected individuals manifest readily apparent symptoms (boils, dysentery, pox, etc.) and can be readily identified and isolated before infecting others.
>
> With AIDS, the lengthy asymptomatic carrier state which initially exists in the majority of those infected enables the disease

to spread swiftly, unrealized, throughout vast numbers of the population. This is what the AIDS virus is now doing in the United States and other Western nations.[27]

Is AIDS a Homosexual Disease?

Although there have been several attempts in the media to downplay the specifically homosexual connection with AIDS, the numbers speak otherwise — and eloquently. In California, more than 92 percent of the 9,000 AIDS victims are homosexuals;[28] if a male heterosexual has the disease, chances are he contracted it through a needle.[29] In the United States as a whole, 23,322 homosexual men contracted full-blown AIDS between June 1981 and June 1987; the next highest category, intravenous drug users, is nowhere near that figure: 5,902 cases. (Another category is that of homosexual men who are also IV drug users, numbering 2,691). Far below that are the cases of those (mostly women) who are presumed to have contracted the disease through heterosexual transmission (1,375), and even that may be an inflated number. According to the report which published these figures, the heterosexual category "includes 661 AIDS victims with no known causes for the disease but who were born in countries where heterosexual transmission is believed to play a major role."[30]

About ten percent of those reported to have caught the disease through heterosexual transmission in this country are males. But some reporters from the homosexual community are disputing whether *any* males in the U.S. have ever contracted the disease from heterosexual activity. "Tiny percentages indicating otherwise are due to lying, they say, and much AIDS press treatment has been a staggering hype."[31] A study of AIDS cases in the military found that "most instances of apparently heterosexual transmission turned out to involve classic risk behavior: homosexuality or IV drug use."[32] We will see in a later chapter how homosexual practices render that group especially vulnerable to the AIDS virus.

The case of Africa, however, seems to confirm the possibility of HIV transmission through heterosexual means. Why is the virus transmitted heterosexually in Africa but not in America? There are several explanations. One is that promiscuity is rampant among Africans to an extent much greater than in the United States. The same is true of Haiti, where "it is quite common for women to have children by several men. Haitian society has a web of sexual interactions not unlike those in the gay communities of New York and San Francisco in the late 1970s — a web that allows a sexually transmitted disease to spread rapidly."[33] Anal intercourse, even between heterosexuals, is a hazardous and destructive practice, a proven channel for numerous infections (especially HIV), and could well account for the higher incidence of AIDS among Africans and Haitians. The restraining effects of Christian ethics have prevented this brutal and unhygienic practice from becoming as prevalent in the U.S. as it is in other cultures. A related and significant factor is that "pre-existing, untreated venereal diseases such as herpes and chancroid appear to be making the disease easier to transmit in Africa and Haiti."[34]

Another factor in the African situation, often ignored, is that homosexuality is common, and is widespread even among those listed as "heterosexuals." According to Frank Polk, professor of medicine at Johns Hopkins, homosexuality in Africa is more frequent than officials there want to admit; also, it is often simply "seen as bisexuality" and thus not characterized as homosexual behavior.[35] It is important to recognize that while "bisexuality" is sometimes useful as a category for sociological purposes, it is really nothing more than part-time homosexuality. Moreover, most homosexuals (over 65 percent in a recent study) *are* "bisexual," at least on occasion; at least 20 percent are or have been married.[36]

"AIDS isn't just a gay disease," proclaims an ad for condoms. "It's everybody's disease." In another ad a handsome young man declares: "I'm a nice guy. I go out with nice girls. These days, some pretty terrible things are happening to some really nice people." Well, not quite. While it is clear that AIDS is not precisely and universally a "homosexual disease," it is also clear that it is an "*immorality* disease," and most of those "really nice" but immoral people contracting and spreading it are homosexuals. In fact, the acronym for AIDS was originally GRID — the Gay Related Immunodeficiency Disease. Under intense political pressure by homosexual activist groups, a more generic title was invented.[37]

Certainly, not everyone suffering from AIDS has contracted it through immoral means. But, just as certainly, the disease would not have spread to them had it not been for the activity of the immoralists, primarily the homosexual fornicators in our culture. Says Dr. Helen Singer Kaplan, who heads the Human Sexuality Program at the New York Hospital-Cornell Medical Center:

> We would stop the spread of AIDS today if these high-risk people, these typhoid Marys, would stop spreading the disease. As a physician and a scientist, I'm appalled at their wildly having sex and spreading AIDS.[38]

There are reasons why heterosexuals—even promiscuous ones—do not contract AIDS as readily as do homosexuals. In the first place, heterosexual intercourse is not nearly as inherently hazardous as is homosexual intercourse. Homosexuality is, by definition, unhygienic, perverse, and violent; sodomy and related practices (to be discussed in Chapter 2) inescapably involve bloodshed, providing channels for infection. Second, as we shall see, homosexual practices damage the immune system even before the introduction of the AIDS virus; the average homosexual is thus much more vulnerable than is the average heterosexual. Third, heterosexuals are not as promiscuous as homosexuals. As one homosexual said to me, "When I was straight, it was hard to get laid. On a good night, if I was lucky, I'd pick up one girl in a bar. Now that I'm gay, it's easy. On a good night, I can have sex with fifteen different partners."

This is not to suggest that heterosexuals are out of danger, however. As pointed out above, HIV is a lentivirus. The infection does not go away, and those who are infected are carriers. The virus remains in the body for life, and if it does not destroy the immune system it will destroy the neurological system instead. It just takes a lot longer. Otherwise healthy heterosexuals may escape AIDS, and fall victim to a slow, fatal brain disease.

Terrorism

"Kill me! Kill me! I have AIDS!" The screams came from Joseph Edward Markowski, a 29-year-old homosexual prostitute, as he grabbed the gun of a security guard at the West Hollywood branch of the Bank of America. After Markowski was overpowered the police were called, and he was taken to Los Angeles County-USC Medical Center's jail ward for observation. Going through his personal effects, police were surprised to find a receipt for a blood donation to Plasma Productions Associates of Los Angeles. The authorities began an investigation, unaware that the county hospital had released Markowski. Within a day of his release, he was back in the office of Plasma Productions, trying to sell his blood again.

Markowski was arrested and charged with ten offenses, including attempted murder, assault with great bodily injury, and attempted poisoning, for repeatedly (twenty-three times) selling his AIDS-tainted blood. "I know that AIDS can kill," Markowski told authorities. "But I was so hard up for money I didn't give a damn."

Asked whether the blood supply had been contaminated, District Attorney Ira Reiner replied: "I'm told by authorities that the screening process is foolproof. I hope for all our sakes that is true."[39]

It isn't.

The blood screening process, as it is currently performed, cannot detect the AIDS virus itself. It can only detect the antibodies attached to the virus. And a person can be infected, and infectious, for up to one year, and possibly *three years,*[40] before those antibodies appear. A process to detect the virus itself has been developed, but it's wildly expensive, about one thousand dollars a shot. A blood bank would go broke in a single day if it applied the more rigorous test to its donations.

Even that is not the worst of it. The AIDS virus is constantly mutating, changing its appearance in order to avoid discovery. There are now *innumerable* strains of the virus, and no guarantees that tests will be able to keep up with them all.[41] The fear of AIDS infection, together with the much greater danger of contracting non-A, non-B hepatitis (which screening tests cannot detect at all), is leading many to contract with private blood banks to store their own blood.[42]

A loose cannon like Markowski is always frightening to think about. Even scarier is the prospect that such "blood terrorism" might be intentional, among a larger group of AIDS carriers.

But that is exactly what some homosexual activists have called for. One suggested that the only way to force funding for AIDS research might be to get the disease into the public at large:

> There has come the idea that if research money is not forth-coming at a certain level by a certain date, all gay males should give blood. . . . whatever action is required to get national attention is valid. If that includes blood terrorism, so be it.[43]

A writer in the *Medical Journal of Australia* found that homosexuals as a group were donating blood at a rate three hundred times higher than the rest of the population.[44]

Sexual terrorism is a threat as well. Stephanie Smith, a suspected drug addict and prostitute in Fresno, California, was diagnosed with AIDS. Her doctor reported her to the county health department, which then called her in for counseling. The workers pleaded with her to stop selling sex. She refused. On June 17, 1987, police interrupted a transaction between Stephanie and a trucker, arresting her along with her alleged pimp on charges of attempted murder. Officials were hoping, one said, that "as long as she is facing a murder charge and is in jail, she will be dead of AIDS before she can get out. She already has a death sentence. The point is not passing that death sentence on to someone else."

That hope changed the next day, when District Attorney Edward Hunt was forced by law to reduce the charges to "willful exposure to a communicable disease," a misdemeanor. Maximum penalty: six months. And then Stephanie Smith will be out on the streets again.[45]

Why would an AIDS victim deliberately seek to infect others? "You have all kinds of people," says Fresno Police Sergeant Jean Coffey. "Some would curtail all sex and try not to spread the disease. Others are so bitter they're going to take as many people with them as they can."

It's called envy, one of the most powerful and deadly emotions in the human breast. Reduced to its most basic element, it is the desire to destroy others because of their perceived blessings, in revenge for one's own perceived misfortunes. As the late seventeenth-century American theologian Samuel Willard observed, "Envy and Malice are inseparable."[46]

How great is the danger of infectious, envy-ridden terrorists seeking to contaminate the rest of us? No one knows for sure. But they are definitely out there in some numbers.[47] And it is not comforting to speculate on the fact that the majority of AIDS victims are already people who have thrown off most social restraints.

Is the AIDS Virus "Frail"?

The AIDS virus has been isolated not only in blood and semen but in saliva, tears, urine, and breast milk. Experts have repeatedly reassured the public that "casual contact" — meaning contact with anything but blood and semen — cannot transmit the virus, because of its frailty. Yet official guidelines for medical workers, such as those published by the American Hospital Association in June of 1987, warn against coming into contact with "other bodily fluids" as well. When Rock Hudson was discharged from the Paris hospital where he had been treated for AIDS,

> all the nurses who had tended him — and this was in a modern hospital, not in a witch doctor's hut — were made to burn their dresses. The patient was fed on paper and plastic plates, with plastic forks and spoons — which were destroyed.
>
> So what, a non-hysterical mother is entitled to ask herself, is a Paris hospital up to, safeguarding the hygiene of nurses and doctors and hospital employees, that she should not also be up to, safeguarding the hygiene of Suzy and Johnny who are asked to go to school and share meals, and games, and rough and tumble, with someone suffering from AIDS?[48]

Is AIDS transmittable by tears and saliva, by sneezing, by mosquito bites? Many health officials are assuring us that such fears are unfounded — while quietly taking more stringent precautions themselves. Certainly, there is some evidence that argues that the AIDS virus is anything but "fragile." Couples have been cautioned against "french" kissing: there is at least one documented case of a woman contracting AIDS from her impotent husband by this means.[49] The prestigious British medical journal *Lancet* warned that there is "a potential risk" of contracting the infection "in contact lens fitting, in cleaning lenses, and in tonometry."[50]

In an earlier issue, the same journal reported that researchers from the Viral Oncology Unit at the Pasteur Institute in France found that *the AIDS virus can remain infectious outside the body for ten days*, at room temperature—even when dried out in a petri dish.[51] Six months later, other AIDS researchers reported even more disturbing results: "in an aqueous environment (e.g., water), infectious virus survived longer than fifteen days at room temperature."[52]

The September 1987 *Atlantic Monthly* carried a lengthy article on the question most publications have been afraid to touch seriously: the possibility of insect transmission of the AIDS virus.[53] Contrary to what we often hear from public health officials, whose calm reassurances give the impression that there is absolutely no danger of contracting the virus from insects, the article shows that the question is far from settled. Many researchers and physicians are extremely concerned—including those who are pretending to dismiss the problem.

> Two years ago an official from the Centers for Disease Control assured an audience in Belle Glade that poverty, the environment, and insects had nothing to do with AIDS. Last May in *Science* magazine's job-advertising pages there appeared a listing for a research entomologist to explore the "possible role of biting arthropods in transmitting human immuno-deficiency (AIDS) virus. . . . Send applications to: . . . Centers for Disease Control."

> People have lost jobs and reputations devising new theories about AIDS. The disease remains one of the greatest medical mysteries of the century. Important headway was made in the first five years of research. Now we are in for the long, long haul. Who's to say that a question that often goes disregarded isn't one that holds an answer everyone is looking for?[54]

The Economics of AIDS

There are two possible scenarios for the future of AIDS. The first, and mildest, is that within the next ten to fifteen years, virtually every homosexual and IV drug addict in the world will be dead; the disease will ravage this relatively small number of a hundred million people or so, and then will burn itself out.

The more severe scenario is that the virus will find ways to survive, infecting the heterosexual population at large, and, over the long haul, wiping out one or two billion. Let us assume, for the sake of argument and the preservation of sanity, that the first scenario will prove to be the case. Let us assume, further, that you, a Christian heterosexual, could somehow be assured of immunity from the disease.

AIDS could still destroy your life.

Have you noticed that there is usually an AIDS story on the evening news or in the papers every day? This is just the beginning. By 1991, there will be 400,000 people dead or dying from AIDS in the United States alone.[55] (Conservative estimates are that fifteen million more will be infected with the virus.)[56] There are varying figures for the cost of their medical care, from $75,000 to $150,000.[57] Let's be optimistic: 400,000 AIDS patients times $75,000 equals $30 billion, only a tiny fraction of which will be covered by Medicaid.

Have you ever thought about how much a billion dollars is? Try it this way, working with more manageable numbers: Say you had started spending one thousand dollars a day, every day, from the day Jesus Christ was born. At that rate, spending one thousand dollars each day for over 700,000 days, you would not yet, today, have spent one billion dollars. By the year 2000, you would have about 270 million dollars to go. And the conservative estimate for 1991's AIDS bill is *thirty* billion dollars. It could be twice that much.

But even that is looking at the problem too optimistically. Sick people need beds. The average AIDS patient stays in a hospital for 167 days prior to his death. At any given moment there are 326,000 unoccupied hospital beds in the United States.[58] But there won't be many unoccupied beds in 1991, because we'll have hundreds of thousands of AIDS patients trying to fill them. Thousands may not be able to find one at all. By the way: according to common sense and millennia of economic history, scarce resources rise in price. This means that the scarce resource of hospital beds will rise in price. As more and more beds become unavailable, as wards become overcrowded, hospital costs will skyrocket—not just for AIDS patients, but for your daughter's tonsillectomy, your father's heart operation, your grandmother's back surgery, your uncle's cancer. (Undoubtedly, someone will try to pass a law controlling prices at a "reasonable" or "fair" level. If such a move is successful, beds will immediately become unavailable, and no new ones will be provided.)

In New York City alone, authorities are expecting that AIDS patients will be using 2,000 hospital beds every day by 1991, at a cost of one thousand dollars per day for each patient. New York State Health Commissioner David Axelrod says, "We are talking about a medical disaster, a catastrophe of major magnitude, no matter what we do now, no matter what vaccines are developed in the next four years."[59] And most experts agree: there will be no vaccine for AIDS.

The trouble has started already. Dr. Anthony Pinching, of London's St. Mary's Hospital Medical School, says that his facility, after having cared for more than 170 AIDS patients, is facing "economic burnout" due to lack of funds. And the numbers keep getting bigger. But even that is not the worst of it.

The people who are dying from AIDS are neither the elderly nor the very young. They are people in the sexually active years—broadly, from the 20s to the 50s, but more specifically from about age 29 to 34. These people must be seen as individuals, but as more than individuals as well, in terms of their interlocking economic relationships to the rest of society. According to health economists Anne Scitovsky of the Palo Alto Medical Foundation and Dorothy Rice of the University of California at San Francisco, the loss of productivity from these AIDS victims will hit $55,600,000 in 1991 alone—and that is a conservative figure.[60]

It doesn't count the fact that for every case of AIDS, as one volunteer put it, "you seriously tie up someone else's activity as well." *Two* people often become unproductive, in economic terms: the patient, and the volunteer, friend, or family member who takes care of him.

Why are all the discussions focusing on 1991? Because nobody wants to talk about 1992, when we really begin running out of beds, or 1993, when there will be close to *one million* people dying of AIDS, or the year 2000, when the figure will reach *ten million* in the U.S. alone.[61] Medical costs will be in the stratosphere by then (perhaps $1.5 *trillion*), and rising. Insurance companies will be bankrupt. The hospital system as we know it could collapse. Productivity will have plummeted to a third-world level.[62] And, remember, this is based on the mild scenario.

Even if you never contract the disease yourself, even if you live some incredibly sheltered existence where no one you know will contract it, AIDS will get you anyway. One way or another.

> Millions upon millions of our nation's men, women and children dying in agony while slowly going mad; our national health care system in shambles; our Social Security programs utterly depleted; the economic and social lifeblood of our nation drained away as our population is decimated: this is the looming specter which will become stark reality if the AIDS epidemic progresses unchecked.[63]

How People Panic

> The AIDS virus shows every sign of being just as deadly as the plague during the Middle Ages. We are on a crash course with reality. This is not a practice run. There is no second chance. AIDS may be to the twentieth century what the Black Plague was to the fourteenth century.[64]

The plague of 1347-50, known to history as the Black Death, was so virulent it appeared to be the end of the world. Close to one-third of Europe's population died, struck down by the millions to suffer an agonizing, tormented end. Some cities lost 80 percent of their inhabitants; within two months over 100,000 died in Florence alone. Contemporaries write of heaps of bodies everywhere, of a shortage of graves and gravediggers, of dogs devouring the corpses—and of utter, abject despair. Some withdrew from all contact with outsiders, hoping to avoid contagion. Others abandoned themselves to the most wanton excesses of debauchery, grabbing for whatever gusto a fleeting life could offer.[65]

In countless ways, the traditional social bonds that had held people together were eroded by the horror. "As the number of deaths increased in Messina," wrote a Franciscan friar, "many desired to confess their sin to a priest and to draw up their last will and testament. But priests and lawyers refused to enter the houses of the diseased. . . . Soon men hated each other so much that, if a son was attacked by the disease, his father would not tend him. If, in spite of all, he dared to approach him, he was immediately infected. . . . Soon the corpses were lying forsaken in the houses. . . ."[66]

Historian Otto Friedrich writes:

Death on such a scale made all the traditional forms of life meaningless. Family responsibilities became meaningless, work became meaningless, money and property became meaningless. Farmers not only failed to plant their fields but failed even to harvest the crops that were already growing there. "Peasants and their families . . . collapsed by the wayside," Boccaccio wrote, "in their fields and in their cottages at all hours of the day and night, dying more like animals than like human beings . . . Moreover, they all behaved as though each day was to be their last, and, far from making provision for the future by tilling their lands, . . . they tried in every way they could think of to squander the assets already in their possession. Thus it came about that oxen, asses, sheep, goats, pigs, chickens and even dogs . . . were driven away and allowed to roam freely through the fields, where crops lay abandoned."[67]

Then came the panic. It was the end of the world. Despairing men and women began wandering around, crazy from fright and hopelessness. They left their jobs and homes, abandoning their possessions. Flagellants marched in processions, hooded and barefoot, to a place of expiation where they would be scourged for their sins. In a single city forty thousand marched, in another eighty thousand.[68]

And then they turned from themselves to other scapegoats, those who, they decided, were the true causes of the Plague: the Jews. Jews were banned from Basel, from Zurich, and from other cities. Massacres began: five hundred Jews were slaughtered by terrified mobs in Worms, two thousand in Strasbourg, a thousand in Mainz. In Mainz, the Jews fought back, killing about two hundred Christians. The Christians took vengeance, annihilating the entire Jewish community of twelve thousand people.[69]

In many areas, people finally stopped killing Jews for only one reason: there were no more left to kill.

Similar instances of irrational frenzy can be documented from the history of other plagues. In terror, people search for someone to blame and punish. It is their way of fighting back against a seemingly invincible peril that is destroying their civilization. Certainly, the Jews were not to blame for the Black Death. But that fact didn't keep them from being slaughtered by the thousands. They were an easy, identifiable target for hysteria. Who will be the target when the panic arrives in our land? Will it be the gay community, assuming there are any homosexuals left? Will the target be the blacks, who, according to the Surgeon General,[70] have a disproportionately high representation in AIDS cases? Or will it be the bureaucrats and public health officials who have misled the American people about the true extent of the crisis and the nature of the danger?

The Coverup: Controlling the Mob

On the day after the committee meeting the fever notched another small advance. It even found its way into the papers, but discreetly; only a few brief references to it were made. On the following day, however, Rieux observed that a few notices had been just put up about the town, though in places where they would not attract much attention. It was hard to find in these notices any indication that the authorities were facing the situation squarely. The measures enjoined were far from Draconian and one had the feeling that many concessions had been made to a desire not to alarm the public.

Albert Camus, *The Plague*[71]

On a Sunday evening in June 1987, KPIX (San Francisco) hosted a live, one-hour program on AIDS, produced by Barbara Lane. A distinguished panel of medical experts was on hand to offer authoritative and reassuring answers to questions about the dreaded disease, from members of the audience and from the viewers. I called the toll-free 800 number. Apparently, a lot of other people had the same idea, so it took me several attempts to get through. Finally, a young woman answered: "What is your question, please?"

I said, "I'm a bit skeptical of the claim that you can't get AIDS from 'casual contact.' Since the virus has been detected in saliva, I'd like to ask your panel members if they really believe their own rhetoric. Would any of them actually be willing to share a drinking glass with an AIDS victim?" My question had a stinger in its tail: One member of the panel actually had AIDS, so I suggested that the experts' willingness to perform the experiment could be tested on the spot.

After a few moments of awkward silence, the woman (let's call her Barbara) told me to hang on, and she put me on hold.

Ten minutes or so later, the phone clicked. I suddenly found myself listening to a dial tone.

I pushed the redial button. Barbara answered. "What is your question, please?"

"Hi. We must have been cut off accidentally. I was waiting to ask my question."

"What was your question?"

"I wanted to know whether anyone on your panel would share a glass of water with an AIDS victim."

A few moments of awkward silence again. Then: "Well, we've decided not to use your question."

"Why not?"

"Because this is a program to inform people about AIDS."

"Uh, right. That's why I asked the question. I want to be informed."

"But we want to give people information. We don't want to scare them."

"But that's the point of my question. Shouldn't people know if it is indeed safe to share a drink with AIDS victims?"

"I'm sorry, we are not going to use that question."

"Well, may I ask another question?"

"No."

"Why not?"

"Because we're waiting for other people to call. I have to clear the line. I'm trying to run a program here!"

"Well, may I call back and ask another question?"

"No!" Click. Dial tone.

I pushed the redial button. Barbara answered again. "What is your question, please?"

"Hi, it's me again. I think you ought to know that I'm a writer. If you suppress my question about sharing drinking glasses, I'll write about it. And I will quote your statement that my question would scare people. Do you understand this?"

"Go ahead and quote me," she snarled.

"Thank you. May I have your name, please?"

"No!" Click. Dial tone.

Something is clearly wrong here. I was asking an entirely reasonable question about an entirely reasonable fear: Can AIDS be transmitted through a drinking glass? The experts have been saying no. But the minute someone poses the question in a personal way — "Would *you* be willing to share a glass with an AIDS victim?" — the question is censored.

Now, there were probably a lot of questions that didn't make it past Barbara's trigger finger. Some would have been uninteresting. Some would have been repetitious, overlapping with other questions that were already being answered. Some would have been embarrassingly religious, having to do with divine judgment and Biblical morality. Some would have been "political," and the show's hosts had made it clear that they didn't intend to answer any political questions. The purpose of the program was to handle health questions.

And the reason they refused to answer my question was not any of the above items, but: "We don't want to scare people."

Let's indulge in a bit of logic for a moment. If AIDS really cannot be transmitted by sharing drinking glasses, wouldn't it have made sense to put my question on the air? The experts could have calmed unnecessary fears simply by demonstrating faith in their own answers.

Instead, the experts were spared the trouble of having to face the question. According to Barbara, we would have been "scared" by their answers, or lack thereof. So Barbara chose to "protect" us from whatever frightening truth might have emerged.

Is it possible that the real purpose of the daily discussions of AIDS in the media is not really to disseminate information but to keep the public from panicking? And if that is true — if there are some questions even the experts are afraid to answer in public — is not panic a rational response?

If the experts themselves are afraid to have certain questions raised — or, at least, raised in a direct and personal, rather than a safe and abstract, manner — then they are not, as they claim, providing the public with the information we need for our own health and safety. They are merely controlling the mob. However laudable such a practice may be, it should be recognized that the physicians who lend their influence and support to it are not really acting in their capacity as health professionals. They are, instead, social psychologists: panic managers, talking quietly and tossing out processed bits of information to keep us at bay.

I am not, of course, advocating panic. I believe AIDS should be dealt with responsibly. But a crucial aspect of responsibility is simple honesty: telling the people the truth. If the experts appear to be dodging hard and practical issues, they will eventually create the very situation they are attempting to prevent.

The Real Plague

When I was a youth pastor in the mid-1970s, a popular TV series ran an episode (since mimicked by numerous other shows) in which the teen starlet faced a moral dilemma: Should I or should I not go to bed with my boyfriend? After twenty-five suspense-packed minutes, she arrived at the conclusion that she shouldn't. The reason? She and her suitor were not yet "mature enough" for such an intimate relationship. "Maybe someday," she informed Mom, her infinitely understanding and sympathetic pal. "But I'm just not ready right now." The parents of my teenage flock were impressed, relieved, and delighted: "Morality" had won the day, and their daughters' virginity was intact.

In truth, what scant virginity still existed in that youth group was now less secure than ever. The question had not been resolved by an appeal to the Standard of morality ("It's wrong because God says so"). It had been decided solely on the basis of this pubescent strumpet's presumptuous assessment of her own "readiness" to disobey God as fully as she and her panting young Lothario would have liked. The real message of the show was not an exhortation to chastity, but a declaration of independence from the law of God. And if you don't suppose most kids who watched that show figured *they* were mature enough to handle a deep and meaningful relationship, you've never been a teenager.

The greatest disease of our age, the most fearful plague of all, is that against which Ralph Venning warned his readers just after the devastation caused by the Great Plague of London in the 1660s. *The Plague of Plagues*, he reminded them, is sin. All other plagues are but its ripened fruit.[72]

There comes an hour in the afternoon when the child is tired of "pretending"; when he is weary of being a robber or a Red Indian. It is then that he torments the cat. There comes a time in the routine of an ordered civilization when the man is tired of playing at mythology and pretending that the tree is a maiden or that the moon made love to a man. The effect of this staleness is the same everywhere; it is seen in all drug-taking and dram-drinking and every form of the tendency to increase the dose. Men seek stranger sins or more startling obscenities as stimulants to their jaded sense. They seek after mad oriental religions for the same reason. They try to stab their nerves to life, as it were with the knives of the priests of Baal. They are walking in their sleep and try to wake themselves up with nightmares.

G. K. Chesterton, *The Everlasting Man*
(Garden City, NY: Image Books,
1955), p. 164

DEATHSTYLE: AIDS AND DIVINE JUDGMENT

As a dog returns to his own vomit,
So a fool repeats his folly. (Proverbs 26:11)

Divine judgment is a touchy subject. Tempers soar in a dozen different directions the minute it's brought up. One irate letter-writer to *Time* summed up the attitude of many:

> Reagan and a number of others insist on referring to individuals infected with the AIDS virus [through birth, blood transfusions, etc.] as "innocent." This term carries the clear implication that the more than 30,000 dead humans who contracted the disease through homosexual activity or intravenous drug use were not innocent and died quite deservedly. It is a cruel injustice to these people and their surviving friends and loved ones.[1]

Are all AIDS victims equally innocent? Are homosexuality and IV drug use merely alternate lifestyles that have no bearing on the fate of their practitioners? The answers should be obvious. Both homosexuals and illicit drug users are willfully and deliberately engaged in dangerous, destructive activities. Their case is radically different from that of the infant born with the AIDS virus, or the unsuspecting wife who contracts the infection from her adulterous husband, or the hemophiliac who receives a transfusion of tainted blood. In a very real sense, these victims are "innocent"; homosexuals and IV drug users are not.

I have already pointed out that homosexuality is far and away the main source of the AIDS virus in this country. There are important reasons for this fact. It is no accident. The popular media version of homosexuality portrays it as little more than a same-sex alternative to normal heterosexuality. As it is actually practiced, however, homosexuality would seem to have more in common with torture and human sacrifice.

I must warn the reader that the following discussion is terribly explicit. There are some, such as a recent writer in *Christianity Today*, who would object to such a frank treatment, going so far as to call it "homophobic." This strikes me as odd: apparently, we should not be squeamish about what homosexuals actually *do*—dear me, that would be homophobic—but we should be squeamish about someone giving an accurate *explanation* of what they do. Such an attitude is, in fact, a standard perversion of our age, which stresses refinement over decency, aesthetics over ethics. Let us not have morality, but please, please, let us have good taste! Again I must emphasize that the standard media portrayal of homosexuality—even in some magazines with the word *Christianity* on the cover—is a lie. Homosexuality is not equal to heterosexuality. Homosexuality is evil. It is a perverse abomination against God.

Unfortunately, in our perverse culture it sometimes becomes necessary to *show* people that perversion is evil. I don't like pictures of aborted babies any more than anyone else does; they make me sick. But sometimes they must be displayed, to help convince confused people that abortion is murder.

I don't like pictures of heaps of bodies of gassed Jews. They make me sick. And I'm certain that they make Jews sick, too. Why do they publish such disgusting pictures? Because people forget how awful the Holocaust really was. Nice, normal people cannot imagine that their neighbors would really do such things. So the pictures become an unfortunate necessity, in order to bring people to reality.

I don't like descriptions of what homosexuals do. It makes me sick to write about it. I hope reading it makes you sick, too.

Homosexuality and Disease

We must begin with a rather basic and obvious point about the difference between heterosexual and homosexual intercourse: God designed the vagina to be penetrated by a penis. The vaginal walls can stretch, and they are naturally lubricated during intercourse. The anus and rectum, in contrast, were not designed for sexual activity. They were created to excrete feces, period. The rectum is neither elastic nor lubricated; consequently, anal intercourse routinely tears the lining of the rectum and causes the anus to split and crack into bleeding fissures. These tears and fissures in turn become channels for HIV to pass into the bloodstream. Studies have shown that "receptive anal intercourse was the specific sexual activity which correlated most strongly with reduced levels of helper T-cells" and the consequent breakdown of the immune system.[2]

Repeated anal intercourse commonly results in other harmful conditions, such as colitis (or colonitis), an extremely painful inflammation of the mucous membrane of the colon; mucosal ulcers in the rectum; and Kobner's phenomenon, a psoriasis of the rectum, penis, and scrotum. Anal intercourse also weakens the sphincter, causing — to put it delicately — "fecal incontinence." The damaged muscle is just unable to hold it in, and the rectum dribbles with bloody feces. This involuntary ooze can leave deposits wherever the homosexual sits: on toilet seats, on benches in saunas and locker rooms, and anywhere else. If the fecal matter is contaminated with the AIDS virus, there is a possibility that others might be infected as well.

Further, anal intercourse has been found — even apart from AIDS — to damage the body's immune system. Large quantities of sperm cells enter the bloodstream of the passive partner. (The thick walls, elasticity, and lubrication of the vagina prevent this from being a problem in normal sexual intercourse.) After repeated instances of sodomy, the body develops antibodies to fight off the invading sperm. These antibodies then circulate throughout the bloodstream, suppressing the immune system itself. Moreover, sperm containing HIV is extremely efficient in communicating the disease: "Leukocytes in the seminal fluid carried the AIDS virus directly to the lymphoid organs of homosexual partners, thus achieving a highly efficient transfer of the infection to most lymphoid cells."[3] A recent study of disease within "monogamous" homosexual relationships revealed that 75 percent of the passive partners "manifested sperm-induced immune dysregulation." Gene Antonio rightly remarks: "From a purely biological perspective sodomy, even apart from the transmission of AIDS, is an intrinsically unsanitary and pathological act. In addition, the practice of sodomy has been a primary reason why AIDS has been so readily transmitted and fostered among homosexuals."[4]

The passive partner is not the only one at risk of disease. Over time, the penis of the active partner can become chafed; various diseases may also cause sores to erupt on the penis. Infected blood and other fluids from the rectum can then enter the body through these abrasions, as well as through the urethra.

But there is much more to homosexuality than anal intercourse. The practice of "fisting" is also common: the active partner shoves his hand and forearm up the other man's rectum and into the colon. Other instruments — dildos, vibrators, and even cola bottles (which occasionally get stuck) — are rammed into the rectum; according to some reports, live rodents (such as gerbils) have been used for this purpose as well. Fisting only further aggravates the problems caused by sodomy: as one "Safe Sex" kit advises, "putting a hand or fist into someone's rectum or vagina is very dangerous because the internal tissue can be easily bruised or torn." (Jeffrey Hart comments on that phrasing: "There is every reason to doubt that heterosexual couples are 'fisting.' The word *vagina* is present in the above sentence only in order to protect the gay practice.")[5]

The same kit provided, along with two brochures, two condoms, and a tube of lubricant, a little latex square called a "rubber dam" to use for hygienic "rimming" — the practice of anilingus (about two-thirds of homosexual men regularly lick or insert their tongue into their partner's anus).[6] Without the rubber dam — or if it breaks, slips, or overflows — the anilinguist ingests his partner's fecal material. In a national study of homosexual practices, 17 percent of the homosexuals admitted to eating their partner's bodily waste, or smearing it on themselves. Twelve percent gave and received enemas as part of their "sexual" activity.[7]

To appreciate this fully one must understand the phenomenon known as "Gay Bowel Syndrome," made up of the following conditions, among others:

- *Amebiasis*, a colon disease caused by parasites, causing abscesses, ulcers, and diarrhea;

- *Giardiasis*, a parasitic bowel disease, again causing diarrhea and sometimes enteritis;

- *Shigellosis*, a bacterial bowel disease, causing severe dysentery; and

- *Hepatitis A*, a viral liver disease, which its victims can spread to others through handling food, and even through the water splashed on toilet seats.

Homosexuals are especially vulnerable to these conditions because of their sexual practices. Between 30 and 50 percent of homosexual males have contracted amebiasis through swallowing fecal matter.[8]

The Safe Sex kit also covers "Golden Showers," or "water sports": "Urinating on skin without open cuts or sores is safe, but urine that enters the mouth, vagina, or rectum can spread viruses such as AIDS or hepatitis-B."[9] Again, one suspects that the word "vagina" is there just for a degree of seeming legitimacy, as if everyone, gay or straight, pees on his partner: some do it into vaginas, others do it into mouths and rectums. The truth is that normal heterosexuals (aside from a few sadomasochistic weirdos), able to find happiness without degrading and humiliating their mates, do not urinate on each other; but "normal" homosexuals do.

All of these perverse practices are invitations to deadly disease. Hepatitis B virus (HBV) has been common to male homosexuals for many years, and is traceable to both anal intercourse and anilingus. In addition to causing hepatitis, cirrhosis, and liver cancer, HBV also results in bleeding rectal lesions—more channels for the AIDS virus to pass through, in either direction.

Then there are the venereal diseases:

- *Syphilis*—Fifty percent of the cases in the U.S. occur in homosexual men, who comprise 4 percent of the population. There is evidence of a connection between a history of syphilis and the contraction of AIDS.

- *Genital herpes*—an incurable condition afflicting virtually all practicing male homosexuals; this is also associated in homosexuals with tongue and rectal cancer.

- *Cytomegalovirus (CMV)*—again, a frequent condition among homosexuals; there is evidence that CMV contributes to both the depression of the immune system and Kaposi's sarcoma (a cancer of AIDS).

- *Venereal warts* — this common affliction among homosexuals appears in large clumps in and around the anus, and can affect the penis as well. The warts itch violently, emit a foul-smelling discharge, and are extremely resistant to treatment.

All of these problems are compounded by the extent of homosexual promiscuity. According to Bell and Weinberg, "in their comprehensive work *Homosexualities*, the majority of homosexual males have scores of homosexual partners in a year. Over a relatively brief period, this may encompass hundreds of encounters. Over an entire lifetime, it involves thousands."[10] The same authors observe that homosexual bathhouses exist primarily "to provide an inexpensive place where homosexual men can engage in frequent, anonymous sexual activities without fear of social or legal reprisal." A single visit can result in up to a dozen sexual encounters.[11]

Anonymous, promiscuous sex is a hallmark of homosexuality, and this can be true even in what are called "monogamous" relationships. *New York* magazine lamented the case of one AIDS sufferer who had had, ironically, a rather stable sex life, staying with the same lover for more than ten years — *except for one night a week*.[12] That makes, at the very least, over fifty partners a year, and possibly five hundred! A heterosexual who acted that way might be called promiscuous.

For the ultimate in anonymity, homosexuals use what is known as a "glory hole" — a hole in the partition between toilet stalls and bathhouse booths, through which they can engage in anal and oral intercourse without ever even seeing each other.

It is not surprising that by the end of 1985, according to an estimate by Dr. James Slaff, Medical Investigator at the National Institutes of Health, between 70 and 90 percent of practicing homosexuals in San Francisco and New York City had contracted the AIDS virus.[13]

Homosexuality and the Bible

Without question, the Bible condemns homosexuality as a sin:

You shall not lie with a male as with a woman. It is an abomination. (Leviticus 18:22)

If a man lies with a male as he lies with a woman, both of them have committed an abomination. They shall surely be put to death. Their blood shall be upon them. (Leviticus 20:13)

There are two points to notice about the Biblical perspective on homosexuality. First, homosexuals are *responsible* for their perverse behavior. God does not regard homosexuality as a person's natural condition, but a deliberate activity in which he engages. Biblically, a person is no more "naturally" a homosexual than he is "naturally" a murderer, adulterer, or thief. Like any sin, homosexuality is a set of attitudes, desires, and actions that are forbidden by the law of God.

Second, the Bible calls homosexuality an *abomination* (the word is *toebah* in Hebrew). It means something that God utterly hates and detests, and something that those who love God will hate and detest also (Psalm 97:10; 119:104, 113, 128; 139:21, 22). The evil perversion of homosexuality is classified in Scripture along with incest, adultery, human sacrifice, and bestiality (it is possible that the AIDS virus was originally contracted and spread to the rest of the human race by men who had sex with diseased sheep)[14] as abominations that defile the very earth (Leviticus 18:6-30). If your reaction to this chapter's descriptions of homosexual behavior was one of revulsion and disgust, your emotions only mirrored God's feelings as He daily beholds His own image degraded and debauched. His holy character abominates such a grotesque monstrosity.

Homosexuality is unnatural. To say this, of course, flies directly in the face of today's neo-pagan sex experts and talk-show hosts—most of whom tend to define whatever people *do* (except, perhaps, the practice of Biblical Christianity) as "natural." But the issue is not my opinion versus theirs. The issue is simply this: What does the Word of God say? Even if it means calling every man on earth a liar, we must maintain that God's Word is always true (Romans 3:4). I can say that homosexuality is unnatural on the basis of this central fact: *Whatever is against God's revealed law is unnatural.* God accused Israel of "unnatural" behavior during a time of apostasy:

> Even the stork in the heavens
> Knows her appointed time;
> And the turtledove, the swift, and the swallow
> Observe the time of their coming.
> But My people do not know the judgment of the LORD.
> (Jeremiah 8:7)

The word *judgment* in this verse is *mishpat*, meaning an ordinance of law ("You shall therefore keep all My statutes and all My *judgments*, and perform them," Leviticus 20:22; cf. Exodus 21:1; 24:3; Leviticus 18:4, 5, 26; 19:15, 35, 37; Deuteronomy 7:11, 12; Jeremiah 5:1, 4, 5; 7:5; 9:24). God is contrasting the instinctive, natural behavior of animals with the disobedience of His people. All His creatures, human and animal alike, should follow His ordinances in every area; it is as "unnatural" (abnormal and pathological) for man to disobey God's *mishpat* in ethics as it is for a fish to forget how to swim. Divine ordinances govern everything, from morals to instincts. Birds *should* fly; man *should* obey.

> The law of the LORD is perfect, converting the soul;
> The testimony of the LORD is sure, making wise the simple;
> The statutes of the LORD are right, rejoicing the heart;
> The commandment of the LORD is pure, enlightening
>   the eyes;
> The fear of the LORD is clean, enduring forever;
> The judgments of the LORD are true and righteous altogether.
> (Psalm 19:7-9)

There are norms for ethical behavior, and God holds us accountable for following these norms. Disobedience is unnatural and deviant—not measured simply by the standards of the culture at any particular moment, but measured by the infallible, immutable standard of God's holy Word. God's ordinance for sexual behavior is stated from the beginning to be heterosexuality within the marital union (Genesis 1:26-28; 2:20-25), and this is true without exception or qualification throughout the Bible. In the absolute sense, there is no such thing as "homosexuality" as a *condition* on a par with heterosexuality. God created the human race to be exclusively heterosexual; any sexuality outside of that is twisted and abnormal.

Some will object that these verses are from the Old Testament. But God and His moral standards do not change. The Lord Jesus and His apostles continually appealed to Biblical law as our unchanging ethical standard (see Matthew 4:4, 7, 10; 5:17-20; 15:1-9; 19:16-19; 22:37-40; 23:23; Romans 13:8-10; 1 John 2:3, 4). The New Testament is unequivocal on this issue: "Sin is *lawlessness*" (1 John 3:4). That is why the Apostle Peter characterizes the homosexuality of Sodom (Genesis 18:20; 19:4, 5) as "filthy conduct" and "lawless deeds" (2 Peter 2:7, 8), for it violated the law of God. In terms of this absolute moral criterion the Apostle Paul vividly describes how God regards the behavior of homosexuals:

> Likewise also the men, leaving the natural use of the woman, burned in their lust for one another, men with men committing what is shameful, and receiving in themselves the penalty of their error which was due. (Romans 1:27)

The apostle goes on to speak of homosexuals as having a "debased mind" (v. 28):

> being filled with all unrighteousness, sexual immorality, wickedness, covetousness, maliciousness; full of envy, murder, strife, deceit, evil-mindedness; they are whisperers, backbiters, haters of God, violent, proud, boasters, inventors of evil things, disobedient to parents, undiscerning, untrustworthy, unloving, unforgiving, unmerciful. . . . (Romans 1:29-31)

"Homosexuality is thus the culminating sexual practice of a culminating apostasy and hostility towards God. The homosexual is at war with God, and, in his every practice, is denying God's natural order and law. The theological aspect of homosexuality is thus emphasized in Scripture. In history, homosexuality becomes prominent in every era of apostasy and time of decline. It is an end of an age phenomenon."[15] That is why God's "righteous judgment" regarding homosexuals in this age remains the same as in the Old Testament era — and they themselves are aware of it, yet rush on headlong into their perversion:

knowing the righteous judgment of God, that those who practice such things are worthy of death, [they] not only do the same
but also approve of those who practice them. (Romans 1:32)

According to both the Old and New Testament, therefore,
homosexuality is absolutely unacceptable. It is condemned
along with all other sinful practices:

Do you not know that the unrighteous will not enter the kingdom of God? Do not be deceived. Neither fornicators, nor
idolaters, nor adulterers, nor homosexuals, nor sodomites,
nor thieves, nor covetous, nor drunkards, nor revilers, nor
extortioners will inherit the kingdom of God. (1 Corinthians
6:9, 10)

Of course, that is not the end of the story. There is forgiveness, and that is what a great deal of the present book is about.
In the very next verse, right after he has listed these categories of
people who cannot inherit the kingdom, Paul says:

And such were some of you. But you were washed, but you
were sanctified, but you were justified in the name of the Lord
Jesus and by the Spirit of our God. (1 Corinthians 6:11)

But we can neither receive forgiveness nor communicate it
to others unless we recognize sin as sin. We are not truly showing love and understanding for the sinner if we minimize his
sin and act as if he has no need of forgiveness. "A faithful witness does not lie" (Proverbs 14:5; cf. 27:6). That is why "the
tender mercies of the wicked are cruel" (Proverbs 12:10). If, in
an attempt to be kind and compassionate, we misrepresent
God's holy standards—if we suggest that God does not really
hate the sinner's sin—we are telling lies about God; and we are
also sealing the sinner's fate, fooling him into supposing that all
is well, intoxicating him with false security in the mouth of destruction. Love for God and neighbor alike is expressed in a
firm commitment to the standards of God's law (1 John 5:2, 3).
The one who proclaims peace when there is no peace is a false
prophet (Jeremiah 6:13-15); and he, too, is hated by the one
true God.

He who justifies the wicked,
and he who condemns the just,
Both of them alike are an abomination to the LORD.
(Proverbs 17:15)

Sin and Judgment

A few years ago, when I worked with the Institute for Christian Economics, a reporter for a national Christian magazine called. He was polling economists and economic writers around the country, asking us a single question: "If you could change only one government policy in order to pull us out of our economic problems, what would that change be?"

"That's easy," I said. "Stop killing babies."

His journalistic instincts keen, he said: "Uh . . . what?"

"Stop killing babies," I repeated. "You know, abortion? In case you've missed the story, over 4,000 unborn babies are slaughtered in this country every day. They're poisoned, chopped in pieces, suctioned, or simply delivered and left to die. Sometimes the doctor strangles or smothers them. . . ."

"Uh, yeah, I know that." He sounded nervous. "But I think you misunderstood the question. I was asking what *economic* policy you would recommend to alleviate the country's problems."

"Yes, I know that. But you misunderstood my answer. I said that if I could change only *one* thing to solve our economic problems, I would stop abortion. That's not the only thing wrong, of course. Many other things should be stopped, such as the government's manipulation of money and credit. Confiscatory taxation should be stopped. Protectionism should be abolished. Fractional reserve banking should be outlawed. We could talk about a lot of things. But you asked for one thing. Life isn't that simple, but I was willing to play along. So I said baby-killing."

"Wait a minute," he said, exasperated. "What has abortion got to do with our economic problems?"

"Maybe that's the real problem," I replied. "Here you are, a writer for a respected Christian publication, and *you* don't get the connection between (a) the legalized murder of one and a half million people every year, and (b) the fact that God is selling us into economic bondage to other nations. It's called Divine

Judgment. And it won't stop with mere economic judgment. Murder is a *capital* crime."

The reporter suddenly discovered he had other calls to make.

All of life is religious. Every aspect of our existence is governed by God. Every ethical choice we make is determined by our religious commitments. And every thought and action bears fruit, not only for ourselves, but for our culture. In the Ten Commandments God's warning against idolatry includes these words:

> For I, the LORD your God, am a jealous God, visiting the iniquity of the fathers on the children to the third and fourth generations of those who hate Me, but showing mercy to thousands, to those who love Me and keep My commandments. (Exodus 20:5, 6)

Your actions, like pebbles tossed into a pond, make ripples throughout the world. Your family, fellow church members, business associates, social acquaintances, even your great-grandchildren—all are affected by the life you lead. God's justice works through history and beyond history to fulfill His purposes. There is no escape. God's law is absolute and universal. Its violation brings inevitable, inexorable consequences.

If this is true, what about the spread of AIDS to the rest of the population? What about the thousands of innocent victims (those who did not contract it through homosexuality, fornication, or illicit drug use)? Why doesn't God keep the disease locked up within the homosexual population? One answer, certainly, is that there are *no* true innocents, in an ultimate sense. "All have sinned and fall short of the glory of God" (Romans 3:23), and "the wages of sin is death" (Romans 6:23). Until the end of the world, death is an unavoidable aspect of our existence. None of us is immune from it, and it will come to us one way or another. The only questions are when and how; the question is not if.

There is a more specific answer, however: Our society has been sentenced to death. Our whole culture is under judgment because of our failure to suppress and outlaw the abominations that are the real plagues of our culture. R. J. Rushdoony summarizes it in his monumental study of Biblical law: "Wherever a society refuses to exact the required death penalty, there God exacts the death penalty on that society. The basic fact of God's law-order is that, from Adam's fall on, the death penalty has been effective. Societies have fallen in great numbers for their defiance of God, and they shall continue to fall as long as their violation of God's order continues. Every state and every society thus faces a choice: to sentence to death those who deserve to die, or to die themselves. But all they that hate God choose death. Certainly, the sin of presumption is total revolution against God and man; all who permit it have chosen death whether they recognize it or not."[16]

"When a people reaches a certain level of moral depravity, punishment ceases to be particular and becomes national. The civil order has lost its ability to act for God, and God then acts against that order. In other words, there is punishment, but the punishment is from God and the people or nation shall fall."[17]

That is why so much of the current discussion in the media about preventing AIDS misses the mark. One quickly gains the impression that the main purpose of the "safe sex" guides is not really to stop AIDS but to make the world safe for perversion. Although male homosexuals make up at least 85 percent of the total sufferers of AIDS, the connection of homosexuality with the disease is often radically downplayed. The tendency is to discuss the danger to heterosexuals first (with statements like "this is an equal opportunity disease"), then the danger to IV drug users, and last, as an afterthought, the vastly overwhelming category of AIDS carriers, the homosexuals. This is not science; it is propaganda.

How do we stop AIDS? "Just Say No!" Why is that slogan acceptable with regard to the use of drugs, alcohol, and tobacco, but not with homosexuality? Think about this one: Go smoke a cigarette. Smoke a whole pack. Smoke a pack a day for a whole year. *Your chances of getting cancer are still infinitesimally small compared to your chance of getting AIDS from a single homosexual encounter.* If our benevolent opinion-molders are truly interested in protecting the public from a health risk, why not outlaw homosexuality? We can be sure that if an industrial corporation were dumping AIDS-causing waste into a river, it would be shut down in a minute. The major networks would have their top journalists screeching and yammering into our televisions around the clock. Environmental activists would break into the offices and smear blood on the files. Congressmen would hold hearings. *Moonlighting* and *ALF* would ridicule the corporation's executives; *Our House* and *L.A. Law* would weep over their cruelty; Mike Hammer would hunt them down, and Crockett and Tubbs would blow them away. Why hasn't this happened with homosexuality?

It has not happened for the same reason that homosexual activity is so often characterized by surreptitious anonymity: Sinful men can't stand the heat. They cannot afford to have their works revealed, for that would reveal the evil nature of their actions. "And this is the condemnation, that the light has come into the world, and men loved darkness rather than light, because their deeds were evil. For everyone practicing evil hates the light and does not come to the light, lest his deeds should be exposed" (John 3:19, 20). This is why the most basic religious motive of unbelievers is suppression of the truth:

> For the wrath of God is revealed from heaven against all ungodliness and unrighteousness of men, who suppress the truth in unrighteousness, because what may be known of God is manifest in them, for God has shown it to them. For since the creation of the world His invisible attributes are clearly seen, being understood by the things that are made, even His eternal power and Godhead, so that they are without excuse. (Romans 1:18-20)

At the most foundational level there are no true atheists, no agnostics. All men *know*. They know the truth about God, about His law, and about His world, but attempt to suppress the truth in order to continue their evil lifestyles. The connection between homosexual behavior and the spread of AIDS is so strong that sinners feel compelled to cover it up, one way or another. So we will hear about hemophiliacs and homosexuals as if they are about equal, when they are emphatically not equal at all. Hemophiliacs make up only 1 percent of those with AIDS. It is noteworthy, in fact, that while virtually 100 percent of hemophiliacs have been infected with the AIDS virus, only about 2 percent are actually coming down with the disease. For some reason, homosexuals in vast numbers are more susceptible to the disease — even though many hemophiliacs have been contaminated repeatedly with tainted blood.[18]

Another tack has been outright denial, as in Harvard Professor Stephen Jay Gould's recent attempt at Christian ethics-bashing:

> This exponential spread of AIDS not only illuminates its, and our, biology, but also underscores the tragedy of our moralistic misperception. . . . We must also grasp the perspective of ecology and evolutionary biology and recognize, once we reinsert ourselves properly into nature, that AIDS represents the ordinary workings of biology, not an irrational or diabolic plague with a moral meaning. Disease, including epidemic spread, is a natural phenomenon, part of human history from the beginning. . . . AIDS must be viewed as a virulent expression of an ordinary natural phenomenon. . . .[19]

You can almost hear him knocking on wood. This is the counsel of a man who is clearly panicked, who has no answers at all. There is, of course, a punchline to all this:

> If AIDS is natural, then there is no *message* in its spread.[20]

That is the great fear paralyzing the experts. For years NASA scientists have been poised at their radios, waiting and hoping for a "message" from outer space, hearing nothing but silence and static. Finally, something has arrived: not a radio signal, but a tiny package invading the bodies of human beings — human beings who just happen to be in flagrant rebellion against the laws of God; human beings who just happen to drink urine, eat feces, and commit all manner of sadomasochistic acts upon each other. Does the package contain a message?

All of a sudden, our scientists begin to betray an unscientific hysteria lying just underneath the professional veneer. Nobody wants to open the package and look inside. Because they already know that it does indeed contain a message.

And they already know what that message says.

One thing I cannot omit here, and indeed I thought it was extraordinary, at least it seemed a remarkable hand of Divine justice, viz., that all the predictors, astrologers, fortune-tellers, and what they called cunning-men, conjurers, and the like; calculators of nativities and dreamers of dreams, and such people, were gone and vanished; not one of them was to be found. I am verily persuaded that a great number of them fell in the heat of the calamity, having ventured to stay upon the prospect of getting great estates; and indeed their gain was but too great for a time, through the madness and folly of the people. But now they were silent; many of them went to their long home, not able to foretell their own fate or to calculate their own nativities. Some have been critical enough to say that every one of them died. I dare not affirm that; but this I must own, that I never heard of one of them that ever appeared after the calamity was over.

Daniel Defoe, *A Journal of the Plague Year* (London: J. M. Dent & Sons Ltd., 1966), p. 202

THREE

ALL THE KING'S HORSES

What is crooked cannot be made straight,
And what is lacking cannot be numbered. (Ecclesiastes 1:15)

As cautious as cats, the international experts at a recent AIDS conference circled their subject like the dangerously elusive prey that it is.

One of the foremost medical research teams concluded its remarks to the group saying, "A cure is nowhere in sight. An effective treatment is remote. Medical relief is at best twenty years down the road. Our best and only weapon in this present crisis is education."[1]

In another presentation, an educator from a prominent university said, "Education is a slow, imprecise, and unreliable process. A crisis may be averted by that process, given enough forewarning. But it is helpless against a crisis already in full swing. It is essential that we implement an educational program with an eye to the long term. For the short term though, we must rely on legal measures."[2]

A professor of jurisprudence argued that "reactionary law is politically and socially volatile. The schism and disruption that would erupt if we adopted strident legal restrictions on AIDS carriers would only add fuel to the fires of panic. Litigation is thus not a viable option."[3]

If the scene had not been so desperate, it might have almost been comical. Each expert passed the buck to the next. No one wanted to accept responsibility for the dilemma at hand. And no one wanted to come right out and say the obvious: *nothing works.*

As I sat in my living room reading the transcripts of the conference I tried desperately to conjure a profoundly devastating response. But the only thing that I could think of was a children's ditty, stuck in my mind like a bad jingle:

Humpty Dumpty sat on a wall.
Humpty Dumpty had a great fall.
All the king's horses and all the king's men
Couldn't put Humpty Dumpty back together again.

In AIDS, modern men have been forced to stare into the hollow eyes of their own inadequacy. *Nothing works*. Not the most formidable medical technologies. Not the most sophisticated educational programs. Not the most ingenious legal formulations. *Nothing works*.

The Medical Failure

The mortality rate for AIDS patients has now been reliably tabulated at just over ninety-eight percent over a three year period.[4] This, despite the fact that for the last seven years, an all-out, world-wide effort by the brightest minds and the finest institutions in the medical field has been marshalled to the task of finding a cure.

Progress toward the development of an effective vaccine has been hampered by a number of complex factors. One issue yet to be resolved is just how many different variations of the AIDS retrovirus actually exist. Dr. Robert Gallo at the National Cancer Institute has already isolated at least eighteen different AIDS contagions.[5] Dr. R. T. Godet at the Sorbonne Medical Research Center in Paris has isolated twenty-two.[6] Although the waters are still quite cloudy, it appears that even those viral isolates are terribly unstable and prone to dramatic and unpredictable mutation and replication. And worse, it is becoming more and more apparent all the time that the virus mutates geographically and chronologically.[7] Thus even if an effective vaccination process could be developed, a number of different, constantly updated serums would have to be utilized. As Dr. William Haseltine of Harvard has said, "Trying to develop a vaccine for AIDS is like trying to hit a moving target."[8] The fact is, no effective vaccine has *ever* been developed for *any* germ of the retrovirus family, of which AIDS is only the most recently discovered member.[9] Most experts agree: a cure is *nowhere* in sight.

Progress toward the development of an effective program of treatment has been equally frustrated. Although dozens of therapeutic procedures have been called upon to combat the sundry clinical manifestations of AIDS, there is *no evidence* to show that treatment improves survival in the least. Patients with Kaposi's sarcoma are treated with chemotherapy. Patients with Pneumocystis carinii are treated with antibiotics like pentamidine. Patients with leukemia are treated with trimethoprisulfamethoxazole. "Wonder" drugs like HPA-23 in France and AZT in the United States are administered to patients with rapidly deteriorating immunological symptoms. But each of these treatments is at *best* palliative.[10]

The bottom line is that medicine has little or no hope to offer us. AIDS is one crisis that man's ingenuity simply cannot overcome.

The Educational Failure

In the Surgeon General's *Report on AIDS*, a mandate for education was issued in no uncertain terms:

> Education concerning AIDS must start at the lowest grade possible as a part of any health and hygiene program. . . . There is now no doubt that we need sex education in schools and that it must include information on heterosexual and homosexual relationships.[11]

Apparently, the assumption of the Surgeon General in issuing this mandate is that sex education in the schools reduces promiscuity, sexually transmitted diseases, and high risk sexual behavior. Sadly, such is not the case.

Sex education *increases* promiscuity. It *increases* teen pregnancy. It *increases* the incidence of sexually transmitted diseases. And it *increases* high risk sexual behavior. Even the most stridently entrenched advocates of sex education, Planned Parenthood, have been forced by the cold, naked facts to admit as much.[12]

In 1986 Planned Parenthood contracted Louis Harris and Associates to conduct a nationwide poll of teen sex attitudes, beliefs, and behavior. The results of the poll, released late that year in a booklet entitled, *American Teens Speak: Sex, Myths, TV, and Birth Control*, were utterly devastating to the ideological position Planned Parenthood has been foisting on the world for the last three generations.[13]

The poll revealed, for instance, that teens who have taken sex education courses are fifty percent *more* likely to engage in promiscuous sexual activity than teens who have had no sex ed classes at all. In addition, sexually active teens who have had sex ed are no more likely to avoid high risk behavior than their entirely unschooled peers. Sixty percent use no contraception. Only ten percent regularly use condoms, despite the vociferous demands of their sex ed curriculums.[14]

When I first saw the following statistic, I couldn't believe it. It seemed too fantastic. So I called Joe Blunt, of the Centers for Disease Control in Atlanta, to make sure. It's true, he said. Not counting the spread of AIDS, *fourteen million cases of venereal disease are contracted by adolescents and young adults in the United States every year.* That translates to *more than 38,000 new cases of sexually transmitted diseases every day!*

In 1980, there were "only" *four million* cases of VD; now there are fourteen million cases per year. Yet the young people of the 1980s are the most sexually educated generation in history. If the Surgeon General wants to slow the spread of AIDS among teens, the *last* thing he should be advocating is *more* sex education. That path is a *proven* dead end.

Moral problems cannot be educated away.

The Legal Failure

The tendency of modern men is to frame every question, every issue, and every crisis in political terms. AIDS has been no exception.

Again and again we are told that "AIDS is shaping up to be a major campaign issue."[15] Candidates build their coalitions, draft their platforms, and plot their strategies in light of the latest developments and statistics. The courts are clogged with cases, the legislatures are grappling with bills, and government agencies are faced with decisions that all revolve around this central question: What do we *do* about AIDS?

The thing is, no matter what we do or don't do politically, the AIDS plague simply will not go away. Mandatory AIDS testing will not slow the scourge's onslaught. Massive quarantining measures will not contain the contagion. Neither job discrimination nor affirmative action can stem the tide of panic. Neither price controls nor support subsidies can salvage the insurance industry. There is *not* a political solution to AIDS. Salvation by law is not only heretical, it is impractical.[16]

The few political measures proposed to deal with AIDS that have Biblical precedent are handicapped by the crippling inconsistencies of the rest of the legal system. It is true that, especially since even the best researchers are not certain about how AIDS is spread, those who are carriers *should* be quarantined, just as those with other communicable diseases have been. There are two problems with that solution, however: first, it is too politically dangerous for most city, state, and federal officials to advocate, and therefore it *will not* be advocated until it is too late; second, a quarantine cannot be successful unless it is accompanied by effective prohibition of homosexual acts, the causes of the disease — and such a measure would definitely be political suicide for any official who supported it. AIDS is a politically protected disease. To stop its spread our leaders would have to have the courage to call sin *sin*. They would have to acknowledge that these abominable acts are truly abominable, that they are polluting the earth. But our leaders are not noteworthy for their courage.

Do you want to know the Biblical perspective on politics? Gideon's son Jotham said it, in Judges 9. He told a story of how all the trees of the forest decided to elect a king. They looked around for the most qualified, and decided on the olive tree. They invited him to reign over them. But he refused: "Should I cease giving my oil, with which they honor God and men, and go to sway over trees?" So next they voted for the fig tree. But he, too, refused: "Should I cease my sweetness and my good fruit, and go to sway over trees?" Then they approached the vine, and offered him the job as king. And the vine also refused: "Should I cease my new wine, which cheers both God and men, and go to sway over trees?" So all these productive trees, trees that were accomplishing something important for God and men, trees that had integrity, were much too busy to hang around a palace all day swaying over their brothers in the forest.

Guess who the trees finally elected: the bramble! *He* wasn't busy; *he* wasn't doing anything of much importance. But he did have an overweening desire to rule over others. And he invited all the trees to come and rest under his shade.

That's politics. Is it any wonder that we have bramble laws and bramble social policies when our leaders are bramble men?

How can we expect them to exercise courageous moral leadership when their primary motive for rule is power over others; when their major concern is not speaking and acting with righteousness and integrity but rather with how they will look on the evening news? The messianic State makes big promises, because the brambles in power desire our worship; but it cannot save us from AIDS because it will not point us away from itself to the true Lord, the true Savior of mankind.

The Tactical Failure

For the last twenty-five years, the birth control experts at institutions like Planned Parenthood and the Alan Guttmacher Institute have been telling us that condoms are an extremely unreliable form of contraception. Effectiveness has been estimated to be at *best* eighty-five percent, due to leaks, tears, breaks, slippage, overflow, incompatibility with lubricants, and inconvenience.[17] An analysis of almost ten thousand clinic visit records from seven different Planned Parenthood affiliates in 1986 showed that 66.8% of all the women who relied on condoms as their primary means of birth control were converted to dependence on the pill as a result of their visit.[18] In other words, Planned Parenthood is actively *dissuading* its clients from condom use. Why? Because they know that condoms *don't work*.

"But if that is true," you may be wondering, "why on earth are Planned Parenthood, the Surgeon General, the Center for Disease Control, and everyone else touting condom use as the cornerstone of safe sex?"

Good question. It's too bad there isn't a good answer.

Condoms, rubber dams, serial monogamy, and other tactical measures are no protection against, and certainly no solution for AIDS. They are instead a dangerous part of the tragic and enticing game of latex roulette.

Arrogance and Impotence

Man cannot function properly outside of God's authority. The essence of sin from the very beginning has been the rejection of God's rule and the idolatrous attempt to substitute the word of the creature in place of that of the Creator. Man had been destined for power and glory, for dominion over the earth in God's image and under God's authority (Genesis 1:26-28). The great irony was that in rebelling against God and seeking to deify himself (Genesis 3:5), man became less like a god and more like an animal. As part of the curse for his disobedience, man received what might be called the original "mark of the beast" on his forehead — *sweat*, the sign of his submission to the serpent (Genesis 3:19). Even in redemption he was clothed with the skins of an animal (Genesis 3:21).

In striking contrast to this imagery, the priests of Israel were forbidden (on pain of death!) to wear animal fabric while on duty (Exodus 28:39-43). The priests were supposed to be living emblems of man fully restored to a proper relationship with God, and so they were prohibited from wearing any official dress that might produce sweat (Ezekiel 44:17, 18). To further emphasize this principle, the high priest even had his forehead covered with a gold plate engraved with the words HOLINESS TO THE LORD (Exodus 28:36-38) — symbolizing, of course, the ethical covering of the law of God over the minds of all the people (cf. Deuteronomy 6:4-6).

A powerful example of man's fate when he seeks to become autonomous from God's authority is in the story of Nebuchadnezzar, king of the Babylonian Empire in the sixth century B.C. The language Daniel uses to describe him is amazing: it could have been applied to Adam instead, in his original state: "You, O king, are a king of kings. For the God of heaven has given you a kingdom, power, strength, and glory; and wherever the children of men dwell, or the beasts of the field and the birds of heaven, He has given them into your hand, and has made you ruler over them all" (Daniel 2:37, 38). What a glorious position — a man as the king of kings, ruler over the earth! But instead of submitting to God's lordship and ruling as His deputy, Nebuchadnezzar fell for the lure of autonomy. Not content with being God's image, he desired to be God instead, demanding that people worship him (Daniel 3:1-7). Because of his proud rejection of God's authority he was transfigured, like Adam before him, from the image of God into the image of a beast: suddenly losing his reason, "he was driven from men and ate grass like oxen; his body was wet with the dew of heaven till his hair had grown like eagles' feathers and his nails like birds' claws" (Daniel 4:33).

Behold great Nebuchadnezzar, "king of kings," ruler of all the known world—a werewolf! In an instant he falls from practical omnipotence (on a human scale) to impotence.

Nebuchadnezzar's story is the story of all men: "because, although they knew God, they did not glorify Him as God, nor were thankful, but became futile in their thoughts, and their foolish heart was darkened. Professing to be wise, they became fools" (Romans 1:21, 22).

Apart from God, man is a fool. Repeatedly the Bible tells us that "the fear of the LORD is the beginning [i.e., the essential part] of wisdom; a good understanding have all those who do His commandments" (Psalm 111:10; cf. Job 28:28; Proverbs 1:7; 9:10). Man was created to have dominion over the earth, to deal successfully with the various problems he would encounter. When he cuts himself loose from the wisdom of God, however, man becomes a drooling, unreasoning animal (cf. 2 Peter 2:12; Jude 10), impotent and helpless as he faces the world. Autonomous man has no sufficient answers. The various non-solutions to the AIDS plague, elaborate in their studied ignorance and avoidance of the obvious, are eloquent testimonies to this magnificent failure.

Secular humanism, man's worship of man, is a dead end.

The Blood

Biblical religion is bloody. When Adam and Eve sinned, they knew they had committed a capital crime: God's law required their blood. Amazingly, when God's judgment caught up with them, a substitute was sacrificed in their place. Animals were slaughtered to provide a covering for themselves. This is the original meaning of the word *atonement* [Heb. *kippur*] in the Bible: a covering. Man needs his sins covered, and that can come about only through death, through the shedding of blood.

From first to last, therefore, the religion of the Scriptures demands that blood be shed for the remission of sins. The very life of the sinner—or that of his appointed substitute—must be poured out in order to satisfy the strict, righteous requirements of God's law. As the sacrificial animal was slain, its blood flowed out and was collected in a basin to be offered up to God and then splashed against the sides of the altar (cf. Leviticus 1:1-17). "In fact, the law requires that nearly everything be cleansed with blood, and without the shedding of blood there is no forgiveness" (Hebrews 9:22).

Of course, those animal sacrifices were never really sufficient. "For it is not possible that the blood of bulls and goats could take away sins" (Hebrews 10:4). Ultimately, a mere animal cannot be a substitute for a man. Our salvation required the sacrifice of the God-Man, Jesus Christ, the true Lamb of God (John 1:29). His sacrifice on the cross was the definitive blood-shedding, that which the Old Covenant sacrifices foreshadowed (Hebrews 9:11-15, 23-28; 10:1-14). His death in our place fully atoned for our sins, procured God's forgiveness, and reconciled us to Him (Romans 3:24, 25; 5:8-11; Ephesians 1:7; 2:13; Colossians 1:14, 20; 1 Peter 1:18, 19). Through His blood our sins are *covered* (Romans 4:7, 24, 25).

Power in the Blood

It is with the blood of Christ, the incarnate Wisdom of God (1 Corinthians 1:24, 30; Colossians 2:3), that our solutions must begin. Man needs redemption, forgiveness, a *covering*. Like Adam, we have tried to hide, we have attempted to paper over our transgressions, we have scrambled frantically for every answer but the Truth. All has been vanity: grasping for the wind (Ecclesiastes 1:14). Nothing works, because the fundamental problems have not been addressed. Unless we recognize that the basic issue in AIDS is *sin*, it will not go away — or it will be replaced by something worse, as Jesus warned (Matthew 12:43-45; John 5:14). If we refuse to listen to the Wisdom of God, judgment will be increasingly severe. Read the following words carefully, the terrifying warning of Wisdom to those who reject God's solutions:

> Because I have called and you refused,
> I have stretched out my hand and no one regarded,
> Because you disdained all my counsel,
> And would have none of my reproof,
> I also will laugh at your calamity;
> I will mock when your terror comes,
> When your terror comes like a storm,

And your destruction comes like a whirlwind,
When distress and anguish come upon you.
Then they will call upon me, but I will not answer;
They will seek me diligently, but they will not find me.
Because they hated knowledge
And did not choose the fear of the LORD,
They would have none of my counsel,
And despised all my reproof.
Therefore they shall eat the fruit of their own way,
And be filled to the full with their own fancies.
For the turning away of the simple will slay them,
And the complacency of fools will destroy them;
But whoever listens to me will dwell safely,
And will be secure without fear of evil.
(Proverbs 1:24-33)

"He who sins against me wrongs his own soul," says Wisdom in a later passage; *"All those who hate me love death"* (Proverbs 8:36).

Is it too late for our death-loving culture? Yes! This is just the beginning of our woes—unless we repent. If we abandon our apostasy, confess our individual and national sins, and seek atonement through the only sufficient covering that God has provided, there is hope (Jeremiah 18:1-10; Ezekiel 33:11-19). But if we love death—if we continue to embrace the contaminating corpse of sin, the rottenness that devours our bodies and souls—there is no salvation.

Salvation is in Christ alone, in His blood shed for the remission of sins (Matthew 26:28). In His blood is cleansing from our filth (1 John 1:7), freedom from our slavery (Ephesians 1:7), and victory over our enemies (Revelation 12:11). This is why He appointed the Sacrament of His body and blood to be observed in His Church until the end of the world, so that His people could continue to appropriate His power throughout their lives. "Most assuredly," He admonished, "unless you eat the flesh of the Son of Man and drink His blood, *you have no life in you*" (John 6:53). C. S. Lewis explained:

> When Christians say the Christ-life is in them, they do not mean simply something mental or moral. When they speak of being "in Christ" or of Christ being "in them," this is not simply

a way of saying that they are thinking about Christ or copying Him. They mean that Christ is actually operating through them; that the whole mass of Christians are the physical organism through which Christ acts—that we are His fingers and muscles, the cells of His body. And perhaps that explains one or two things. It explains why this new life is spread not only by purely mental acts like belief, but by bodily acts like baptism and Holy Communion. It is not merely the spreading of an idea; it is more like evolution—a biological or super-biological fact. There is no good trying to be more spiritual than God. God never meant man to be a purely spiritual creature. That is why He uses material things like bread and wine to put the new life into us. We may think this rather crude and unspiritual. God does not: He invented eating. He likes matter. He invented it. [19]

The cup of blessing is the very communion in Christ's blood, the bread the very communion in His body. Apart from Him we exist in death; with Him alone is the fountain of Life.

This is not merely some pious platitude. It is, literally, the very foundation of the world, of life itself. The world, the whole universe, is centered on Christ, and is dependent upon Him for every atom of its being, every moment of its continuance. Until we understand that absolute fact we will not understand the true nature of the AIDS crisis. The solution to this great tragedy, and the reason why all other "solutions" are bankrupt, is in knowing how the world works.

The Bible shows us a personalistic world, not impersonal law. What we call scientific law is an approximate human description of just how faithfully and consistently God acts in ruling the world by speaking. There is no mathematical, physical, or theoretical "cosmic machinery" behind what we see and know, holding everything in place. Rather, God rules, and rules consistently.

A miracle, then, is not a violation of a "law of nature," and not even something alongside laws of nature, but is the *operation* of the only law that there is — the word of God. What God says is the law.

Vern S. Poythress, *Symphonic Theology:*
The Validity of Multiple Perspectives in Theology
(Grand Rapids: Zondervan Publishing House,
1987), p. 107

FOUR

HOW THE
WORLD WORKS

The earth is the LORD's, and all its fullness,
The world and those who dwell therein. (Psalm 24:1)

As a child growing up in a Christian home, I was quietly puzzled for years by a familiar phrase used in prayer at mealtime:

Heavenly Father, bless this food to the nourishment of our bodies.

I thought: Sure, we can *thank* God that Dad has a job, so we can have enough money to buy the food. But once it's on the table, God doesn't have to give it any special blessing, does He? Why should we ask God to make it nourish us? If it has vitamins and minerals, it'll nourish us all by itself, won't it?

Miracles and the "Laws of Nature"
As I later discovered, I was wrong — and the grownups (whether or not they knew the meaning of their words) were right. Food *does* need God's blessing. How else can it give life? Food itself is dead; like a corpse, it must be either refrigerated or embalmed with preservatives to retain the appearance of the life it once had. Apart from the grace of God, we are eating death. Unless God works immediately and personally in our food, it cannot nourish us. In the sense of an autonomous, self-sustaining process, there is no such thing as "nature" or "natural law."

That may seem to be a shocking statement. But it is completely in accordance with the Biblical worldview. And it makes all the difference as we consider the various implications of AIDS to our faith and to our society.

The Apostle Paul tells us that our Lord Jesus Christ is the Ruler of the universe: "For by Him all things were created that are in heaven and that are on earth, visible and invisible, whether thrones or dominions or principalities or powers. All things were created through Him and for Him. And He is before all things, and in Him all things consist" (Colossians 1:16, 17). "The Son is the radiance of God's glory and the exact representation of his being, sustaining all things by His powerful word" (Hebrews 1:3, NIV).

"Nature," as the word is commonly used, is merely a collective term for "reality." But then — and here is the sleight-of-hand illusion — this reality is implicitly assumed to have a life of its own. Those who profess not to believe in God often sneak another god in through the back door, capitalizing *Nature* and speaking as if the creation were the Creator instead. To Nature are ascribed attributes of personality, and of deity as well: purpose, order, creativity, sovereignty, the ground of all being, the ultimate Source.

But the Biblical worldview insists that God the Creator rules every aspect of reality. Holy Scripture never uses the term *nature* in the sense of an autonomous entity, with unity in and of itself. The unity of the created order is in the Creator alone. The world works in terms of its Creator's acts and decrees. The pagan concept of Nature must be discarded.

This means that we must also toss out much of the traditional distinction between "natural" and "supernatural." For too long it has been assumed that "nature" runs along under its own steam, occasionally interrupted by "the supernatural" — God (or the unknown) breaking down the walls, violating the normal laws of nature. But, again, the Biblical worldview is radically different from all this. The Bible does not draw the natural/supernatural distinction. It simply asserts that God created the world, and that He and His messengers manage it. The same God who brings miracles also brings the "normal" events of life: sunshine, darkness, heat and cold, seasonal changes, wind and rain, thunder and lightning. These things do not happen on their own. Note the intimate, personal relationship between God and His creation:

He covers the sky with clouds;
He supplies the earth with rain
    and makes the grass grow on the hills.
He provides food for the cattle
    and for the young ravens when they call. . . .
He sends his command to the earth;
    His word runs swiftly.
He spreads the snow like wool
    and scatters the frost like ashes.
He hurls down his hail like pebbles.
Who can withstand his icy blast?
He sends his word and melts them;
    He stirs up his breezes, and the waters flow.
(Psalm 147:8, 9, 15-18, NIV)

The Bible indicates that the rain which we take for granted as normal and natural was once regarded as a miracle: until God sent the Flood, apparently, there was no rain (and, consequently, no rainbows, either; cf. Genesis 2:5, 6; 7:11, 12; 9:12-17).[1] Why don't we regard rain as miraculous now? Because it happens regularly, and somewhat predictably. But this does not mean that "normal" rain is any less the direct action of God than "miraculous" rain. The difference is only in its frequency; it has become somewhat "habitual," and consequently seems less mysterious to us. (Take a moment to think about it, however; isn't it astonishing that water actually falls out of the sky? Isn't it surprising — the last thing we might have expected — that food grows out of the earth, that birds can sing and fly, that fish can breathe underwater, that strawberries taste the way they do? Once we forsake our arrogant attitude of taking the world for granted, we can begin to realize that our world is an enchanted, magical place. We are surrounded with eye-popping wonders.) The first stories of Yellowstone seemed like tall tales; everyone knew that there were no such things as geysers in the real world. Then, as more people saw Old Faithful for themselves, it acquired approved status as a "natural" occurrence.

What is a miracle, in the Biblical sense? A miracle is not God bursting into history, breaking established laws. A miracle is simply an *exception* — an exception to God's ordinary, usual way of doing things. French theologian Auguste Lecerf wrote: "The constant relations which we call natural laws are simply 'divine habits': or, better, the habitual order which God imposes on nature. It is these habits, or this habitual process, which constitute the object of the natural and physical sciences."[2] God is constantly active throughout His creation, bringing all things to pass. He "works out everything in conformity with the purpose of his will" (Ephesians 1:11). Usually—*so* usually and regularly that you stake your life and occupation on it hundreds of times a day—God works according to a pattern. His angels have habits. Creation works according to a great cosmic liturgy; and there is nothing necessarily wrong with calling this liturgy *law* as long as we recognize that it is intensely personal—and, in a real sense, arbitrary. God could have done it differently. And, sometimes, He does.

> The miracle, in its form, is nothing but a deviation from the habitual course of natural phenomena, provoked by the intervention of a new factor: an extraordinary volition of God. There is, thus, no violation of law, as scientifically defined, since every scientific law supposes this restriction, explicit or implicit: all things being equal in all respects. . . .

> If . . . God confers extraordinarily on any[thing] . . . a quality which it does not possess habitually, or if He withdraws one from it, things are no longer equal in all respects. But science has no means of knowing whether this takes place or not. Philosophy cannot place any limit at all on the divine liberty. On the other hand, science is not concerned with the eventuality of the miracle. Its object is to enable man to foresee, in order that he may have power. In order that the prevision may be practically possible, it is sufficient that the natural order should be practically invariable. Now, this is presupposed by the very concept of miracle. What renders it astonishing is its extreme rarity. For the natural order itself, in a broad sense, may be described as a perpetual "miracle," and should always excite the astonishment which lies at the foundation of all ontological science, and at the same time, the admiration and fear which are among the elements of religion.[3]

How Bread Works

Orthodox Christianity has always stood in firm opposition to both pantheism and deism, of every variety. Against pantheism Christianity has always and everywhere insisted that God must never be *identified* with the world: the creation is absolutely distinct from the Creator; the world is not an extension of His being or essence. Against deism Christianity has always and everywhere insisted that God must never be *separated* from the world: the creation is absolutely dependent upon the Creator, and by His holy, wise, and powerful providence He preserves and governs all His creatures, and all their actions. As the great Dutch theologian Herman Bavinck observed, "the point is not that He *lets* the world exist but that He *makes* it exist. This is maintenance in the true sense of the word. Very beautifully the Heidelberg Catechism describes this providence as the almighty and everywhere present power of God, whereby, as it were by His hand, He still upholds heaven, earth, and all creatures. Virtue, strength, almighty and Divine strength, proceeds from God, goes out from Him, quite as much in causing the world to continue to exist, as at first in causing it to exist. Without receiving such strength no single creature could for a moment be. The moment God removed His hand and withheld His strength the creature would sink back into nothingness."[4] This was beautifully and powerfully expressed by Moses when he explained to the Israelites why God had miraculously provided manna for them during their forty-year wilderness wandering:

> So He humbled you, allowed you to hunger, and fed you with manna which you did not know nor did your fathers know, that He might make you know that man shall not live by bread alone; but *man lives by every word that proceeds from the mouth of the LORD*. (Deuteronomy 8:3)

All too often this verse has been radically misinterpreted, as if Moses (or Jesus, in His quotation of the text against Satan in Matthew 4:4) were simply making the point that man needs spiritual food in addition to physical food. Emphatically, that is not the meaning of the text. Rather, the meaning is that bread *alone*, in and of itself, has no power to nourish us whatsoever.

There is no inherent nourishment in bread, or in any food. God can feed us with it or without it. Usually, He chooses to use bread, and our Lord taught us to ask Him for it daily (Matthew 6:11). But God is not limited or restrained by any "laws of nature." The bread He usually uses to nourish us is simply a *means*, nothing more. To put it another way: God did not choose to use bread because bread is good for us; rather, bread is good for us because God chooses to use it. By His almighty creative Word, He constantly imparts nourishing power to bread. Without God's Word, bread cannot feed us: we could stuff ourselves with food and still die of hunger. Apart from God's blessing, nothing works. With God's blessing, anything can do the job— even *whatchamacallit* (the literal translation of *manna*) falling out of the sky.

That is why God sent the manna. He did it to demonstrate to the Israelites that all things are governed, at every point of their existence, by His Word of power. He did it to convert them from their deistic faith in "Nature," as John Calvin pointed out: "The majority of mankind think of God as if banished afar off, and dwelling in inactivity as if He had resigned His office in heaven and earth; and hence it arises, that trusting in their present abundance, they implore not His favor, nay, that they pass it by as needless; and, when deprived of their accustomed supplies, they altogether despair, as if God's hand alone were insufficient for their succor. . . . Although there be some harshness in the words, yet the sense is clear, that men's life consists not in their food, but that God's inspiration suffices for their nourishment. . . . The animating principle, which is diffused by the Spirit of God for sustenance, proceeds out of His mouth."[5]

Life in the Spirit

From the beginning, orthodox Christians have recognized that our lives utterly depend, moment-by-moment, on God's grace: "He gives to all life, breath, and all things. . . . For in Him we live and move and have our being" (Acts 17:25, 28). "For of Him and through Him and to Him are all things" (Romans 11:36). Christians confess together, in the words of the Nicene Creed, that the Holy Spirit is "the Lord and Giver of life." The psalmist offers praise to God for His personal providence toward the creatures of the earth:

These all wait for You,
That you may give them their food in due season.
What You give them they gather in;
You open Your hand, they are filled with good.
You hide Your face, they are troubled;
You take away their breath,
They die and return to their dust.
You send forth Your Spirit, and they are created;
And You renew the face of the earth. (Psalm 104:27-30)

That closing verse is very significant. It tells us two important things. First, as the Creed states, the Spirit gives life to all creatures, including animals. Second, this is a creative act. God did not just wind up the creation and leave it on its own, as the deistic "absentee landlord" view of God holds. He continues to work with His creation, and life exists because He continues to create it. His Spirit continues to breathe life into His creatures; and without the Spirit's breath, they die (cf. Genesis 2:7; 7:22). God is the "God of the spirits of all flesh" (Numbers 16:22). He actively and personally gives life to everything (Nehemiah 9:6), and "in His hand is the life of every living thing and the breath of all mankind" (Job 12:10). At death, says Solomon, "the dust will return to the earth as it was, and the spirit will return to God who gave it" (Ecclesiastes 12:7).[6]

But there is a spirit in man,
And the breath of the Almighty gives him understanding. . . .
The Spirit of God has made me;
And the breath of the Almighty gives me life. . . .
If He should set His heart on it,
If He should gather to Himself His Spirit and His breath,
All flesh would perish together,
And man would return to dust. (Job 32:8; 33:4; 34:14, 15)

God is in control of the world, at every moment. This doesn't mean that we are to be fatalistic, resigned to everything life dishes out on the grounds that "it's God's will." There is sin in the world. There are disasters and tragedies. There are evils that we must fight, as we will see in later chapters. But the point to be stressed here — the base for what follows — is this: the Christian acknowledges, even in the greatest catastrophes, that "the LORD has established His throne in heaven, and His kingdom rules over all" (Psalm 103:19); that "our God is in heaven; He does whatever He pleases" (Psalm 115:3); that "He does according to His will in the army of heaven and among the inhabitants of the earth. No one can restrain His hand or say to Him, 'What have you done?' "(Daniel 4:35).[7]

The Wings of the Wind

It is important to recognize in all this that God doesn't just sit in heaven and push buttons on a control panel. He uses "messengers," better known to us by the Greek word: *angels*. The Biblical view of the universe is not the modern one of vast reaches of barren space interrupted every couple of million miles or so by flying dead boulders. The Biblical view of the universe is that it is teeming and throbbing with life everywhere. The cosmos is heavily populated with "legions" and "myriads" of angelic beings, of various ranks (Colossians 1:16) and "species" (see, for instance, the descriptions in Ezekiel 1:5-25 and Revelation 4:6-8). Angels are associated with astronomical phenomena throughout the Bible (Judges 5:20; Job 38:7; Isaiah 14:13; Matthew 24:29; Jude 13; Revelation 1:20; 8:10-12; 9:1; 12:4) as well as with the activity of the weather: wind, storms, and lightning are spoken of in connection with the actions of God and the angels in both blessing and curse (Genesis 8:1; 41:27; Exodus 10:13,19; 14:21; 15:10; 19:16; Numbers 11:31; Psalm 18:10; 104:3, 4; 107:25; 135:7; 147:18; 148:8; Ezekiel 1:4ff.; Matthew 24:31; John 3:8; Acts 2:2; Revelation 7:1-3; 8:5, 7; 16:8, 17, 18). Clearly, the Biblical worldview does not attribute changes in weather to impersonal "forces" or "processes":

> He makes the clouds his chariot
> and rides on the wings of the wind.
> He makes winds his messengers [*angels*],
> flames of fire his servants. (Psalm 104:3, 4, NIV)

"God controls the government of the universe," said Calvin. "No wind ever arises or increases except by God's express command."[8] Further, "since angels are the powers of God, it follows that they never cease from their office of working. For God never can rest; he sustains the world by his energy, he governs everything however minute, so that not even a sparrow falls to the ground without his decree (Matthew 10:29). . . . God works continually by angels . . . so that all creatures are animated by angelic motion: not that there is a conversion of the angel into an ox or a man, but because God exerts and diffuses his energy in a secret manner, so that no creature is content with his own peculiar vigor, but is animated by angels themselves."[9] Martin Luther, as usual more pithy and direct, took seriously the psalmist's statement that the wind has *wings*. After a particularly severe and violent storm, he offered his opinions on the subject: "The devil provokes such storms, but good winds are produced by good angels. Winds are nothing but spirits, either good or evil. The devil sits there and snorts, and so do the angels when the winds are salubrious."[10]

The Biblical worldview is uncompromising: God is running the world. Every atom in the universe is under His command. His Word created and sustains all things, and all things are held together in Him. That is why He can assert His power and authority in such absolute terms:

> I form the light and create darkness,
> I make peace and create calamity,
> I, the LORD, do all these things. (Isaiah 45:7)

> Who can speak and have it happen
>   if the LORD has not decreed it?
> Is it not from the mouth of the Most High
>   that both calamities and good things come?
> (Lamentations 3:37, 38, NIV)

It was this understanding of the absolute God—infinitely transcendent, above His creation, and at the same time wholly immanent, nearer to us than we are to ourselves—that enabled Job, in the midst of terrible sufferings, to trust Him with implicit confidence and assurance. Informed that his oxen, donkeys, and camels had been stolen by marauding enemies, his sheep destroyed by fire, and his servants and children killed, he did not blame these events (in their ultimate significance) on either the devil or the devil's human agents, even though they were certainly responsible. Over and through it all, Job recognized the sovereign hand of God. Falling to the ground in worship, he cried:

> The Lord gave, and the Lord has taken away;
> Blessed be the name of the Lord. (Job 1:21)

As Calvin observed, Job's confession was no mere anomaly. It was rooted in a thoroughly Biblical understanding of how the world really works[11] — an understanding that we've lost despite such cataclysmic demonstrations as the reality of AIDS.

Blessing and Cursing

God's providence — His personal activity in everything according to His eternal plan — is the foundation for the Biblical teaching of blessing and cursing. Perhaps the best summary of this is found in the Book of Deuteronomy, where Moses outlined for the Israelites the covenant that God the King had made with them. Throughout his discourses Moses stressed that the covenant is *ethical*. God imposed His ethical standards of living upon Israel, promising them His blessings for obedience and warning of His curses for disobedience.

It is important to note that these ethical laws were never intended for Israel alone; God is "the great King over all the earth" who "reigns over the nations" (Psalm 47:2, 8); indeed, "the earth is the Lord's, and all its fullness, the world, and those who dwell therein" (Psalm 24:1). Psalm 2 is addressed to the kings and rulers of all nations, commanding them to submit to God under the rule of His Son. Christ, the "Anointed One" (cf. Acts 4:25-27), declares:

> I will declare the decree:
> The Lord has said to Me,
> "You are my Son;
> Today I have begotten You.
> Ask of me, and I will give You
> The nations for Your inheritance,
> And the ends of the earth for Your possession.
> You shall break them with a rod of iron;
> You shall dash them in pieces like a potter's vessel."
> Now therefore, be wise, O kings;

Be instructed, you judges of the earth.
Serve the LORD with fear
And rejoice with trembling.
Kiss the Son, lest he be angry
  and you perish in the way,
When His wrath is kindled but a little.
Blessed are all those who put their trust in Him.
(Psalm 2:7-12)

An important part of Israel's calling was to serve as a "model community" during the provisional period of waiting for the Messiah. Moses commanded the people to observe God's laws carefully, "for this will show your wisdom and understanding to the nations, who will hear about all these decrees and say, 'Surely this great nation is a wise and understanding people.'. . . What other nation is so great as to have such righteous decrees and laws as this body of laws I am setting before you today?" (Deuteronomy 4:6, 8, NIV). Moreover, the heathen nations which God would drive out of Canaan were being punished precisely because they had disobeyed the laws God gave Israel through Moses!

> Do not defile yourselves in any of these ways, because this is how the nations that I am going to drive out before you became defiled. Even the land was defiled; so I punished it for its sin, and the land vomited out its inhabitants. But you must keep my decrees [lit. *statutes*] and my laws. The native-born and the aliens living among you must not do any of these detestable things, for all these things were done by the people who lived in the land before you, and the land became defiled. And if you defile the land, it will vomit you out as it vomited out the nations that were before you. . . . Keep my requirements and do not follow any of the detestable customs [lit. *statutes*] that were practiced before you came and do not defile yourselves with them. I am the LORD your God. (Lev. 18:24-30, NIV)

God's ethical standards are the same for all nations. He warned Israel that she would meet the same fate meted out to the heathen nations if she disobeyed Him. So the blessings and curses listed in Deuteronomy are not intended to apply to Israel alone. They apply to the people of any nation or culture. The nations that are obedient to God will be blessed; those that are disobedient will be cursed.[12]

The most comprehensive account of God's covenantal sanctions is contained in Deuteronomy 28. The first 14 verses describe the blessings, and verses 15-68 record the curses — sometimes in horrifying detail. What should not be missed is the exceedingly mundane, "economic" quality of the sanctions. The personal and cultural blessings are refreshingly earthly: "You will be blessed in the city and blessed in the country. The fruit of the womb will be blessed, and the crops of your land and the young of your livestock — the calves of your herds and the lambs of your flocks. Your basket and your kneading trough will be blessed. . . . The LORD will send a blessing on your barns and on everything you put your hand to. . . . The Lord will open the heavens, the storehouse of his bounty, to send rain on your land in season and to bless all the work of your hands. You will lend to many nations but will borrow from none . . ." (NIV).

Just as earthly — and painfully physical — are the curses for rebellion against God: "You will be cursed in the city and cursed in the country. Your basket and your kneading trough will be cursed. The fruit of your womb will be cursed, and the crops of your land, and the calves of your herds and the lambs of your flocks. . . . The LORD will send upon you curses, confusion and rebuke in everything you put your hand to, until you are destroyed and come to sudden ruin because of the evil you have done in forsaking him. The LORD will plague you with diseases until he has destroyed you from the land you are entering to possess. The LORD will strike you with wasting disease, with fever and inflammation, with scorching heat and drought, with blight and mildew, which will plague you until you perish. . . . The LORD will cause you to be defeated before your enemies. . . . The LORD will afflict you with the boils of Egypt and with tumors, festering sores and the itch, from which you cannot be cured. The LORD will afflict you with madness, blindness and confusion of mind. . . . The sights you see will drive you mad. The LORD will afflict your knees and legs with painful boils that cannot be cured, spreading from the soles of your feet to the top of your head . . ." (NIV).

It is clear, therefore, that God punishes nations and cultures, as well as individuals, for flagrant rebellion against His commandments. When we see a fearful disease manifesting itself primarily among homosexuals, as a direct result of the abominations they practice, we have no option but to acknowledge it as divine judgment on sinners. The greatest danger—for our culture as a whole and for the victims of AIDS in particular—would be for the Church simply to accept the secularist and deistic medical model. If we approach AIDS as if it were not God's judgment, it will only increase.

The Christian Response to AIDS

Our only hope is in God. Numbers 21 tells of a plague of deadly serpents sent by God against the rebellious Israelites. Many people died from the poisonous snakebites. When at last the Israelites came to Moses, confessed their sins, and asked for mercy, God instructed Moses to set up a bronze serpent on a pole: "Then when anyone was bitten by a snake and looked at the bronze snake, he lived" (Numbers 21:9, NIV). The point is that the response that saved the victims was oriented toward God—not primarily toward the plague. The saving response was an admission that the plague was under the control of God, not Nature. Further, the saving response meant confessing and forsaking the sin that had brought on the plague in the first place; certainly, no one would have been helped by well-meaning liberals claiming that a loving God would never punish sinners. (In fact, the very existence of the judgment demonstrated the love of God, because it brought people to repentance and thus to salvation. If God had allowed them to continue in sin without suffering the consequences, no one would have been saved.) Finally, the saving response required coming for salvation in the appointed way: the victims had to look at the bronze snake in order to be healed. There was no other way.

So what is the proper Christian response to the plague of AIDS? As in the case of the plague of serpents, our primary response must be toward God, recognizing His sovereignty over the disease. In the final analysis, AIDS has come from His holy and loving hand. Sinners must confess their acts of rebellion against His law; they must repent and forsake the ungodly deathstyles that have provoked God's anger. And they must trust in Jesus Christ for salvation, acknowledging Him as Lord of their lives. Jesus explicitly drew a parallel between Himself and the bronze serpent: "And as Moses lifted up the serpent in the wilderness, even so must the Son of Man be lifted up, that whoever believes in Him should not perish but have eternal life" (John 3:14, 15). *The saving response—for individuals and for our whole culture—is faith in the Lord Jesus Christ.*

This will mean absolutely and utterly abandoning homosexual activity in any form, along with all heterosexual intercourse outside of a strictly monogamous marriage. There are only two sexual options for the Christian: absolute chastity and faithfulness within the bounds of marriage, and absolute celibacy outside of marriage. As the Apostle John warned in his first letter to the churches, "faith" apart from obedience is empty and worthless: "Now by this we know that we know Him, if we keep His commandments. He who says, 'I know him,' and does not keep His commandments, is a liar, and the truth is not in him. But whoever keeps His word, truly the love of God is perfected in him. By this we know that we are in Him. He who says he abides in Him ought himself also to walk just as He walked" (1 John 2:3-6).

The answer to AIDS is repentance—not merely treatment, or a kind of prophylactic prevention that does not address the root causes. The answer is not in condoms, "rubber dams," and so-called "safe sex." The answer is, as God commands, simply obedience to His Word. Because many in our culture have disobeyed God's commandments, the curses of His law have come upon us instead. Our nation is under the judgment of heaven.

Who's To Blame?

It would be very easy at this point—and very wrong—merely to point our fingers at the homosexuals and the drug addicts and blame them for what has happened. Certainly, they bear a great deal of responsibility for this terrible plague, and many of them are reaping what they have sown. Yet they are not the major villains of this drama being played out in our culture. If we are faithful to the Bible, we cannot say that AIDS is primarily their fault. The real blame for this plague rests elsewhere.

AIDS is the fault of the Christian Church.

What a grandeur of spirit it is to struggle with all the powers of an unshaken mind against so many onsets of devastation and death! What sublimity, to stand erect amid the desolation of the human race, and not to lie prostrate with those who have no hope in God; but rather to rejoice, and to embrace the benefit of the occasion; that in thus bravely showing forth our faith, and by suffering endured, going forward to Christ by the narrow way that Christ trod, we may receive the reward of His life and faith according to His own judgment!

Cyprian, *On the Mortality*, 14
(written during the plague
of A.D. 252)

FIVE

THE FAILED PRIESTHOOD

The earth is also defiled under its inhabitants,
Because they have transgressed the laws,
Changed the ordinance,
Broken the everlasting covenant. (Isaiah 24:5)

What is the Church's relationship to the world—a world buffeted by sin, sickness, depravity, and now AIDS? The Apostle Peter summed it up in a letter he wrote to encourage a group of first-century Christians: "You . . . are being built into a spiritual house to be a holy priesthood, offering spiritual sacrifices acceptable to God through Jesus Christ. . . . You are a chosen people, a royal priesthood, a holy nation, a people belonging to God, that you may declare the praises of him who called you out of darkness into his wonderful light" (1 Peter 2:5, 9). The Apostle John wrote similarly to the churches of Asia Minor, assuring them that Christ "has made us to be a kingdom and priests to serve his God and Father" (Revelation 1:6).

The notion that God's people are a united kingdom of priests was not original with the apostles. They adopted it from the story of Israel's encounter with Yahweh at Sinai. God had pronounced the new nation to be His special people, declaring: "Now if you obey me fully and keep my covenant, then out of all nations you will be my treasured possession. Although the whole earth is mine, you will be for me a kingdom of priests and a holy nation" (Exodus 19:5, 6). The priesthood had belonged to Israel; now, said the apostles, in the Messianic era brought in by Jesus' resurrection and ascension, the priesthood belongs to the corporate Body of Christ.

What does it mean for the Church to be a priesthood? The answer begins, as many answers do, at the very beginning, in the Garden of Eden with Adam. Eden was originally organized as a special sanctuary, a temple in which God could meet with the creatures He had created in His image.[1] Into this garden sanctuary He placed Adam, a priest, giving him two responsibilities (Genesis 2:15):

1. to *work* the garden [the Hebrew verb is *'abad*, meaning *to serve, tend,* or *till*]; and

2. to *take care* of the garden [the verb is *shamar*: *to keep* or *guard*].

The force of these terms is made clear by way of contrast a few verses later, after Adam's rebellion, when we read that the disobedient priest was kicked out of the sanctuary: "So the LORD God banished him from the Garden of Eden to work [*'abad*] the ground from which he had been taken" (Genesis 3:23). Adam remained a tiller of the soil. But the judgment altered his status in one very important respect. Adam was defrocked. God removed him from office as Eden's guardian, replacing him at the gateway with angelic guardians: "After he drove the man out, he placed on the east side of the Garden of Eden cherubim and a flaming sword flashing back and forth to guard [*shamar*] the way to the tree of life" (Genesis 3:24). No longer was Adam allowed to be a priest-warrior. He had forfeited the privileges of his position, and his office was given to others.

It is significant that these same two terms appear later in the job descriptions of the Aaronic priests. For example, the LORD says to the high priest:

> And you shall *attend to* [*shamar*] the duties of the sanctuary and the duties of the altar, that there may be no more wrath on the children of Israel. . . . Therefore you and your sons with you shall *attend to* [*shamar*] your priesthood for everything at the altar and behind the veil; and you shall serve [*'abad*]. I give your priesthood to you as a gift for service, but the outsider who comes near shall be put to death. (Numbers 18:5, 7)

As this theme is developed throughout the Bible, the responsibility of "guarding" turns out to be preeminent among the tasks of the priests. The word *shamar* is used frequently in describing their basic duty (cf. Numbers 1:53; 3:5-8, 32; 8:26; 18:3-7; 31:30, 47; 1 Samuel 7:1; 2 Kings 12:9; 1 Chronicles 23:32; 2 Chronicles 34:9; Ezekiel 44:15-16; 48:11; Zechariah 3:7). Priests were to regard themselves as on duty at a military post, guarding the sanctity of their charge against all dangers and against unlawful intruders.

The priests of Israel came from the tribe of Levi, and from a particular family within that tribe, the House of Aaron. They and the other Levites had the sole responsibility for working in the temple and guarding it. They constituted the special priesthood for the nation of Israel. But, in addition to this special priesthood, there was what we might call a "general" priesthood as well. At Sinai, as we have seen, all the tribes of Israel were forged into one great priestly nation.

Israel was a kingdom of priests to the other nations of the world. God intended the whole nation to exercise a ministry of guarding and teaching the surrounding peoples, and interceding with Him on their behalf. In order to emphasize this vital calling, God used numerous reminders throughout Israel's experience. For example, Israel's priestly ministry was beautifully portrayed as the people traveled from the Red Sea and camped at an oasis known as Elim. On two occasions Moses took the trouble to record the fact that Elim had twelve springs and seventy palm trees (Exodus 15:27; Numbers 33:9). *Twelve springs*, corresponding to the twelve tribes of Israel: as the people were refreshed with the cool spring water they were reminded of their calling to bring the water of life to the world. But what of the seventy palms? They, too, were part of this unmistakable visual lesson being taught to Israel. For their own leader, Moses, was compiling and editing an account of the early history of the world, leading up to God's choice of the patriarch Abraham. In that book of beginnings was the story of how the descendants of Noah's sons were divided into the nations of the earth. From Japheth came fourteen nations; from Ham came thirty; and from Israel's own ancestor, Shem, came twenty-six: *Seventy nations* in all. And out of all peoples of the earth, God had chosen Israel to be the priests, to provide divine protection for the nations and feed them with the water of life. Grace coming through

Israel—culminating in the work of the Messiah, the great High Priest of the order of Melchizedek—would make the world develop and bear fruit.

Another strong reminder of her calling was given to Israel in the great national festival called the Feast of Tabernacles. In this week-long festival the nation of priests enacted the drama of redemption, as a way of keeping alive the hope that someday all nations would come to know the true God. At the close of one of these feasts, the prophet Haggai spoke of its symbolic meaning: " 'I will shake all nations, and the desired of all nations will come, and I will fill this house [the Temple] with glory,' says the LORD Almighty" (Haggai 2:7). His contemporary Zechariah explained that the menacing heathen nations surrounding Israel would someday be converted to the true faith, so that they would participate in this time of joy and gladness with Israel: "Then the survivors from all the nations that have attacked Jerusalem will go up year after year to worship the King, the LORD Almighty, and to celebrate the Feast of Tabernacles" (Zechariah 14:16).

What was it about this feast that spoke of Israel's priestly duty toward the nations? The feast lasted seven days, and on each day the priests were commanded to sacrifice a number of bulls as whole burnt offerings, for the atonement of sin (Numbers 29:12-32). On the first day they were to sacrifice thirteen bulls; on the second day, twelve bulls; on the third day, eleven bulls; on the fourth day, ten bulls; on the fifth day, nine bulls; on the sixth day, eight bulls; and finally, on the seventh day, seven bulls were sacrificed. *Seventy bulls.* Again, Israel was being reminded of its exalted, priestly status in the world. God's special people were to intercede for the nations.

All the men of Israel wore special priestly garments as visible reminders of their status (Numbers 15:37-41). The rite of circumcision, too, was a symbol not of "salvation" as such (many uncircumcised people outside of Israel were saved), but of the priesthood. Only those who were members of the "kingdom of priests" could receive the covenant sign of circumcision.[2] Even Israel's political and social organization spoke of its priestly calling: as a model for the nations, a microcosm of the whole world, Israel was led by a council of seventy elders—a dramatic picture that someday all nations would serve God and rule with Him. In a type of the future blessing of all nations (Joel 2:28-29; Acts 2:1-18), the seventy elders received the gift of prophecy when the Holy Spirit came upon them (Numbers 11:24-29).

God's kingdom of priests to the world possessed a great responsibility indeed. Israel was to be, in the words of the Apostle Paul, "a guide for the blind, a light for those who are in the dark, an instructor of the foolish, a teacher of infants," because the law they had received from God was "the embodiment of knowledge and truth" (Romans 2:19, 20). The law was not intended for Israel alone; rather, the law was considered a sacred trust deposited with the royal priesthood (Romans 3:1-2), to be proclaimed before the rulers of the earth (Psalm 119:46) in order that the whole world might walk in the light of God's justice (Isaiah 51:4; cf. Proverbs 14:34). Israel was called to be a guide to all nations.

The surrounding nations often recognized Israel's priestly ministry; in the tenth century B.C., "the whole world sought audience with Solomon to hear the wisdom God had put in His heart" (1 Kings 10:24). Ezra records that over four hundred years later, King Cyrus of Persia openly acknowledged the religious leadership of Israel (Ezra 1:1-10; 6:3-5). When Israel was faithful in this calling, the world was at peace; when Israel failed to protect the nations, the world was plunged into the darkness of sin and the curse.

The ninth-century B.C. prophet Azariah understood this. He explained the national and international social consequences of the failure of the priesthood: "For a long time Israel was without the true God, without a priest to teach and without the law. . . . In those days it was not safe to travel about, for all the inhabitants of the lands were in great turmoil. One nation was being crushed by another and one city by another, because God was troubling men with every kind of distress" (2 Chronicles 15:3-6). On every level of responsibility — whether of the "special" or the "general" priesthood — when the priests neglect their duty to bring God's Word to the world, they render the socio-political body defenseless against attack, and evils of all kinds will invade the culture to seduce and destroy the people.

That is why the Apostle Paul, in the passage cited earlier, rebuked first-century Israel for abandoning its responsibility:

"You, then, who teach others, do you not teach yourself? You who preach against stealing, do you steal? You who say that people should not commit adultery, do you commit adultery? You who abhor idols, do you rob temples? You who brag about the law, do you dishonor God by breaking the law? As it is written: 'God's name is blasphemed among the Gentiles because of you.' Circumcision has value if you observe the law, but if you break the law, you have become as though you had not been circumcised" (Romans 2:21-25).

The Church: God's New Royal Priesthood

When the nation of Israel apostatized from the Biblical faith in the first century through its rejection of Christ, its position as the kingdom of priests was taken away and given to another "nation." Jesus had warned that this would happen: "Therefore I tell you that the kingdom of God will be taken away from you and given to a people who will produce its fruit" (Matthew 21:43). That is the significance of the Apostle Peter's statement, with which we began this chapter. The Church has inherited the mantle of the priesthood. Israel has been deposed from office, and the priestly role of guidance and protection has been bestowed upon the people of the New Covenant.

This means that the Church has the responsibility to lead the world in righteousness. In fact, the Church's responsibility is even greater than that of Old Covenant Israel's, for we have been given a specific commission from Christ to disciple the nations: "Go and make disciples of all nations, baptizing them in the name of the Father and of the Son and of the Holy Spirit, teaching them to obey everything I have commanded you" (Matthew 28:19-20). "You are the light of the world," Jesus told His disciples. "Let your light shine before men, that they may see your good deeds and praise your Father in heaven" (Matthew 5:13, 16). In a familiar passage, the Apostle Paul exhorts the Church to "be strong in the Lord and in his mighty power. Put on the full armor of God, so that you can take your stand against the devil's schemes" (Ephesians 6:10-11; cf. Romans 13:12). He then goes through the various items in the soldier's armor (vv. 14-17; cf. 1 Thessalonians 5:8), using them to illustrate the ethical defenses in the Christian's life — the belt of truth, the breastplate of righteousness, the helmet of salvation, and so on. While these have often been understood in terms of the Roman soldier's military garb, a study of the origin of this imagery (cf. Exodus 28; Isaiah 59:17ff.; 61:10) reveals that the Apostle Paul is thinking instead of the "military" uniform of the High Priest, God's holy warrior. The Bible uses similar images to depict the Lord Jesus Christ at the head of an army of warrior-priests, doing battle with the forces of darkness and winning decisive victories throughout the world (cf. Psalm 110; Revelation 19). It is clear that the Church, as the royal priesthood, is the divinely ordained institution to protect the world "against principalities, against powers, against the rulers of the darkness of this age, against spiritual hosts of wickedness in the heavenly places" (Ephesians 6:12, NKJV). In this great cosmic battle, only the Church is equipped with the proper armor: Jesus Christ Himself (Romans 13:14; Galatians 3:27).

The Church and its program of discipling the world to the obedience of Christ are thus central to the world; from the strictly Biblical point of view, Church history is the key to world history, and history is inexplicable apart from such an understanding. Historian Philip Schaff wrote, in the introduction to his magisterial *Church History*: "The central current and ultimate aim of universal history is the KINGDOM OF GOD established by JESUS CHRIST. This is the grandest and most important institution in the world, as vast as humanity and as enduring as eternity. All other institutions are made subservient to it, and in its interest the whole world is governed. . . . Secular history, far from controlling sacred history, is controlled by it, must directly or indirectly subserve its ends, and can only be fully understood in the central light of Christian truth and the plan of salvation."[3]

A Vacant Office

All Christians, then, have a priestly role to fulfill within their culture. But the great tragedy of our era is that Christians have been engaged in a steady retreat. Having been installed in office, seated on the throne with Jesus Christ (Ephesians 2:6), we have abdicated. Once upon a time, Christians assumed they had a duty to lead the world, to set the standards for society. Christians founded universities, built hospitals, and were at the forefront of scientific activity and social action. Yet the twentieth century has witnessed the Church taking a back seat to the secular humanists, allowing our enemies to steer us according to their maps and their itineraries, toward their destinations. When today's Church does venture to speak out on social issues, it usually produces little more than a weak echo of the humanist agenda. Only rarely do we issue manifestos; our feeble bleatings merely serve as evidence of the new Babylonian captivity—dressed up with jargon-laden justifications for our bondage to alien worldviews and pagan standards. Instead of fulfilling Christ's command to be light and salt in the world, we embrace the darkness and assure our neighbors that life is much healthier on a "salt-free" diet.

This retreat has been absolutely inexcusable. There is no internal logic in Christianity that requires it to wind down or run out of steam. There is nothing in the nature of the world that makes a flight from victory necessary. There is no eschatological imperative that predetermines the defeat of the Church. On the contrary, our Lord infallibly promised us victory if we are faithful to Him. Jesus declared: "I will build my Church, and the gates of Hades will not overcome it" (Matthew 16:18). This is much more than a mere guarantee of protection for His people. Jesus is giving a picture of His Church as a mighty army, besieging the fortress of evil—and defeating it! According to Christ's own infallible Word, the forces of the evil one cannot stand against the determined assault of God's warrior-priests. James told his early Christian readers the same thing: "Submit yourselves, then, to God. Resist the devil, and he will flee from you" (James 4:7). Why, then, do we not see the devil fleeing in terror from the advances of God's people? The answer is, unfortunately, all too easy: Christians have not been resisting. The priests have abdicated.

Many factors have contributed to this loss of Christian influence. I believe that the following seven items are particularly significant:

1. False Spirituality

The Bible views man as a unit, and teaches that salvation is the reconciliation of the whole person to God. True "spirituality" in the Christian life really has a capital S, for it means being enabled by the Spirit to live according to God's ethical requirements in every area of life (John 14:15; 1 John 1:7; 2:3-6; 3:22; 5:3). The one who is Spiritual focuses his attention on the law of God (Romans 8:4-9) and meditates in its instructions day and night (Psalm 1:2; 119:97). Spirituality is living as the Spirit commands us; and we discover the Spirit's commands by referring to the law which He authored. "The law is Spiritual" (Romans 7:14); it is "holy, just, and good" (Romans 7:12). It is the believer's continuing standard of right living in every area.

The last two centuries or so have witnessed the rise of a counterfeit "spirituality" in the West. Often this has been accompanied by a great deal of discussion about the Holy Spirit — much of it by those who neglected the holiness of the Spirit and advocated a disregard of His law. Some groups popularized the notion that the "spiritual" person is one who transcends the actual teachings of God's Word and lives on a higher plane (a corollary of this view was that the one who is preoccupied with the details of Biblical teaching is carnal and unspiritual). In this pietistic perspective Christianity was seen increasingly as a religion of the "heart" as opposed to the "head"; emotional fervor rather than doctrinal understanding was considered the key to one's relationship with God. (It was a false dilemma. The Bible never opposes emotions and intellect, and the metaphorical term *heart* in Scripture refers not to man's feelings but to the "control center" of his whole person, the root of the mind as well as the tear ducts.) Sermons took on a more "feminine" cast as preachers appealed to the affections — or, more directly, to the "will" — and specifically rejected any attempt toward an intelligent, informed faith. Pietism's anti-intellectual bias led in turn to a practical despising of God's creation. God, it was said, is not interested in matters of this world, but only in otherworldly things.

This notion about God is absolutely unbiblical, and foreign to any recognizable Christian orthodoxy. As the historic creeds state, the true God is the "Maker of heaven and earth"; *of course* He cares about the world. That is why He sent His Son: not to abandon the world but to redeem it. And the very first time the Holy Spirit is mentioned in the Bible is at the Creation, in Genesis 1:2, where we find the Spirit hovering over the primordial waters, blazing forth light upon the darkness, fashioning the earth into a suitable environment for His very image. Biblical Spirituality takes the world seriously as the scene of God's greatest acts of creation and redemption. The false spirituality, drawing more from pagan mythology than from Christian truth, rejects the world and seeks to flee from it.

2. Dualism

A corollary of this false spirituality has been the restriction of Christian activity to "soul-saving," with little or no regard for the older Christian goal of sanctifying every area of life to the glory of God. When God created the first man and woman, He commanded them to rule the whole earth under His lordship. His purpose was that man should develop the world as a consecrated offering to Him, bringing its created potential to fruition. And even though sin, death, and destruction invaded the world, God's central goal has not changed. He has not abandoned His creation. He sent His Son into the world in order to save man, to re-create him in His image, and then to make all things new. Man has been granted dominion again, in Jesus Christ; and through Him God's original plan will be infallibly fulfilled. The salvation of souls is the beginning of this process, not the end. In fact, the salvation of souls does not take place in isolation: The Apostle Paul wrote, "May God himself, the God of peace, sanctify you through and through. May your whole spirit, soul, and body be kept blameless at the coming of our Lord Jesus Christ. The one who calls you is faithful and he will do it" (1 Thessalonians 5:23-24). The doctrine that "salvation concerns only the soul" comes not from Christianity, but from an early antichristian heresy known as gnosticism; and it was roundly condemned by the entire Christian Church.[4] God's Cultural Mandate for the sanctification of all of life is basic for the Christian worldview. Jesus commissioned us not only to witness to the nations but to *disciple* the nations, teaching them to bring every area of their lives into conformity to His commandments (Matthew 28:19-20).

The loss of this Christian perspective among some groups resulted in a practical dualism, a position that held (implicitly, if not explicitly) that the world belongs to the devil, and must not be claimed and captured for Jesus Christ. Where earlier generations had vigorously proclaimed the "Crown Rights of King Jesus," those infected by the false spirituality declared that "you don't polish brass on a sinking ship." A new monasticism set in, seeing the Church as a place of retreat from the world, rather than as a training camp for guerrillas. (This was, incidentally, very different from traditional Christian monasticism, in which monasteries were really frontier missions working for the advance, not the retreat, of the Church.)[5]

3. Rationalism

Not all Christians were taken in by the seductions of false spirituality and dualism. Some, especially in the Reformed tradition, valiantly attempted to stand against these errors. But they were undermined by their own misguided commitment to a rationalistic theology which had little room for mystery, for miracle, for liturgical richness, and for eucharistic worship. In the name of emphasizing the Word of God, what they really emphasized was the attainment of theological knowledge. A new legalism was established: salvation by intellect. The historic Christian doctrine of the Real Presence of Christ in the Eucharist was jettisoned in favor of a Zwinglian view, amounting in practice to a virtual neglect of the sacrament altogether. Instead of weekly communion—the pattern in the New Testament and throughout most of Church history—the Holy Supper was observed annually or quarterly, or at best monthly. Jesus had expressed His own attitude when He said: "I tell you the truth, unless you eat the flesh of the Son of Man and drink His blood, you have no life in you" (John 6:53). In light of such an authoritative declaration, any assumption that we can live apart from the sacraments—or that we can earn the right to partake them by demonstrating our intellectual comprehension of their meaning—is shocking in its arrogance. In His institution of the Supper, Jesus did not say: "Understand this in memory of me," but: "*Do* this as my memorial" (Luke 22:19).

The barren, lifeless, intellectualistic Church produced a reaction of irrationalism among many. People abandoned the lecture-hall atmosphere and turned toward religious carnivals and freak shows instead. Seeking the holistic expression of devotion denied them in the rationalistic, communionless communions, they invented the "dry eucharist" known as the "altar call." Wild, frothy excesses of enthusiasm replaced the staid emotionlessness of the Reformation Church, whose description of God in her creeds would have served well, instead, as a self-portrait: "without body, parts, or passions." Rather than counteracting pietism, in a perverse way rationalism actually nurtured it. A proper theological perspective was sorely needed in our culture; the irony was that the very tradition that could have provided it was driving people away. Instead of giving bread and wine, they tried to feed the hungry with catechisms.

4. Naturalism

One far-reaching consequence of the retreat into false spirituality, dualism, and rationalism was widespread unbelief. The modern heresy of Naturalism (sometimes known as theological liberalism) became entrenched in our theological schools. Whenever orthodox Christians fail to provide leadership, the vacuum is filled by their enemies. The eighteenth century pietistic retreat, in the name of greater spirituality, made way for the invasion of Deism — a Baalistic, absentee-landlord view of God that denied His Personal activity in the world. Even the most orthodox circles were infiltrated by this insidious but eminently respectable and "reasonable" form of unbelief. It was not long before the even more blatantly apostate doctrines of Kant and Hegel made inroads into the seminaries and churches, followed by Darwinism and Marxism (parading as a "Social Gospel"). All these amounted to the increasing secularization of the Church, and therefore of the culture as a whole. In a memorable passage, Herbert Schlossberg has defined the essence of secularization as idolatry: "Western society, in turning away from the Christian faith, has turned to other things. This process is commonly called *secularization*, but that conveys only the negative aspect. The word connotes the turning away from the worship of God while ignoring the fact that something is being turned *to* in its place."[6] The secularization of Christianity cut it off at the knees and ripped out its guts: the Church lost its aggressive character. The time-honored (and Biblical) notion of "the Church Militant" was regarded as a "triumphalistic," and rather impolite, relic of our medieval, Dark-Ages past.

5. Feminization

Several books have been published over the last few years documenting one of the most appalling aspects of our cultural fall from grace. Christianity became sentimentalized and romanticized, and Jesus Himself became identified with feminine characteristics. No longer was He regarded as the Almighty Lord, the Judge with fire blazing from His eyes, waging war in righteousness (Revelation 1:13-18; 19:11-21) as the Bible represents the glorified Christ; instead, He became "gentle Jesus, meek and mild," a pale, effeminate, pathetic figure. The doctrine of the Atonement changed from the traditional, Biblical view — Christ suffering the full punishment of the broken Law in place of His people, and defeating the devil, sin, and death — to a new, moralistic theory that Christ suffered simply as an example of love.

In her landmark study of this transformation in American theology and philosophy, Ann Douglas points out the result: the feminized Church lost its position of leadership. "Between 1820 and 1875, the Protestant Church in this country was gradually transformed from a traditional institution which claimed with certain real justification to be a guide and leader to the American nation to an influential *ad hoc* organization which obtained its power largely by taking cues from the non-ecclesiastical culture on which it was dependent."[7]

It should come as no surprise that a feminized Church has produced a feminized culture in which homosexuality, impotence, exhibitionism, and general sexual *angst* are rampant, and our male role models are either Phil Donahue and Boy George at one end of the spectrum, or Rambo and Conan the Barbarian on the other.

6. Defeatist Eschatology

A new eschatology (doctrine of "last things") came into prominence during this period, a theology that held that "Satan is alive and well on planet earth" rather than having been defeated through the death, resurrection, and ascension of Christ. Earlier generations of Christians had believed that Christ's victory and exaltation as King of kings authorized them to disciple all nations in His name, looking forward to the conversion of all nations by the power of the Gospel. A Biblically and historically unprecedented theory known as Dispensationalism came into being, which openly repudiated the goal of world conversion — and repudiated most of the Bible as well. Only the New Testament (and only selected portions of it) was regarded as authoritative for the Church. Having lost anywhere from 69 percent to 98.2 percent of Scripture (depending on which Dispensationalist theory was adopted),[8] Christians gave up hope in the promises of God and the power of the Holy Spirit to overcome opposition to the Gospel.

A partial Bible created a partial Christianity, one that expected earthly defeat rather than victory.

7. Ethical Compromise

Because Christians bought into pagan theologies of spirituality, because we abandoned the Biblical worldview, because we conceded ground to neo-pagan Naturalism, because we became effeminate, and because we gave up hope for victory, we were helpless to fight back when the moral crisis unleashed its fury on the world. We had lost "the full armor of God" and were unable to stand our ground in the evil day, the day of battle. Soon we beheld the disgusting spectacle of Christian leaders condoning, and even advocating, premarital sex, extramarital affairs, "therapeutic" divorce, "compassionate" abortion, and "Christian" homosexuality. Christian leaders had been so used to compromise that they no longer were sure about standards even in the most obvious areas. Pastors, counselors, and theology professors united in their endorsement of degenerate behavior that would make a godly man vomit. Christianity became synonymous with moral cowardice, unable to confront evil. Confused by a false notion of love, Christian opinion-molders sought peaceful coexistence with the devil, becoming alarmed only when that ungodly peace was threatened by the lonely voice of an occasional prophet or a phenomenal plague.[9]

No list such as this can hope to be exhaustive, but these seem to be the major causes within the Church for the rampaging secularism of our day. The priesthood has not been faithful to its charge. We have failed to guard our society from sin. And because of our failure, God's judgment is falling upon the world.

Consider Sodom: completely given over to homosexual perversion, its sins raising a stench to heaven, it was utterly annihilated by God with fire and brimstone. The judgment was completely righteous; according to God's immutable moral law, the Sodomites utterly deserved to be destroyed. The great tragedy, however, is that it did not have to turn out that way. Sodom could have been saved from this disaster. God would rather redeem than destroy, and He assured Abraham that if He could find but ten men standing up for righteousness in that city, Sodom would be spared (Genesis 18:20-33). Ten faithful priests could have protected the city and its inhabitants from that awful doom. But there were not ten righteous men in the city. There was only one, Abraham's nephew Lot—who had chosen the easy route of "personal peace and affluence," of "going along to get along" in that depraved and decadent culture. The result was that Lot lost his wife and family, except for two daughters who had been corrupted by their degraded moral environment. Instead of having a leavening effect for righteousness, Lot and his household had themselves been leavened by Sodomite morality. He had not been faithful to his calling and so was unable to protect his society from destruction.

This pattern is repeated again and again throughout Biblical history: God provides a priest; the priest fails to protect his charge; someone else commits a crime; and the earth is crushed under God's judgment. Adam failed to protect his bride in the Garden of Eden, and so she fell into temptation and the whole world was cursed. Aaron the high priest morally deserted his post and became responsible for Israel's lapse into idolatry; three thousand people died as a direct result of his sin. The whole book of Judges illustrates this problem repeatedly, as the priests and Levites abandon their role as the guardians of society against sin and judgment.

The failure of the priesthood is thus the theological equivalent of AIDS: the breakdown of a culture's moral immune system leaves it vulnerable and helpless against attack and eventual destruction. As George Gilder points out, "The liberal journalists, compassionate churchmen, tolerant sociologists, pliable psychologists, pandering politicians, and valuefree sex educationists who condoned the most extreme homosexual behavior as an acceptable lifestyle are *the true sources of the AIDS epidemic*. That gay liberationists were killing themselves in a mad gadarene rut was evident to many doctors long before the new plague struck. By the early 1980s gays comprised 41 percent of all cases of syphilis and 21 percent of cases of gonorrhea. According to various surveys, they showed a rate of infectious hepatitis eight to twenty-five times higher than heterosexual males. Some 78 percent had contracted at least one venereal disease, and at any one time perhaps a fifth suffered from some stage of gonorrhea. Over the last decade of liberation in San Francisco, infectious hepatitis A more than doubled, infectious hepatitis B quadrupled, amoebic colon infection rose 25 times. Yet gays turning to churches and other institutions for help all too often were told not to worry. Seeking redemption for their sins they were treated as sinless. Denied repentance they could not attain expiation."[10]

We must not be complacent about the AIDS crisis. To a great extent, it is our own doing. We have failed to speak the truth to our culture. Our trumpet too often has had "an uncertain sound." We have quenched the ministry of the Spirit, who was sent by the Son to "convict the world of sin, and of righteousness, and of judgment." We have been silent about the demands of God's law over every area of life. And by that silence we have brought God's curse into our land instead of His blessing.

Even as a practical matter, we cannot afford to ignore the crisis. By all accounts, it is only the very beginning. The Plague is spreading like a forest fire, and its effects will be felt by us all. Apart from the mercy of God, AIDS will kill millions, perhaps tens of millions of people over the next decade. You may be one of them. And if you are fortunate enough to avoid the disease, its economic ramifications will get you. The medical costs of dealing with the victims, already skyrocketing beyond belief, will break the back of Western culture. We have reached the end of our age.

One advantage Christians had over their pagan contemporaries was that care of the sick, even in time of pestilence, was for them a recognized religious duty. When all normal services break down, quite elementary nursing will greatly reduce mortality. Simple provision of food and water, for instance, will allow persons who are temporarily too weak to cope for themselves to recover instead of perishing miserably. Moreover, those who survived with the help of such nursing were likely to feel gratitude and a warm sense of solidarity with those who had saved their lives. The effect of disastrous epidemic, therefore, was to strengthen Christian churches at a time when most other institutions were being discredited.

William H.McNeill, *Plagues and Peoples*
(Garden City, NY: Anchor Press/Doubleday,
1976), p. 121

SIX

GOSPEL ETHICS: HOLINESS AND LOVE

Mercy and truth have met together;
Righteousness and peace have kissed each other. (Psalm 85:10)

We are the true priesthood. Let us never forget that. But there are other priesthoods seeking domination, and if we continue to abdicate our high position of responsibility, God will allow false priests to triumph for a time. It would be easy to take the comfortable, seemingly safe route of non-resistance, of allowing the secularists to handle the situation. There's only one problem: we have the solutions, and they don't. We possess authoritative answers to the questions asked by one honest physician:

> If we act as empirical scientists, can we not see the implications of the data before us? If homosexuality, or even just male homosexuality is "Okay," then why the high prevalence of associated complications both in general and especially in regard to AIDS? *Might not these "complications" be "consequences"?* Might it not be that our society's approval of homosexuality is an error and that the unsubtle words of the Bible are frightfully correct?[1]

In 1979 there appeared one of the most significant Christian books ever published: *Whatever Happened to the Human Race?* Accompanied by a film series of the same name, it was primarily the work of two Christian leaders — Dr. Francis A. Schaeffer, the American missionary to Switzerland whose books had already defined the intellectual agenda for a generation of Christians, and Dr. C. Everett Koop, an outstanding pediatric surgeon from Philadelphia. *Whatever Happened* shook the slumbering evangelical Christian world into its senses with an aggressive message on the evils of abortion and infanticide. If there is a single book that is responsible for creating an army of Christian pro-life activists, it is that book. It positively rings with the affirmation of the Lordship of Jesus Christ over every area of life:

> When we accept Christ as Savior, we must also acknowledge and then act upon the fact that if He is our Savior, He is also our Lord in *all* of life. He is Lord not only in religious things and not just in cultural things such as art and music, but in our intellectual lives and in business and our attitude toward the devaluation of people's humanness in our culture. Acknowledging Christ's Lordship and placing ourselves under what is taught in the whole Bible includes thinking and acting as citizens in relation to our government and its laws. We must know what those laws are and act responsibly to help change them if they do not square with the Bible's concepts of justice and humanness. The Biblical answers have to be lived and not just thought.[2]

After Ronald Reagan became President of the United States, he appointed Dr. Koop to the office of Surgeon General, largely on the strength of his work as a foe of abortion and infanticide. It was one of the most crucial if symbolic positions a passionate and articulate evangelical Christian could be in, a national podium from which Koop could speak prophetically to his country. Installed just as the AIDS threat was bursting upon the American consciousness, Dr. Koop seemed to have been providentially placed by God to be a spokesman for righteousness. And few could doubt that he would acquit himself honorably at his post. Surely, if in the interests of health he could call for a "smoke-free society by the year 2000," he would have the courage, in the interests of health, to call for a "sexual perversion-free society" as well.

Obviously, such a stand would demand tremendous courage. Dr. Koop would be vilified in the press, he would become the object of scorn and ridicule, and would probably get fired from his job. But he would have spoken the truth. He would have made a stand. He would have drawn national attention to the root cause of a dangerous epidemic destroying the people he had sworn to protect. He would have created a national, public debate on the real issues about AIDS. He would have, perhaps just once, forced the American people to face the facts. Dr. Koop, a great man, would have gone out in a blaze of glory worthy of his Lord.

No one could doubt that Dr. Koop was courageous enough to meet the challenge. He had demonstrated courage throughout his entire career. And, with Dr. Schaeffer, he had issued an inspiring call to other Christians to stand for the truth no matter what the personal price might be:

> We must live under the Lordship of Christ in all the areas of life — at great cost, if need be. It is moving to think of the Christians in China, paying a great price for their loyalty to Christ, but that does not relieve each of us from being under the Lordship of Christ in regard to our own country.[3]

Strong words. Koop and his co-author knew that readers who took them seriously might be called upon to make great sacrifices for the sake of the truth. Faithfulness to Christ can mean losing one's job, livelihood, influence, and reputation. Still, these leaders agreed with the Apostle Paul, who declared: "But what things were gain to me, these I have counted loss for Christ. But indeed I also count all things loss for the excellence of the knowledge of Christ Jesus my Lord, for whom I have suffered the loss of all things, and count them as rubbish, that I may gain Christ" (Philippians 3:7, 8). Koop and Schaeffer clearly threw down the glove to all of us in terms of the all-or-nothing demands of loyalty to Jesus Christ. After brave language like this, American Christians could be certain that Surgeon General C. Everett Koop would stand boldly and firmly for God's law, regardless of the personal cost to himself:

> Who is on the cutting edge here? The doctor who pays the price of having certain hospitals closed to him because he will not perform abortions. The businessman who knows he is forfeiting advancement in his company because he will not go along with some inhuman practice of his company. The professor of sociology who is willing to lose his post because he will not teach sociology on the basis of determinism. The pastor who loses his church rather than follow the dictates of a liberal

theology or a "trashy Christianity." Or the pastor who preaches
the Bible, stressing that today's people are called to sacrificial
action, rather than keeping his congregation comfortable
while death, spiritual and physical, is built up year after year
for their children and grandchildren. Examples could be end-
lessly multiplied.[4]

In words which have as much relevance for issues surrounding AIDS and homosexuality as for abortion and infanticide, the
book ended with a stirring appeal for self-sacrifice in view of the
heritage we are creating for those who will come after us:

> Future generations will look back, and many will either scoff or
> believe in Christ on the basis of whether we Christians of today
> took a sacrificial stand in our various walks of life on these over-
> whelmingly important issues. If we do not take a stand here
> and now, we certainly cannot lay any claim to being the salt of
> the earth in our generation. We are neither preserving moral
> values and the dignity of the individual nor showing compas-
> sion for our fellow human beings.

> Will future generations look back and remember that—even if
> the twentieth century *did* end with a great surge of inhuman-
> ity—at least there was one group who stood consistently,
> whatever the price, for the value of the individual, thus pass-
> ing on some hope to future generations? Or are we Christians
> going to be merely swept along with the trends—our own
> moral values becoming increasingly befuddled, our own
> apathy reflecting the apathy of the world around us, our own
> inactivity sharing the inertia of the masses around us, our
> own leadership becoming soft?[5]

Clearly, Christians had a Champion, a Defender of the
Faith, sitting in the Surgeon General's chair. We waited for a
sterling affirmation of Christian values, a call to national repentance, a moral manifesto. And this is what we got, *ex
cathedra*:

> Unless it is possible to know with *absolute certainty* that neither
> you nor your sexual partner is carrying the virus of AIDS,
> you must use protective behavior. . . .

If you suspect that [your partner] has been exposed by previous heterosexual or homosexual behavior or use of intravenous drugs with shared needles and syringes, a rubber (condom) should always be used during (start to finish) sexual intercourse (vagina or rectum).[6]

From one perspective — that of, say, Planned Parenthood, or the National Gay Task Force, or the National Education Association — there is nothing wrong with these and other recommendations by the Surgeon General. Indeed, any one of those groups could have written it. That, sadly, is precisely what is wrong with the report. Instead of prophecy we got pap; we needed a Moses and ended up with a Milquetoast instead. It doesn't take much courage to pass out condoms. Any secularist can do as much. But Dr. Koop isn't just any secularist: he is an unusually intelligent and articulate Christian, one who had been brought to the Kingdom "for a time such as this."

America doesn't need rubbers; it needs ethics.

At best, Dr. Koop has done nothing more than to keep sexual immorality a bit safer than it might have been otherwise. There is no hint in the report that people should not engage in anal sex: it is treated as equivalent to vaginal intercourse. Dr. Koop does not suggest that homosexuality is wrong and harmful, but rather that people should practice it with greater ecological efficiency. A Christian Surgeon General has no business giving that sort of advice. The result can only be more fornication, more venereal disease, more unwanted pregnancies, more abortions, and, yes, more cases of AIDS. Dr. Koop has become little more than a "Trojan Horse" for the sexual revolution. By his refusal to speak out, by allowing his nation's "moral values to become increasingly befuddled," as he himself so eloquently put it in his book, he has betrayed his trust. And, because this priest has abdicated, people will die.

Author Gene Antonio says what Dr. Koop should have said: "It is time for people to realize that society stands on the brink of an imminent self-induced AIDS holocaust. Pecksniffian advisories on therapeutic techniques of perversion and promiscuity are a base deception. Saccharine platitudes about pansexual 'serial monogamy' (coupling with only one partner for weeks and months at a time) are intellectually dishonest. With two million or more persons already infected with the AIDS virus, a little promiscuity will go a long way toward spreading mass contagion.

"Only those who intransigently abide by Biblical standards of sexual morality will be able to guard themselves effectively against sexually transmitted AIDS virus infection. Avoidance of homosexual behavior, abstinence before marriage and fidelity afterwards are the only truly reliable means of safe sexual interaction."[7]

Dr. Koop might object that Ronald Reagan did not hire him to preach about ethics; after all, Dr. Koop is a government official, not a minister. Wrong, on both counts. First, President Reagan *did* hire him to preach about ethics. Koop was chosen specifically because of his ethical stand on abortion and infanticide. Moreover, it is the Surgeon General's job to warn and protect the American people against health hazards, and homosexuality is a health hazard, both to its practitioners and to all of us non-consenting adults and children who are placed in danger because of their activities.

Second, Dr. Koop, as a government official, *is* a minister of God. The Bible says so: "For there is no authority except from God, and the authorities that exist are appointed by God. . . . For he [the government official] is God's minister to you for good. . . . For because of this you also pay taxes, for they are God's ministers attending continually to this very thing" (Romans 13:1, 4, 6). Before Dr. Koop considers what President Reagan wants him to say, he must consider his prior obligation to God, the One who really appointed him. It is true that a clear ethical statement might cost Koop his job. But the price this nation will pay for his silence is far more expensive.

Why do Christians exist, anyway? Does that question ever bother you?

Dominion Through Service

It was just about one week before the Crucifixion. Jesus was making His way toward Jerusalem, where He would face His darkest period of conflict. Two of His disciples, the brothers James and John, approached Him with a request: "Grant us that we may sit, one on Your right hand and the other on Your left, in Your glory" (Mark 10:35-37). It would be easy to criticize this request, and we will in a moment; but first, we ought to give the disciples some credit: they did have faith, they did expect the coming of the Kingdom, even at a time when opposition to the King was increasing. This is commendable. But, as is the case so often with ourselves, their true faith was mixed with corruption and selfishness (cf. James 4:1-3). They were not aware of what they were really asking of Jesus. All they were thinking of was the glory of the Kingdom—not the necessary suffering beforehand. In fact, they were ignoring what Jesus had just told them a moment before: "Many who are first will be last, and the last first" (Mark 10:31).

To pray for glory is to pray for suffering. James and John were quite prepared, in their own minds, to "start at the top"; they wanted the prize before the contest was over. Of course, it's a good thing to be confident of victory. Confidence enables us to be courageous against opposition. But the confidence of the disciples made them forget that there was a battle at all. They had turned aside, losing sight of the very real dangers and temptations that lay ahead of them.

It's always easy to find people who want superiority and status; what's difficult is finding people who want to *work*. But the throne is given to the overcomer (Revelation 3:21); the Kingdom is for those who share in the sufferings of Christ (Acts 14:22; Colossians 1:24; 1 Peter 4:12-14). That is why Jesus said, in response to the disciples' request, "You do not know what you ask. Can you drink the cup that I drink, and be baptized with the baptism that I am baptized with?" (Mark 10:38). Immediately, as usual, the disciples misunderstood. "We can!" they exclaimed. In all likelihood, they were thinking that Christ would soon be anointed ("baptized") as King, and that they would share the cup of victory with Him at the inaugural celebration afterward. Self-confident and secure, presuming their own strength, they did not realize that when the actual moment of testing arrived they would all forsake Him. "Without Me," Jesus would soon admonish them, "you can do *nothing*" (John 15:5).

But in speaking of His "baptism" and His "cup," Jesus was referring to His own sufferings. To share these would mean for the disciples to share in martyrdom. In the ancient world, the cup symbolized one's destiny: to share a cup meant to share the same experience. The cup can signify happiness, as in the Twenty-third Psalm ("my cup runneth over"); it can symbolize a destiny of judgment, as when the Harlot Queen in the book of Revelation is forced to drink a cup of blood (Revelation 18:6); and, for Jesus, the cup speaks of His sacrifice, His passion and death: trembling in Gethsemane, He prayed, "O My Father, if it is possible, let this cup pass from Me; nevertheless, not as I will, but as You will" (Matthew 26:39).

It is no mere coincidence that when we see these words *Baptism* and *Cup* we are inevitably reminded of the Sacraments of the Church. That association was undoubtedly intended by both our Lord and the Gospel writers. The Sacraments, intimately involved with our sanctification in Christ, are also connected with suffering. Baptism calls us to self-denial, to crucifixion; we are baptized, says the Apostle Paul, into death (Romans 6:3). Baptism — a ritual death by drowning — is our once-for-all initiation into a life of cross-bearing. And that sacrificial life is carried on with a repeated memorial of death, of the broken body and shed blood of Him whose Name we bear. The eucharistic Cup is a continual, weekly reminder of Christ's sufferings, and of our communion with Him in them.

Suffering can be the lot of any Christian. One way or another, "all who desire to live godly in Christ Jesus will suffer persecution" (2 Timothy 3:12). "If they persecuted Me," Jesus said, "they will also persecute you" (John 15:20). The Apostle Paul told the church at Philippi, "To you it has been granted on behalf of Christ, not only to believe in Him, but also to suffer for His sake" (Philippians 1:29). In fact, the apostle regarded his own sufferings in the light of Christ's sacrificial offering: "I now rejoice in my sufferings for you, and *fill up in my flesh what is lacking in the afflictions of Christ*, for the sake of His body, which is the church" (Colossians 1:24). There is certainly a sense in which Christ's suffering for us is unique, a once-for-all vicarious sacrifice on behalf of sinners (Hebrews 10:12-14). But there is also a sense, the Apostle Paul admonishes us, in which Christ continues to suffer through the sufferings of those who are in communion with Him. Back when he had been Saul the Persecutor, he had been forced to acknowledge Christ's union with

His people in their tribulations. On the Damascus Road the risen Lord had confronted him in blazing glory: "I am Jesus, whom you are persecuting!" (Acts 9:5). "All our afflictions," said Puritan theologian John Owen, "are His in the first place, ours only by participation."[8] So our Lord went on to assure James and John that they would indeed suffer for His sake: "You will indeed drink the cup that I drink, and with the baptism I am baptized with you will be baptized; but to sit on My right hand and on My left is not Mine to give, but it is for those for whom it is prepared" (Mark 10:39, 40). At this, the other ten disciples became angry with James and John for requesting preferential treatment. The truth is, they were all thinking the same thing! Each of them desired a position of honor above the rest. Each of them envied the real or imagined benefits the others had received.

Gently, Jesus gathered His proud and foolish disciples around Him and corrected their selfish misunderstanding about the kind of "dominion" that would characterize His Kingdom. "You know that those who are considered rulers over the Gentiles lord it over them, and their great ones exercise authority over them. Yet it shall not be so among you; but whoever desires to become great among you shall be your servant. And whoever of you desires to be first shall be slave of all" (Mark 10:42-44). The Lord's point here—and this must be understood with absolute clarity—is not that His Kingdom works by different standards than those necessary for success in business and government. Jesus is not saying that Christians should be inept in sound principles of management. The issue is the difference between Christianity and heathenism. Jesus Christ forbids His followers to attempt to get ahead in life by pagan standards.

This goes all the way back to the sin in the Garden of Eden. Adam and Eve were created for dominion; they were commanded to rule over all creation under God (Genesis 1:26-28). Clearly, God fully intended them for greatness. He wanted them to have power and glory—on His terms. But they refused to submit to His lordship. Instead, they tried to seize His position for themselves. They were seduced by the temptation to "be like God, knowing [determining for themselves] good and evil" (Genesis 3:5). Ever since their terrible fall, which plunged the whole world into sin, their rebellious descendants have chosen the same false route to success: trying to be Gods. The ungodly method of dominion is to dominate, to throw our weight around, to tyrannize those under our authority, to crush the powerless under our heels. Pagans seek honors and awards, not so much for the sake of the awards as such, but in order to demonstrate superiority over others. The heathen concept of rule is oppression of the weak, terrorizing the defenseless.

"It shall not be so among you," Jesus says. Instead He commands us to get ahead God's way: not by saving our life but by losing it. "If anyone desires to come after Me, let him deny himself, take up his cross, and follow Me. For whoever desires to save his life will lose it, and whoever loses his life for My sake will find it" (Matthew 16:24, 25). How do Christians rule? *Christians rule by serving.* Dominion is not domination; far from it. Biblical dominion is *ministry* to the needs of others. "Whoever desires to become great among you shall be your servant. And whoever of you desires to be first shall be slave of all." In a sense, Jesus is telling us how to *truly* "look out for Number One." Our desire for dominion and rule — if it is really a desire for godly authority — will be demonstrated in our degree of service toward others. The true ruler, in our Lord's terms, is the one who puts himself most at the disposal of others. Our level of greatness is shown in our degree of submission and ministry.

The Bible is replete with examples of this: Joseph, whose uncomplaining spirit and habitual service made him ruler over the most powerful nation on earth; Moses, who became the mediator and deliverer of God's people; Daniel, who was raised to dominion through a lifetime of service, retaining his post through not only succeeding administrations but also succeeding empires. The supreme example, of course, is that of our Lord Himself, who came into His glory and dominion through service, through emptying Himself for others (Philippians 2:5-11). And this is the point that Jesus made in concluding His discussion with the disciples: "For even the Son of Man did not come to be served, but to serve, and to give His life a ransom for many" (Mark 10:45). To understand the force of this statement we must grasp what the term *Son of Man* meant to Jesus' followers. Literally, it means *Son of Adam*: a second

Adam. It might help to think of it as a movie and its sequel: First we have *Man*—a hit at the box office, perhaps, but a critical flop. Next comes *Son of Man*, a remake. That is exactly what went through the minds of first-century Israel when Jesus spoke of Himself (some eighty times in the Gospels) as the Son of Man. They were all familiar with the vision Daniel had of a new Adam, ascending to the dominion that God had promised our first parents in the beginning:

> I was watching in the night visions,
> And behold, One like the Son of Man
>   coming with the clouds of heaven!
> He came to the Ancient of Days,
> And they brought Him near before Him.
> Then to Him was given dominion and glory and a kingdom,
> That all peoples, nations and languages should serve Him.
> His dominion is an everlasting dominion,
> Which shall not pass away,
> And His kingdom the one
>   which shall not be destroyed. (Daniel 7:13, 14)

This passage, a prophecy of Christ's ascension to heaven, was well-known to the disciples. It was the definitive Old Testament text on the Son of Man. So when Jesus applied the title to Himself, all the disciples could think of was "dominion and glory and a kingdom"—and they were in on the ground floor of His administration! They would go from being poor laborers and country rubes to being the inner circle, the ruling elite of the Messianic Empire! All nations would be at the feet of the Messiah and His junta; the very prospect was thrilling, intoxicating. But then Jesus Himself reversed their expectations. Yes, He was the Son of Man, He said; but His rule was to be manifested in service, in ministering to the needy, in lifting up the weak, in binding wounds, in healing. The Son of Man didn't come to be waited on by admirers, but to wait on others. He did not come to acquire slaves, but to ransom people out of slavery.

A few days later, after they had arrived in Jerusalem, Jesus provided a magnificent demonstration of His teaching by washing His disciples' feet. "I have given you an example, that you should do as I have done to you. Most assuredly, I say to you, a servant is not greater than his master; nor is he who is sent greater than he who sent him" (John 13:15, 16). We cannot presume to have greater dignity or more extensive rights than our Lord and Master. If He humbled Himself to such an extent, we have no excuse for doing any less. His followers are supposed to enjoy dominion, rule, and authority. We are to be leaders. But our leadership must be exercised according to the pattern He set forth in His own life. We must rule as He did, by "washing the feet" of our brothers. We must rule by ministering the Spirit to the world around us. Genuine, Biblical dominion means serving, helping, making ourselves available to others, as our Lord gave Himself for us.

The Dilemma

There is an important character in Camus' novel *The Plague* who dramatically illustrates a problem with which many people wrestle. An old priest, Father Paneloux, seeks to come to terms with the agony, suffering, and death that surround him (of children especially). Theologically, he knows that all things ultimately come to pass because of God's will. Practically, the priest hates to see a child suffer. Yet, if the suffering is ordained of God, it must be *right*. If we deny this, he felt, we deny the sovereignty, the very Godhood, of God. The only way to honor God must be by a full acceptance of His will.

> He was saying that the total acceptance of which he had been speaking was not to be taken in the limited sense usually given to the words; he was not thinking of mere resignation or even of that harder virtue, humility. It involved humiliation, but a humiliation to which the person humiliated gave full assent. True, the agony of a child was humiliating to the heart and to the mind. But that was why we had to come to terms with it. And that, too, was why—and here Paneloux assured those present that it was not easy to say what he was about to say— since it was God's will, we, too, should will it. And thus only the Christian could face the problem squarely and, scorning subterfuge, pierce to the heart of the supreme issue, the essential choice. And his choice would be to believe everything, so as not to be forced into denying everything.[9]

A young deacon later summarizes Father Paneloux's position:

It's illogical for a priest to call in a doctor.[10]

After preaching his sermon the priest surrenders to the will of God so completely that without actually contracting the disease he himself dies of the plague.

The logic is completely understandable: God is good, and cannot will what is evil; God wills and ordains all things; therefore, all things are good. We cannot fight a plague, because God has ordained it; and we have the duty to love the plague as we love God, for it is one of His good works.

Before we analyze this, let us take it a step further. The plague that is the subject of the present book is AIDS, a disease that has arisen and spread specifically as a result of flagrant disobedience to the law of God. It is an obvious instance of divine punishment for sin. Logically, therefore, must we say that we cannot fight this plague, not only because it is the will of God, but also because its victims (by and large) are sinners who have brought it upon themselves? To put it another way: Is it wrong to try to help those under judgment?

The answer is an emphatic "No!"

The answer is no because the dilemma is a false dilemma. The dilemma is false, not because God is not sovereign (He is), not because AIDS is not divine judgment against sinners (it usually is), but because a logical syllogism is being exalted over the revelation of God's Word. In an ultimate sense, all suffering is because of disobedience: "through one man sin entered the world, and death through sin, and thus death spread to all men, because all sinned" (Romans 5:12). On that basis we could argue that we should never fight against death, never even seek to postpone it, because it comes as God's righteous judgment against all men for their sins. Obviously, such a conclusion would be ridiculous and wrong. It flies in the face of God as He has revealed Himself in the Gospel.

Imitating the Gospel

When in doubt about how to act, look at the Gospel. We all are sinners, deserving only the eternal wrath of God (John 3:36), yet He has had mercy on us. Since we have received freely, our Lord said, we are to give freely as well—a text in which Jesus specifically commands His disciples to destroy disease and death:

> Heal the sick, cleanse the lepers, raise the dead, cast out demons. Freely you have received, freely give. (Matthew 10:8)

Far from setting before us an insoluble dilemma, it is Christianity that has the only answer to the problem. The Christian approach to death and disease is utterly opposed to the pagan worldview. The Apostle Paul makes an astounding statement in 1 Corinthians 15, one completely foreign to paganism. He says:

> But now Christ is risen from the dead, and has become the first-fruits of those who have fallen asleep. For since by man came death, by Man also came the resurrection of the dead. For as in Adam all die, even so in Christ all shall be made alive. But each one in his own order: Christ the firstfruits, afterward those who are Christ's at His coming. Then comes the end, when He delivers the kingdom to God the Father, when He puts an end to all rule and all authority and power. For He must reign till He has put all enemies under His feet. The last enemy that will be destroyed is death. (1 Corinthians 15:20-26)

Pagan religion accepts death as natural, an unpleasant but necessary condition of human existence, and seeks to be reconciled to it. Pagan religion and secularism have this in common, that both seek to "help" people to die, to be reconciled to death: since this world is all there is, death and disease are natural and we must make the best of them. Christianity, however, stresses that what is important isn't "help" but *truth*; Christianity condemns paganism precisely because it helps—because it enables people to act as if death is acceptable. In total antithesis to all this, the Apostle Paul speaks of death not as an overpowering, invincible reality to which we should become reconciled and accustomed, but as an enemy to be destroyed. Christianity proclaims that death is the very farthest thing from being normal and natural. Death is abnormal and horrible.[11]

This is powerfully set forth in the story of Jesus' friend Lazarus, whom He raised from the dead. John's Gospel tells us that when Jesus saw Lazarus' sister Mary wailing with grief,

He *raged* in spirit and was troubled (John 11:33); a few moments later, when some of the Jews noticed His tears and expressed surprise that this Healer had been unable to prevent the death of His friend, we are told again that Jesus *raged* within Himself (John 11:38). Benjamin Warfield commented: "The spectacle of the distress of Mary and her companions enraged Jesus because it brought poignantly home to his consciousness the evil of death, its unnaturalness, its 'violent tyranny' as Calvin (on verse 38) phrases it. In Mary's grief, he contemplates—still to adopt Calvin's words (on verse 33)—'the general misery of the whole human race' and burns with rage against the oppressor of men. Inextinguishable fury seizes upon him; his whole being is discomposed and perturbed. . . . It is death that is the object of his wrath, and behind death him who has the power of death, and whom he has come into the world to destroy. Tears of sympathy may fill his eyes, but this is incidental. His soul is held by rage: and he advances to the tomb, in Calvin's words again, 'as a champion who prepares for conflict.' The raising of Lazarus thus becomes, not an isolated marvel, but—as indeed it is presented throughout the whole narrative (compare especially verses 24-26)—a decisive instance and open symbol of Jesus' conquest of death and hell."[12]

Jesus was *angry* at death, *enraged* at the abnormality of the world, a world that is not the way it was created to be. God had fashioned the world as the stage on which He would display Life in its fullness. That is the terrible reality of sin. Sin is the destroyer of everything good, of God's very image; and Jesus stands at the tomb of Lazarus overcome with the most profound realization that in the deepest sense this death, every death, is *wrong*.

The next point is absolutely crucial. The late Francis Schaeffer observed it several times throughout his teaching: "The Christian never faces the dilemma posed in Camus' book *La Peste*. It simply is not true that he either has to side with the doctor against God by fighting the plague, or join with the priest on God's side and thus be much less than human by not fighting the plague. If this were an *either/or* choice in life, it would indeed be terrible. But the Christian is not confined to such a choice. . . . Jesus, standing in front of the tomb of

Lazarus, was *angry* at death and at the abnormality of the world—the destruction and distress caused by sin. In Camus' words, Christ hated the plague. He claimed to be God, and *He could hate the plague without hating Himself as God.*"[13]

Do you understand what this means? This is absolutely powerful for Christian ethics! Jesus Christ is the sovereign Lord of all, the almighty Word of God through whom all things came into being. And He could be angry. He was able to fight against the evil in the world. He came to transform the world, to reverse the disorder caused by sin. The Good News of the Gospel contains this message, that death has been conquered in principle at Christ's resurrection, and will be defeated in finality at His Second Coming. Death is not the victor; Jesus Christ is the Victor.

Can we fight against AIDS, even if we understand it as God's judgment against sinners? Can we have mercy and compassion on those who suffer under the righteous judgment of God? Perhaps it comes down to this question: Does God love homosexuals?

Our answer to that question is absolutely critical for our view, not only of homosexuals and AIDS, but of God and salvation. It is a crucial question for our view of the basis on which *we* have been saved. Does God save us on the condition that we are not guilty, or at least on the condition that we have not committed really gross sin? No: God saves sinners; He justifies the ungodly; He reconciles His bitterest enemies to Himself.

Ponder a mystery: the Lord Jesus Christ, in one of the final discourses of His earthly ministry, pronounced an awful, horrifying judgment against first-century Israel for her apostasy and rejection of Him. *At the same time*, He was able to weep over her: "O Jerusalem, Jerusalem, the one who kills the prophets and stones those who are sent to her! How often I wanted to gather your children together, as a hen gathers her chicks under her wings, but you were not willing!"(Matthew 23:37).

The Christian Response

We must begin to think and act redemptively, living every moment in terms of the Gospel ethic. This means being able to carry around more than one thought in our heads at the same time. I have seen two unbiblical reactions to the AIDS crisis among Christians. The first wrong reaction is to say that these people are under judgment and deserve what they get; to assist them, to have compassion on them, is to fight against God. The major flaw in this theory is that it directly contradicts the ministry of Christ and the apostles. The objection of the Pharisees against Christ was also a marvelous summary of the Gospel ethic: *This man receives sinners and eats with them!* (Luke 15:2). "Why do You eat and drink with tax collectors and sinners?" they demanded (Luke 5:30). Tax collectors were especially despised by all honest Israelites, because they were collaborators with the hated, oppressive Roman government, mercenaries whose income was often based on fraud and deception; in fact, tax collectors as a class were excommunicated from the temple and the synagogues (cf. Matthew 18:17). Yet our holy Lord associated with them, welcoming them to Himself and sharing meals with them. Jesus answered the Pharisees' objection, and ours, with these familiar words:

> Those who are well do not need a physician, but those who are sick. I have not come to call the righteous, but sinners, to repentance. (Luke 5:31, 32)

Like a doctor confronted with a loathsome disease that frightens and nauseates others, Jesus ministered to people's needs. He had to get close to the sick in order to heal them. One component of true religion, James the Just reminds us, consists in doing mercy (James 1:26, 27). If we are to be conformed to the image of Christ, we must bring His mercy to the world.

James mentions a second component of true religion, however, one which answers the second erroneous response of many Christians to the AIDS crisis.

> Pure and undefiled religion before God and the Father is this: to visit orphans and widows in their trouble, *and to keep oneself unspotted from the world.* (James 1:27)

This means that true religion, as well as showing compassion, must demonstrate a firm commitment to Biblical standards. We must not allow ourselves to capitulate to pagan ways of thinking and acting. This speaks directly to the second error into which well-meaning Christians can fall. Unlike the first group, who would ignore the plight of homosexual AIDS sufferers, the second group would go to any lengths to avoid being seen as "pharisaical." I have heard it again and again: "We just want to minister to their needs; we aren't supposed to judge." This is used as an excuse not to share with these needy people the Biblical message of the holiness of God and the reality of His judgment. Nothing could be clearer than that AIDS has fallen upon our world as a direct result of disobedience to the law of God. We cannot communicate the Gospel to sinners if we withhold from them the fact that they are sinners. And that would be the greatest act of hatred and injustice that we could ever do.

Let's be honest: the real reason why we don't want to "judge" is that we are afraid. "There is no fear in love; but perfect love casts out fear" (1 John 4:18). It is time to follow our Lord in His ministry of compassionate confrontation, of holiness and healing.

> We must realize that love alone is not the end of the matter. It rests upon the character of God, and God is the God who is holy and the God who is love. We must not choose between love and holiness, for to forget either is equally vicious. But we do have to realize that the talk of love which so surrounds us today is often a love without tracks. Therefore, when we begin to deal in practice with God's holiness, we must always remember that simultaneously there must be the reality of His love. And when we begin to deal in practice with God's love, we must remember that simultaneously there must be the reality of His holiness. It is not that we do one and then the other, like keeping a ball in the air with two Ping-Pong paddles. Both God's holiness and His love must be exhibited simultaneously, or we have fallen off one cliff or the other.[14]

The life and work of the Church is to be redemptive, a ministering to the world of the once-for-all redemption wrought by the Lord Jesus Christ. We are called to do this after His example, showing forth both the love and the holiness of God. There is no philosophical dilemma in this. That is not to say that we can satisfactorily explain how the two pieces fit together; we can no more comprehend that answer than we can comprehend how the one God exists eternally as three distinct Persons who are equal in power and glory, or how the all-glorious God can be glorified by His creatures (how can you add water to a full bucket?), or how the eternal and unchangeable God can respond in history to our prayers, or how God's sovereign election of the redeemed harmonizes with His genuine, sincere, free offer of salvation to all men. The glorious thing is that we do not have to understand these things in a comprehensive sense. They are *true*: All we have to do is believe and obey them.

We do not have to be God. We don't have to worry about how all these things fit together. It is enough to be assured that they do fit together, perfectly, in His infinite understanding (Psalm 147:5; Isaiah 55:8, 9). We can leave the philosophical problems with Him, because His knowledge, unlike ours, is comprehensive and absolute. There will always be a contradiction in our knowledge about ultimate questions, because we are finite. We can be content to be creatures. The problems are resolved in God, and that is sufficient.

Deuteronomy 29:29 is perhaps the most liberating verse in the whole Bible in this regard:

> The secret things belong to the LORD our God, but those things which are revealed belong to us and to our children forever, that we may do all the words of this law.

God Loves Homosexuals

Can this really work? Is it possible for Christians to demonstrate observable love for people and confront them with the truth of God's holiness?

In April 1978 Mr. Kevin Walker applied for the position of organist at the First Orthodox Presbyterian Church of San Francisco. Walker gave a credible testimony of faith in Christ, and he was hired (although he was not required to become a member of the church, which the leaders later realized was a mistake). After a few months Walker informed Pastor Charles McIlhenny that he was a practicing homosexual. The church fired him.

A week later a lawyer from the Gay Rights Advocates called the Reverend McIlhenny and told him that the church had better retain a lawyer of its own. Walker was going to sue on the basis of San Francisco's Gay Rights Ordinance prohibiting discrimination against homosexuals. The ordinance had been passed a month before Walker was hired. In June 1979 the church was served with a summons, which contained formal complaints against Pastor McIlhenny, against the congregation, and against the Northern California Presbytery of the Orthodox Presbyterian Church.

McIlhenny decided to fight the suit on First Amendment grounds, and on the advice of theologian R. J. Rushdoony obtained the services of the respected Christian defense lawyer John Whitehead. Some members of the congregation as well as some of McIlhenny's fellow presbyters opposed him at first, frightened at the prospect of a court battle, but McIlhenny would not be budged on his convictions: the church and the presbytery eventually agreed to hire Whitehead to defend them too. The case went to court for summary judgment in March of 1980, and the judge ruled in the church's favor. Walker appealed, but dropped the suit in July. The church then filed for recovery of their costs (which had amounted to $100,000), and eventually got $700 back. Final disposition of the case came in December 1980. Since then the church has withstood several attacks of vandals and one attempt to burn the church and the Reverend McIlhenny's home. The First Orthodox Presbyterian Church of San Francisco has suffered greatly for their Biblical stand. It is a small church, not at all powerful politically. Members have been placed in physical danger and exposed to public ridicule. In addition, this church subscribes to a rigorous theological creed which, it may be argued, they interpret even more strictly than do most other churches in what is widely considered a rather strait-laced and puritanical denomination. They would perhaps be able to witness of Biblical law and God's righteousness, one would think; but would they be inclined to show love for homosexuals as well?

"God loves homosexuals," says the Reverend McIlhenny flatly, "and so do we." His church has taken the lead in their area (no other churches have responded to their appeals to join them) in seeking to minister the Gospel to the homosexual community. In particular, they have organized food drives throughout their neighborhood to provide dried and canned goods to the San Francisco AIDS Foundation (one popular program is a "scavenger hunt" in which the young people find enumerated items for the food box). Church members, including the kids, then take the food to the AIDS Foundation and visit the patients. Often, the children will tape Bible verses about the Gospel and God's standards onto the boxes: John 3:16, Romans 10:9, 10, and so on; one child even came up with this one:

> And the LORD God said, "It is not good that man should be alone; I will make him a helper comparable to him.". . . Then the rib which the LORD God had taken from man He made into a woman, and He brought her to the man. (Genesis 2:18, 22)

Chuck and Donna McIlhenny have invited AIDS patients into their home. Church members have continued to carry on friendly but forthright conversations with homosexuals, seeking to demonstrate God's love and holiness at the same time. It is not easy. Mistakes are made, in one direction or another. But this church has discovered that it is possible to set before the world a substantial witness to the truth of Scripture—not just part of the truth, but all of it. The people have made a hard ethical stand, one that can easily be misunderstood by opponents on both side of the fence. They have taken their position, based neither on "homophobia" nor on standardless, contentless "love," but on the character of God and the redemptive work of Jesus Christ: a Gospel Ethic.

"The Christian has no other option but to say, 'I love you for Christ's sake,'" Donna told me. "A fatalistic concept of God's love is wrong. It leads to a dual gospel, in which God's love in Christ is not really offered to sinners. But the pragmatic concept of love—'love for love's sake'—is wrong too. In the end, love for love's sake brings only death and destruction. It cannot provide a solution because it tries to deny the existence of the problem. Love for Christ's sake is based on the person and work of Christ. That makes it an impenetrable love, not based on circumstances. It is a love that tells the truth with compassion. Love for Christ's sake brings life."

It was indeed a lamentable thing to hear the miserable lamentations of poor dying creatures calling out for ministers to comfort them and pray with them, to counsel them and to direct them, calling out to God for pardon and mercy, and confessing aloud their past sins. It would make the stoutest heart bleed to hear how many warnings were then given by dying penitents to others not to put off and delay their repentance to the day of distress; that such a time of calamity as this was no time for repentance, was no time to call upon God.

Daniel Defoe, *A Journal of the Plague Year*, (London: J. M. Dent & Sons Ltd., 1966), pp. 117f.

SEVEN

IS CHANGE POSSIBLE?

And do not be conformed to this world, but be transformed by the renewing of your mind, so that you may prove what is that good and acceptable and perfect will of God. (Romans 12:2)

Gospel Ethics do not end with evangelism and conversion. The Great Commission commands discipleship as well. Converted homosexuals desperately need to be fully incorporated into the life of the Church. And this means counseling—particularly, a personal, pastoral ministry of counseling—what used to be called the "cure of souls." In one sense, this is the valid ministry of the whole body, not just the leaders (Romans 15:14). But it is *especially* the duty of the leaders. Any leader who refuses to engage in it is not worth his stripes. The Apostle Paul characterized his own ministry as one of "warning every man and teaching every man in all wisdom, that we may present every man perfect in Christ Jesus" (Colossians 1:28). As he was about to leave Ephesus after an extended ministry there, he reminded the elders that "for three years I did not cease to warn everyone night and day with tears" (Acts 20:31; see also v. 20).

The Reformer John Calvin held that pastoral negligence of counseling is "inexcusable":

For Christ hath not appointed pastors upon this condition, that they may only teach the Church in general in the open pulpit; but that they may take charge of every particular sheep, that they may bring back to the sheepfold those which wander and go astray, that they may strengthen those which are discouraged and weak, that they may cure the sick, that they may lift up and set on foot the feeble (Ezekiel 34:4), for common doctrine will oftentimes grow cold, unless it be helped with private admonitions.[1]

Where to Start

How should we counsel the homosexual? The following is necessarily nothing more than a brief outline. It must be supplemented by more detailed studies (some of which I have included in the endnotes). But it is of crucial importance to understand at the outset that counseling a homosexual is no different, *in principle*, than counseling anyone else. The reason for this is simple: *homosexuality is a sin*, and must be dealt with as a sin.

To many, that will seem to be a cruel, insensitive attitude, a "homophobic" response of condemnation rather than concern. But the truth is that it is the beginning of true freedom and joy for the homosexual. For if homosexuality were either an inescapable human condition (like height and skin color) or an incurable disease, there would be no hope. The homosexual would be locked into his lusts forever, with no possibility of escape. Once we see clearly that homosexuality is a sin, we can also see the way of deliverance.[2]

That homosexuality is a sin means that it is *only* a sin — nothing more. It is not some mystical force within the person, some genetic or psychological programming that cannot be overcome. It is a transgression of God's law, a form of self-love that expresses itself in a particularly heinous attack on God's image. Like every sin, it is not ontological (having to do with a person's *being* as such); it is ethical. It is not rooted in the essential nature of humanity as God created us; it is rooted in the fall of man in the Garden of Eden, when man became alienated from God, from himself, from his society, from the world around him.

Jay Adams properly observes: "One is not a homosexual constitutionally any more than one is an adulterer constitutionally. Homosexuality is not considered [in the Bible] to be a condition, but an act. It is viewed as a sinful practice which can become a way of life. The homosexual act, like the act of adultery, is the reason for calling one a homosexual. (Of course, one may commit homosexual acts of the heart, just as one may commit adultery in his heart. He may lust after a man in his heart as another may lust after a woman.) But precisely because homosexuality, like adultery, is learned behavior into which men with sinful natures are prone to wander, homosexuality can be forgiven in Christ, and the pattern can be abandoned and in its place proper patterns can be reestablished by the Holy Spirit. Some homosexuals have lost hope because of the reluctance of Christian counselors to represent homosexuality as a sin."[3]

The Cure: A New Identity

The liberating fact is this: *Jesus died for sins.* There is a cure for homosexuality, as there is a cure for every other sinful practice. The cure for homosexuality is the Gospel of Jesus Christ. The Apostle Paul had a profound appreciation for this. Notice how he juxtaposes the most severe condemnation of homosexuality (along with other sins) with a recognition of its solution, and a full acceptance of his brothers in Christ who had been delivered from it:

> Do you not know that the unrighteous will not inherit the kingdom of God? Do not be deceived. Neither fornicators, nor idolaters, nor adulterers, nor homosexuals, nor sodomites, nor thieves, nor covetous, nor drunkards, nor revilers, nor extortioners will inherit the kingdom of God. And such were some of you. But you were washed, but you were sanctified, but you were justified in the name of the Lord Jesus and by the Spirit of our God. (1 Corinthians 6:9-11)

The Apostle Paul tells the Christians in Corinth three things that have given them a new identity in Christ:

1. You were washed. The Christian's baptism has created a definitive break with the past. The Apostle Paul observes elsewhere that the Israelites were "baptized into Moses" in the crossing of the Red Sea (1 Corinthians 10:2). As they stood on the shore looking back at the raging waters surge and foam over the bodies of the Egyptian army, they knew there was no going back: from now on, they were "baptized into Moses," identified with him as his people. Their bondage had been irrevocably broken off. That is the way our baptismal washing is viewed in Scripture: it places us into union with Christ, identifying us with him. There is no turning back.

> Or do you not know that as many of us as were baptized into Christ Jesus were baptized into His death? Therefore we were buried with Him through baptism into death, that just as

Christ was raised from the dead by the glory of the Father, even so we also should walk in newness of life. (Romans 6:3, 4)

2. You were sanctified. The term *sanctification* is often used in theology to speak of the Christian's growth in grace, his gradual, increasing conformity to the image of Christ. The *Westminster Shorter Catechism* says: "Sanctification is the work of God's free grace, whereby we are renewed in the whole man after the image of God, and are enabled more and more to die unto sin, and live unto righteousness." This is certainly true, and the Bible teaches it clearly. But the Bible does not generally use the term itself in this sense. Rather, sanctification is spoken of in a more *definitive*, once-for-all sense: from the moment of baptism, the Christian is sanctified—literally, "constituted a saint."[4] He is consecrated to God's exclusive service, and is called henceforth to consider himself "dead indeed to sin, but alive to God in Christ Jesus our Lord" (Romans 6:11).

> Therefore do not let sin reign in your mortal body, that you should obey its lusts. And do not present your members as instruments of unrighteousness to sin, but present yourselves to God as being alive from the dead, and your members as instruments of righteousness to God. For sin shall not have dominion over you, for you are not under law but under grace. (Romans 6:12-14)

Note what the Apostle Paul provides as a motive for refusing to surrender to lust. We do not yield our physical members to God as "instruments of righteousness" in order to *become* something, but because we already *are* that something: We have already been consecrated to God! We obey, not in order to receive approval from the law, for we are not "under law" and its condemnation; rather, we have been placed "under grace" as our means of justification. John Murray explains the tremendous force of that statement: "It is necessary to state what law *can* do and what it *cannot* do, and it is in the light of what it cannot do that the meaning of 'under grace' will become apparent. (1) Law commands and demands. (2) Law pronounces approval and blessing upon conformity to its demands (cf. Romans 7:10; Galatians 3:12). (3) Law pronounces condemnation upon every infraction of its demands (cf. Galatians 3:10). (4) Law exposes and convicts of sin (cf. Romans 7:7, 14; Hebrews 4:12). (5) Law excites and incites sin to more aggravated transgression (cf. Romans 7:8, 9, 11, 13). What law *cannot* do is implicit in these limits of its potency. (1) Law can do nothing to justify the person who has violated it. (2) Law can do nothing to relieve the bondage of sin; it accentuates and confirms that bondage.

"It is this last feature of the impotency of the law that is particularly in view. . . . The person who is 'under law,' upon whom only law has been brought to bear, whose life is being determined by the resources of law, is the bond-servant of sin. Hence to be 'under law' is to be the bondservant of sin. It is in this light that 'under grace' becomes significant; the word 'grace' sums up everything that, by way of contrast with law, is embraced in the provisions of redemption. Believers have come *under* all the resources of redeeming and renewing grace which find their epitome in the death and resurrection of Christ."[5]

The logic of the Apostle Paul's position is this: (1) the believer is no longer under that which cannot relieve the bondage of sin, i.e. *law*; (2) the believer *is* under that which *does* deliver from the bondage of sin, i.e. *grace*; (3) therefore, it follows that the believer cannot be dominated by sin. God's sanctifying, consecrating grace guarantees the Christian's life of holiness. Freed from his slavery to sin, he is now enslaved to righteousness (Romans 6:17, 18).

3. You were justified. Again the Apostle Paul emphasizes the Christian's objective standing as the ground of his subjective ethical action. God's justification of the sinner is a judicial act in which He declares the believer to be righteous, solely on account of the righteousness of Christ worked out on his behalf.

Here is the problem that the Biblical teaching of justification addresses: God's standard for acceptance with Him is total, absolute righteousness. Anyone who has a record of having lived a perfect, sinless life will be declared righteous; anyone who has broken even a single commandment will be condemned. "Cursed is everyone who does not continue in all things which are written in the book of the law, to do them" (Galatians 3:10). "For whoever shall keep the whole law, and yet stumble in one point, he is guilty of all" (James 2:10). The problem? "All have sinned and fall short of the glory of God" (Romans 3:23).

How can a just and holy God *justify* — declare righteous — those who have broken His law? If you are a thief, a murderer, an adulterer, a homosexual, how can He possibly declare (without lying and being unjust Himself) that you have met His standard perfectly and are worthy of entering His presence? How can God be both just *and* the justifier of the ungodly? Some will answer, "Because I repented for my sins and trusted in Christ." That is all well and good, but it doesn't solve the problem. The fact that you change your ways (even assuming that you could now live a sinless life, which you can't) doesn't erase the crimes you have committed. Those have to be paid for; and even that is not enough. For the standard of acceptance with God is not simply that your sins are paid for, but that you actually have a record of living a perfectly righteous life. Without that, you will never see God. Do you begin to understand the problem? You are unjustifiable!

This is why the Gospel is such good news. The Son of God became man in order to live out the righteous life we failed to live. He created a record of a perfect life. Then He died on the cross, paying for the sins we committed. The record of our evil works was legally charged to His account; officially, before God's court, He became guilty of everything we had done against God's law. When we believe in Him, God does not pardon us on account of our faith, as if our faith makes up for what we had done wrong. Our faith is an *instrument*, not a *cause*, of our justification. Faith is saying to God, "I want Christ's righteous record charged to my account. He took the blame for what I did wrong; I want to get the credit for what *He* did *right*!" And when God answers that prayer — when He legally imputes to us the righteousness of Christ — *that* is justification.

The judicial substitution of Christ for us solves the problem I mentioned a moment ago. This is how God can "be *just* and the *justifier* of the one who has faith in Jesus" (Romans 3:26): "For He made Him who knew no sin to be sin on our behalf, that we might become the righteousness of God in Him" (2 Corinthians 5:21). This is why the Bible says that "God imputes righteousness apart from works" (Romans 4:5). In a sense, we *are* justified by works—*Christ's* works, not ours. We are declared righteous on account of what Jesus did in His righteous life and atoning death, plus nothing.

> But God demonstrates His love toward us, in that while we were still sinners, Christ died for us. Much more then, having been justified by His blood, we shall be saved from wrath through Him. For if when we were enemies we were reconciled to God through the death of His Son, much more, having been reconciled, we shall be saved by His life. And not only that, but we also rejoice in God through our Lord Jesus Christ, through whom we have now received the reconciliation. (Romans 5:8-11)

We rejoice! Once a person begins to grasp the magnitude of what God has accomplished for him through Christ, the psychological release is boundless. One young man who had struggled with homosexuality and guilt because of repeated failure describes how a new understanding of justification radically changed his life and gave him a fresh perspective on the person of Christ:

> He was no longer merely my example whose victory I was to imitate. He was now *my* Victor, whose victory I could boast about and claim as my own. He was now no longer my *means* to righteousness; He *was* my righteousness. Before, I saw Him as the justification for all my past sins. Now I saw Him as my justification for past, present, and future sins. Before, I saw Him as the author of my salvation and the Holy Spirit as the Finisher. Now I saw Jesus as both the Author and Finisher, the Alpha and the Omega. He was no longer the *means* to the death of self. He *was* my death of self. And He was now no longer my *means* to the resurrection life, He *was* the resurrection life. Before, I saw Him dying for my sins; now I saw Him as dying for my sinful nature. Before, I saw salvation as dependent on the strength of my faith in Jesus; now, I saw it dependent on the strength of Jesus, in whom I placed faith. . . .

The book of Romans showed me that the Gospel provided me with a righteousness from God—the life of Christ (see chapter 3:21). I needed to know so desperately how to be righteous be-

fore God, and I found it written in Romans 4:3 that all of
Christ's goodness was charged to my account. I was treated as
righteous, even when I was wicked, as long as I clung to Christ
(see chapter 4:5). I needed to know that He wasn't displeased
with me anymore, and I found that Christ was my propitiation
(see chapter 3:25). He was my peace before God, a peace produced not by the depth of my surrender, which faltered so
much through homosexual desire, but a peace created by His
sacrifice that reconciled me while I was still an enemy (see
chapter 5:1, 10). I needed to know that my sinful nature, with
all its homosexual condition, would not be charged against me,
and I read it in Romans that my sinful body was reckoned as
dead in His so that I need never feel condemned by the law (see
chaps. 6:3, 6, 11; 7:4; 2 Corinthians 5:14). . . .

I know that's an idea that frightens some people, particularly
perfectionists, because they think it implies a person can do
what he wants. But it's actually the very opposite of that. By
faith we accept that God looks upon us as if our sinful nature
had already died, and we say to God, "You mean you're not
charging all my feelings and urges against me?" "No," says
God, "I'm setting you free from the guilt and the fear of them."
And you respond, "Well, God, that gives me freedom to get up
and try again with dignity and to believe I'm accepted. Now, I
feel I can walk more willingly with You in the right way."[6]

Helping Homosexuals Change

"It's impossible for a homosexual to change!" Is that oft-
repeated statement true? Not according to the Apostle Paul:
"Such *were* some of you. . . ." Many homosexuals throughout
history have found that there is hope.

A friend of mine who was struggling with this issue had
despaired of the possibility of change. He felt that his desires toward men could not be overcome. Not wanting to sin against
God, he had resigned himself to a celibate life, on the assumption that God must have given him the "gift" of celibacy
(1 Corinthians 7:7). Then he went to a Biblical counselor, who
gave him the shock of his life: "You're wrong, Jim. You obviously haven't been given such a gift. Otherwise you wouldn't be
tormented with sexual desires! Paul goes on in that same passage
to say, 'It is better to marry than to burn with passion'! God's will

for your life is not for you to be a frustrated Christian homosexual. He commands you to *change*. You, of all people, should realize that God has given you the gift of *marriage!*"

That stopped Jim dead in his tracks. The very thing that he had supposed disqualified him for marriage was the strongest evidence that he *should* get married! He was so shocked that he began to giggle and couldn't stop. Possessed with a new sense of freedom and joy, he laughed all the way home in the car. Within months he met and then married a wonderful and sensitive woman — the *real* gift God had in store for him. And, a year later, God gave Jim another gift, something he never in his wildest dreams imagined he'd see: a child.

This is not to suggest that change is easy. Far from it: genuine, radical, long term change is not easy at all. It requires conscious, determined discipline, without letting up. But the point is that it is possible. It can be done. At its root, homosexuality is like any other habitual sin against God; and, like any other sin, it can be rooted out and replaced.

Molded into Christ's Image

In his second letter to Timothy, the Apostle Paul outlines four basic steps in the Biblical program of change, of transfiguration into the image of Christ:

> All Scripture is God-breathed and is useful for teaching, rebuking, correcting and training in righteousness, so that the man of God may be thoroughly equipped for every good work. (2 Timothy 3:16, 17, NIV)

Note that it is Scripture that is the counselor's essential resource. God made us; He comprehensively understands us and our problems; and His Word — the Manufacturer's "instruction manual" for proper operations — gives us the answers to every problem we face. The late Cornelius Van Til said it: "The Bible is the final authority on everything of which it speaks; *and it speaks of everything.*"[7]

Biblical revelation makes a man *complete*, says the Apostle Paul; it *thoroughly equips* him for *every* good work. I am not, of course, defending the screaming, foam-spitting Bible-thumper who ignores Biblical language, context, and proper application. But the fact is that the Bible remains *the* infallible resource for the Christian counselor. "The entrance of Your words gives light," confessed the psalmist (Psalm 119:130). Isaiah exhorted his people to acknowledge the supreme authority of inspired Scripture over all supposed experts and authorities: "To the law and to the testimony! If they do not speak according to this word, it is because there is no light in them" (Isaiah 8:20) — literally, the Hebrew text reads *they have no dawn*: there is not even a glimmer of light in those who contradict the revealed, God-breathed, written Word of God.

> For the LORD gives wisdom;
> From His mouth come knowledge and understanding;
> He stores up sound wisdom for the upright;
> He is a shield to those who walk uprightly;
> He guards the paths of justice,
> And preserves the way of His saints.
> Then you will understand righteousness and justice,
> Equity and every good path. (Proverbs 2:6-9)

Let's consider, then, the four steps the Apostle Paul sets forth in 2 Timothy 3:16 as the essential factors in the Biblical process of change.[8]

First, he lists *Teaching*. Counseling necessarily, inescapably involves teaching. At every moment, one way or another, we are communicating doctrine to those whom we seek to help. And if we really are to help them, that doctrine must be Biblical. We must teach the law, God's righteous requirements for every area of life. With regard to the issue of homosexuality in particular, we must teach God's standards for marriage and sexuality. And here it must be acknowledged that, notwithstanding a virtual explosion of Christian books, tapes, and films on the subject, the Church has dropped the ball. Of course, there are those non-evangelical churches which have capitulated entirely to the sexual revolution. For more than a decade they have taught that premarital sex, adultery, divorce, and homosexuality are acceptable lifestyles. To a great extent, AIDS is the harvest of the crops they planted. But even many proudly evangelical, "Bible-believing" churches have failed.

I recently attended a closing service for a Vacation Bible School program, which attracted many unchurched parents. Here was a golden opportunity to present a living, relevant, vibrant Christianity to many who would seldom otherwise be reached by the Gospel. The evening's "entertainment" was provided by a husband-and-wife duet. Technically, they were highly accomplished performers who put on a good show. But the songs they sang, without exception, were syrupy, weepy little ditties about what one theologian has termed "pious gush." Those scant notes of praise that entered the music had only to do with God's helping us hurdle one emotional breakdown after another. The wife had nothing resembling the capable, competent "Proverbs 31 woman" about her; the man's voice continually cracked and broke (on cue) as he bleated about his inner struggles. There was nothing about the objective work of the Son of God; nothing about the power of God's grace to overcome sin; nothing about the strength of righteousness. To top it all off, the parson got up and delivered a wimpy little sermonette on the "sweetness" of Christianity. I looked around at the men in the audience. Here were carpenters, contractors, businessmen, engineers, mechanics, doctors — men who were accomplished in their fields; what was in this for them? What possible interest could this brand of "loser religion" hold for them? A vague *let-me-out-of-here* look was evident on their faces. The church's message had been all too clear: Become a Christian, lose your masculinity. Church is *Mister Roger's Neighborhood* with Bible verses. Only Dagwood Bumsteads need apply.

The story of how the American Church lost its muscle and became feminized has been documented, as I noted earlier, in Ann Douglas's superb book *The Feminization of American Culture*.[9] Her work is important for an understanding of the decline of Biblical masculinity in our society. How do we regain it? An excellent beginning would be for every pastor and Christian leader to read, and teach through, Weldon Hardenbrook's *Missing from Action: Vanishing Manhood in America*.[10] The Biblical study in his chapter "A Model for Manhood" alone would make a good ten-week course for a men's breakfast or Sunday School class.

Another point that should be stressed under the subject of teaching is that men should be involved in theological thought in general, not only in studying the specific subject of manhood. One important way to develop a Biblically sound manhood is to teach a strong theology from the pulpit. Too often our sermons have failed to attract and hold men's attention because there is simply nothing to them. If our services are merely larger versions of "Junior Church," where can adults go to worship? Why would a real grownup want to be babysat?

Christianity was not always considered the domain of wimps. There was a time, even in American history, when, as Hardenbrook observes, "theology was the most popularly discussed topic in the marketplace . . . ; it was even more popular than politics." He quotes Peter Stearns: "Patriarchal Christianity was of course a man's religion. Men were its principal priests. Men were not only the leading but the most numerous church members in societies such as seventeenth-century New England."[11] Ann Douglas states that "until roughly 1820, this theological tradition [Calvinism] was a chief, perhaps the chief, vehicle of intellectual and cultural activity in American life."[12] And Calvinism made rigorous intellectual demands upon its adherents, as historian Perry Miller pointed out in his study of Puritanism:

> A Puritan preacher never surrenders to feeling; he does not celebrate the glories of religion in sustained paeans or bring home its terrors by shouting, but argues his way step by step, inexorably disposing of point after point, quoting Biblical verses, citing authorities, watching for fallacies in logic, drawing upon the sciences for analogies, utilizing any information that seems pertinent. He proceeds thus not only in controversies with scholars, but also in composing sermons for the populace. As far as possible he simplifies his explanations, avoids abstruse issues, demands no more of his auditors than he thinks necessary; even so, he demands a degree of close attention that would seem staggering to modern audiences and is not to be paralleled in modern churches. He does not hesitate to put his congregation through the most difficult dialectical paces and take them over lofty metaphysical hurdles.[13]

The clergy were so far successful that by the time of the [English] Civil Wars the mass of those who had come under Puritan influences were generally familiar with a marvelously large body of thought. The ability of Cromwell's soldiers to debate intricate theological issues around their campfires was a wonder to all beholders; so in later times the proficiency of New England farm hands in threading the mazes of free will, fore-ordination, and fate around the kitchen fire was a never-ending source of admiration to visitors. The evidence would seem to show that whenever a people were taught for any length of time by a Puritan ministry the level of their information was definitely raised. . . . The average church member, during most of the century, acquired a good portion of this information by attending sermons and reading not only Scripture but many commentaries, histories, and solid treatises.[14]

The result was, as Hardenbrook says, that "there was no tolerance for heresy. Sin was openly exposed and evil boldly confronted. Discussions in pastoral get-togethers resembled the New Testament account of the heated debates over circumcision at the Jerusalem council; the don't-intimidate-or-challenge-anyone conversations held in ministerial associations today are nothing like that. Colonial men were not shy about the prospect of entering into intense doctrinal discussions. They sharpened their faith by courageous public debate. It was part of being a man!"[15]

Hardenbrook's conclusion is blunt but right on target: "Men are going to have to get theological—something their passive minds do not want to do—to come back to the truth of manhood. Theology, remember, is a manly discipline. When men forsake the discipline of thinking theologically, they trade the church for commerce and surrender it again to feminine piety. So, rather than just being comfortable and unscholarly, men need to think, even if it hurts."[16]

Returning to the Apostle Paul's outline of the steps in Biblical change, his second point is *Rebuke*, or, better, *Conviction*. The Greek word is *elegcho*, a legal term, meaning to prosecute a case against a lawbreaker in such a way as to convict him of his sin. The Biblical teacher and counselor must use the Scriptures to demonstrate, both objectively and to a person's conscience, the sinfulness of his sin. The goal, certainly, is not to manipulate him into a long, drawn-out, morbid period of introspection. But he must be confronted directly regarding the righteous requirements of God's law and his rebellion against that standard. To do anything less is cowardice and rebellion on the part of the counselor himself.

The counselor who seeks to convict of sin will have to be prepared to refute objections and excuses:

"It's not my fault!" the counselee may say.

Yes, it is your fault. God holds you responsible, you respond.

"But that's just the way I am!"

Perhaps; but God commands and expects you to change.

"But I don't feel that it's a sin!"

The issue isn't your feelings or mine; the issue is what God's Word says. Besides, God says in Romans 1 and 2 that you do know in your own conscience that it is a sin.

"What you're asking me to do is impossible!"

No, it's just very difficult. But by God's grace you can do it.

"But I'm not strong enough!"

Of course you aren't strong enough. But Jesus Christ is, and by His Spirit He makes us strong enough for anything He tells us to do.

"It's just too hard!"

No, it isn't. God says that His commandments are not burdensome.

"You aren't being very loving toward me!"

Is it "loving" to allow you to continue in sin and face the wrath of God? The Bible says that true love means keeping God's commandments.

And so on. The point is to hold his feet to the fire, not conceding an inch, until he is *convicted.*

The third step in the process of Biblical change is *Correction.* This means repentance, a change of mind about beliefs, attitudes, and behavior that produces a change of action and lifestyle. It involves restitution, setting right what was wrong—as in the case of Zacchaeus, who resolved to restore fourfold to those from whom he had stolen (at that point, Jesus announced: "Today salvation has come to this house," Luke 19:9). Jay Adams considers how this works in the case of Bill, a professed Christian and homosexual who has come to you for help:

> To help him you first must convict him of his sin. There can be no acceptable change of life without a corresponding change of heart. God wants truly repentant people. So, the first thing is to make out a solid, convincing, biblical case against homosexual-

ity. Bill's expressed concern may be only about the consequences of his lifestyle to himself. There may be regret but no repentance, no change of mind of the sort that God requires. When that "change of mind" takes place, and Bill sees homosexuality not just as a dangerously unhealthy way of life, but as sin against God and his neighbor and is willing to confess it as such, forsake it in thought and deed, and begin a new way of life pleasing to God, he will be on his way toward making the change that God requires of him.

Along with seeking God's forgiveness, Bill may also need to seek the forgiveness of others, such as his wife or parents. He must then forsake all alliances to those with whom he has been committing homosexual acts. Abandoning such connections indicates the early growth of outward fruit appropriate to repentance. Likewise, according to 1 Corinthians 15:33, he must rid himself of every influence that might lead him back into homosexuality. That is the idea behind the doctrine of radical amputation, in which Jesus ordered us to eliminate the right hand, foot, or eye if it presents a temptation to sin. (Matthew 5:29; 18:18ff.; Mark 9:42-48)[17]

Finally, the Apostle Paul tells us of the fourth step in Biblical change: *Training in righteousness.* This is the really hard part, the step that requires the most determined effort from both the counselee and his counselor. Real, lasting change has not been accomplished until training takes place. This means the complete restructuring and reprogramming of a person's habits in the image of Christ.

The ability to be habitual is one of the greatest gifts God has bestowed upon the human race. Our habits are regular rituals that we perform, more or less unconsciously, in order to go about our duties in life efficiently. In fact, life would be virtually impossible without habits. How terrible and frustrating it would be to have to learn, all over again every day, how to walk, eat, talk, brush our teeth, dress, drive a car, use a telephone, and so on. Apart from habits, we would be helpless babies. In themselves, habits are wonderful blessings from God.

But sin changed all that. With the entrance of rebellion against God, the possibility of bad habits arose. And most of the problems dealt with by Christian counselors are rooted, not only in specific acts of sin, but in sinful habits—lifestyles that are characterized by sin. If someone comes to you with a problem of anger, you must deal not only with the particular occasions on which his anger erupted, but with anger as a *habitual* response to pressure. Gossip, lying, theft, envy, and other sins must often be handled both as isolated instances *and* as patterns of behavior.

That is why the Bible does not simply tell us to stop doing something wrong. That would be an extremely insufficient way of dealing with sin, and would almost always result in failure. God, who created us with the capacity for habitual behavior, perfectly understands that we need not only to abandon bad habits; we also need to develop good habits in their place. Righteous patterns of living must replace sinful patterns. Notice how the Apostle Paul encourages his readers to replace sinful habits with godly ones—what Adams has called the "put off-put on dynamic":

> You were taught, with regard to your former way of life, to *put off* your old self, which is being corrupted by its deceitful desires; to be made new in the attitude of your minds; and to *put on* the new self, created to be like God in true righteousness and holiness. (Ephesians 4:22-24, NIV)

This dehabituation and rehabituation pattern is carried on throughout the passage with respect to particular areas of sin:

- *Lying:* "Therefore each of you must put off falsehood and speak truthfully to your neighbor, for we are all members of one body" (v. 25).

- *Anger:* "In your anger do not sin: Do not let the sun go down while you are still angry, and do not give the devil a foothold" (v. 26, 27).

- *Theft:* "He who has been stealing must steal no longer, but must work, doing something useful with his own hands, that he may have something to share with those in need" (v. 28).

- *Evil speech:* "Do not let any unwholesome talk come out of your mouths, but only what is helpful for building others up according to their needs, that it may benefit those who listen" (v. 29).

- *Hatred:* "And do not grieve the Holy Spirit of God, with whom you were sealed for the day of redemption. Get rid of all bitterness, rage and anger, brawling and slander, along with every form of malice. Be kind and compassionate to one another, forgiving each other, just as in Christ God forgave you" (v. 30-32).

In each of these instances, appropriate, godly behavior is substituted for the sinful behavior that is forbidden. And, in each of these instances, the issue is not merely a certain action but a lifestyle, a habitual pattern, that is addressed.

The problem, of course, is that habits are not easily replaced. Jeremiah recognized this as he rebuked his contemporary Israelites for their habitual acts of apostasy from the true faith: "Can the Ethiopian change his skin or the leopard its spots? Then may you also do good who are accustomed to do evil" (Jeremiah 13:23; cf. 22:21). The Apostle Peter speaks of sinners who have habituated themselves in sinful behavior, possessing "a heart trained in covetous practices" (2 Peter 2:14). It is not enough simply to tell a person who has trained himself in evil habits to stop. Certainly, he must stop; but he must also be trained and disciplined, exercised and practiced, in righteousness. "Train yourself to be godly," the Apostle Paul advised (1 Timothy 4:7).

Jerry Bridges, bestselling Christian author, tells of the crucial importance of practice in the Christian life: "It is practice, where the skill is developed, that makes the athlete competitive in his sport. And it is the practice of godliness that enables us to become godly Christians. There is no shortcut to Olympic-skill level, there is no shortcut to godliness. It is the day in and day out faithfulness to the means which God has appointed and which the Holy Spirit uses that will enable us to grow in godliness. We must *practice* godliness, just as the athlete practices his particular sport."[18]

The Christian struggling with sinful habit patterns must not be abandoned by his spiritual leaders after step three, the initial correction of the problem. He must be assisted in reprogramming his lifestyle, restructuring major patterns of living. Pastors, elders, and others in responsible positions need to see themselves not just as lecturers handing down wisdom, but as coaches training spiritual athletes to be a winning team. For, like coaches — but with a much stricter judgment — they will be held accountable for their team's performance (Hebrews 13:17; James 3:1).

From Glory to Glory

The goal of the four-point program of change and growth we have considered is righteous living, conformity to the image of Christ. For every Christian this means continual transfiguration into His likeness, "from glory to glory . . . by the Spirit of the Lord" (2 Corinthians 3:18). There are three aspects of Christian growth which should always be kept in view as the target, the direction in which we are being transformed.[19] First, the Christian is to grow in *spontaneity*: he must internalize God's law in such a way that he automatically, instinctively knows what to do in a given situation. This takes a long lifetime of practice (cf. Hebrews 5:13); it is what the Book of Proverbs calls "wisdom," and is attained not simply by memorizing a stack of Bible verses but by gaining weathered, tempered experience in living by Biblical principles.

Second, the Christian is to grow in *stability*, a self-conscious determination to obey God. As someone once put it, the mature Christian has "a gyroscope in his heart," keeping him on course, preventing him from veering off into false doctrines and heretical practices (cf. Ephesians 4:14). This means perseverance, the very opposite of the flightiness and spiritual nomadism characteristic of the spiritual baby. Again, the development of this trait will summon all the resources of a steady-handed, even-tempered coach. The Christian needs to be characterized by both spontaneity and stability — a combination that is unfortunately as rare as it is indispensable.

Third, the Christian is to grow in *momentum*. He must be characterized not only by a spontaneous and stable obedience, but also by an increasing capacity for such obedience. He is supposed to get better and better at it as he goes along. Christianity is like yeast (Matthew 13:33): it has progressive, compounding effects. The Apostle Paul knew that the Christians in Thessalonica were characterized by love for one another, yet encouraged them to increase their momentum: "And may the Lord make you increase and abound in love toward one another and to all, just as we do to you, so that He may establish your hearts blameless in holiness before our God and Father at the coming of our Lord Jesus Christ with all His saints. . . . But concerning brotherly love you have no need that I should write to you, for you yourselves are taught by God to love one another, and indeed you do so toward all the brethren who are in all Macedonia. But we urge you, brethren, that you increase more and more" (1 Thessalonians 3:12, 13; 4:9, 10).

Is change possible for a homosexual? Certainly! There is no doubt about it. Such a transformation is difficult, for homosexuality is generally a habitual pattern of sinful attitudes, desires, and actions that must be rooted out and replaced with a godly set of habits. But if the homosexual has been given a new identity in Christ, and if he is being taught, convicted, corrected, and discipled in the context of the Body of Christ, there is every reason to expect his spontaneous, stable, and progressive growth into the image of Christ. We can be "confident of this very thing, that He who began a good work in him will complete it until the day of Jesus Christ" (Philippians 1:6).

Therefore, my beloved brethren, be steadfast, immovable, always abounding in the work of the Lord, knowing that your labor is not in vain in the Lord. (1 Corinthians 15:58)

Jesus Christ attests to us and seals in the sacrament that participation in His flesh and blood by which he pours His life into us, just as if he were entering into the very marrow of our bones. He does not present us with an empty frustrating sign, but displays in it the power of His Spirit to accomplish what He promises. . . . This is why the apostle says that the bread we break is the communion of the body of Christ, and the cup we consecrate by the words of the Gospel and the prayers, is the communion of the blood (1 Cor.10:16). No one should object that this is a figure of speech. . . . We can deduce from the fact that the sign is given to us, that the *substance* is also conveyed *in its truth*. . . . In fact, the faithful should make it a hard and fast rule, that every time they see the signs God has ordained, they can know for certain that *the truth* of the thing represented is incorporated. . . . We should be confident beyond all shadow of doubt that *when we take the sign of the body we are taking the body itself.*

John Calvin, *Institutes of the Christian Religion*, 4:17:10; translation in Max Thurian, *The Mystery of the Eucharist: An Ecumenical Approach* (Grand Rapids: William B. Eerdmans Publishing Co., 1984), pp. 55f.

EIGHT

MINISTRY AND SACRAMENTS: RESTORATION TO TRUE ORDER

*Behold, I stand at the door and knock. If anyone hears
My voice and opens the door, I will come in to him and
dine with him, and he with Me. (Revelation 3:20)*

Dan is a converted homosexual. Raised in what was for all practical purposes a broken home (although his parents were never legally divorced), he was introduced to the Gospel in his early teens through attending Campus Life meetings. He made a commitment to Christ, but "it didn't work," he says. "I guess I didn't really mean it. I think I was using Jesus as a way to get away from Dad. And to try to get help for the way I was feeling sexually."

But he didn't find help. While there were many group discussions about dating and sex, no one ever approached the subject of homosexuality. So Dan drifted away. In college, away from home, he "came out" as a homosexual. "At first, it was very exciting, liberating. I was accepted. I was part of a group—a *movement* that was changing history." He shrugs. "Then it just seemed ridiculous. And dirty. All this high moral talk about rights and the Constitution and liberty. For what? A sick little orgy in a bathhouse with people you'd be ashamed to be seen with if regular people were around."

Late one night, angry and miserable, Dan watched the "700 Club" on TV and tearfully prayed to receive Christ. "This time,

I *know* I meant it," he says with conviction. He rifled through his boxes of books until he found his New Testament and began to read. Realizing his need for fellowship, he began attending a church and a Bible study group. He cut off his homosexual relationships, stopped visiting the gay bars, even got an unlisted telephone number. Everything went well for five or six weeks. Then disaster struck, in the form of a newcomer to the Bible study. "As soon as we caught each other's eye across the room, we *knew*," Dan says. "It was like Fate. I went home with him after the Bible study; in fact, we didn't even make it three blocks down the street." Everything Dan thought he had escaped came back in a flood.

"I don't understand it," he mourns. "Why didn't it work? Why can't I stick with it? Isn't Jesus supposed to *save* us from our sins?"

I told Dan there were several answers to his question. For one thing, a fall into sin does not mean the end. As one of the Puritans said, "A sheep may fall into a ditch, but it's the swine that wallows in it." The point is to cast yourself on the grace and mercy of God and get going again.

But that's not the end of the story. Another part of the solution is that Dan needs to understand the nature of the Christian life. It's not just a matter of knowing the right doctrines, having the right emotional experiences, determining to do the right things, and spending time with Christian friends — as necessary as all those things are. The different items in the Christian life need to be bound together in a context, a covenant, an *order*.

From Disorder to Order

When God created man in His image, He placed him into an orderly, structured environment that would provide the proper surrounding for stability, growth, and momentum in his relationship with God. Adam's person was perfectly integrated with himself; his mind, body, senses, will, emotions, energy, and character all worked in harmony. His social life was structured right from the beginning, defined from the outset in terms of marriage to his wife. There never existed, even for one fleeting moment, what the philosophers used to call "the state of nature," in which man lived autonomously and atomistically from others.

No, from the moment of his existence man found himself in a hierarchy of relationships, a covenantal law-order which framed his development. The covenant—the "contract" imposed by God which bound Him to man by promises, stipulations, and conditions—formed the context for man's entire world of relationships, for all human action.

Adam and Eve were expected to extend this law-order throughout the world, beginning from the Garden. The creation already existed in harmonious order under its Creator; man's task was to make it even more complete and glorious, bringing all potentiality into its fullest realization. Man would more and more reflect the image of God in his being, in his relationships with others, and in his every activity. The whole creation would be transformed into the New Creation, according to God's plan: the first creation preceding and anticipating the transfigured, consummate creation of the Spirit (cf. 1 Corinthians 15:44-49).

But Adam and Eve rebelled. They fell from glory and became a naked image, a broken icon. They began to experience guilt, shame, and fear; their relationship with each other became twisted by blame-shifting, distrust, and betrayal. The world fell into chaos, disorder, and death, cut off from Life in the Presence of God. But this is not the end; it is, instead, the backdrop of redemption.

The Son of God became Man in order to remedy the effects of the Fall. The Bible announces Him as Son of Man, the Second Adam, whose mission is to get the derailed creation back on track, restoring man and his environment to true order, and then fulfilling God's original mandate to bring the world into its consummate state as the New Creation. Definitively, this took place in Christ's death, resurrection, and ascension (Ephesians 1:20-22), when He defeated and disarmed the devil (Colossians 2:15; Hebrews 2:14; 1 John 3:8), remade us in His image (Romans 8:29; Ephesians 4:24; Colossians 3:10), raised the Church to heaven (Ephesians 2:6), and began the New Creation (2 Corinthians 5:17). Progressively, this restoration to true order streams from the Cross and the Throne, proceeding through history until the final restoration of all things at the last day (2 Corinthians 3:18; Philippians 3:20, 21; Acts 3:21). From the perspective of God's sovereignty, this process takes place through the regenerating, sanctifying, and glorifying work of the Holy Spirit, who is constantly at work to transform us into Christ's image. From the perspective of human responsibility, this process is known as discipleship.

Discipleship and Discipline

As we have seen, the goal of Christian counseling (as indeed of all Christian teaching) is to produce a disciplined life in Christ's image. Indeed, one of the most basic descriptions of a Christian in the New Testament is that he is a "disciple"—one who is being disciplined, learning obedience to Christ. How does one become a disciple? By baptism: the rite of initiation into the Church. Jesus commanded the apostles: "Go therefore and make *disciples* of all the nations, *baptizing* them in the name of the Father and of the Son and of the Holy Spirit, *teaching* them to observe all things that I have commanded you" (Matthew 28:19, 20). Once a person is baptized he is a disciple, a learner in the school of Christ. And his goal is to become *self*-disciplined, a mature Christian who can stand on his own and handle his problems without someone always coming to the rescue, picking him up, dusting him off, drying his tears, and leading him by the hand.

Everyone starts off in the Christian life as a baby, regardless of his physical age. The new Christian often needs the constant attention and assistance of others in order to grow and develop as he should. But it is an indication of abnormality, of stunted growth, if a Christian remains in such a helpless condition all his life. Self-control is the fruit of the Spirit's work in the believer's life (Galatians 5:22, 23). God wants His child to grow up into the maturity of spontaneous, stable, and increasing self-government and discipline, knowing how to apply practical, Biblical wisdom to the various issues of life (2 Peter 3:18; Ephesians 4:13-16).

When a Christian fails to exercise self-discipline, God brings other forces into his life to produce the desired changes. Some of these forces are events and circumstances by which God directly chastises us, as the writer to the Hebrews reminded his readers, many of whom had become discouraged under their various trials, and so were tempted to forsake their new-found faith:

And you have forgotten the exhortation which speaks to you as to sons:

My son, do not despise the chastening of the Lord, nor be discouraged when you are rebuked by Him; for whom the Lord loves He chastens, and scourges every son whom He receives. [Proverbs 3:11, 12]

If you endure chastening, God deals with you as with sons; for what son is there whom a father does not chasten? But if you are without chastening, of which all have become partakers, then you are illegitimate and not sons. Furthermore, we have had human fathers who corrected us, and we paid them respect. Shall we not much more readily be in subjection to the Father of spirits and live? For they indeed for a few days chastened us as seemed best to them, but He for our profit, that we may be partakers of His holiness. Now no chastening seems to be joyful for the present, but grievous; nevertheless, afterward it yields the peaceable fruit of righteousness to those who have been trained by it. (Hebrews 12:5-11)

This shows us that *every* Christian, at one time or another, receives discipline. Discipline is an inescapable fact of covenantal life. The only question is what form the discipline will take, and what our response will be. But in every case the discipline has as its goal the "profit" of the believer, enabling him to partake of God's holiness and enjoy "the peaceable fruit of righteousness" which comes to those who have been *trained* by God's disciplining action.

Discipline, therefore, is not supposed to be a scary subject. Granted, church discipline has erred in the past, and will in the future—as is true of family discipline. But we do not abandon the concept of proper child-rearing just because of the existence of foolish and wicked parents who have abused their children. Nor do we give up hope just because we ourselves have sinned and made mistakes in disciplining our own children. We resolve to do it right. In the same way, the erroneous practices of some churches should make us more determined to conform our practices to the Word of God. The alternative—no discipline at all—is horrendous: it would bring about the same result for the Church as an undisciplined household produces in its children.

We can see what the lack of Biblical discipline has created in the modern Church. Apostasy has triumphed. Once-faithful congregations have become, in the words of Jesus, "synagogues of Satan": ministers commit adultery and homosexuality (according to some reports, half the urban ministers in one large denomination and twenty percent in another are homosexuals),[1] and teachers regularly deny the basic articles of the Christian faith (one pastor told me, with pride, that his denomination would ordain a Buddhist or an outright atheist "as long as he's good with people"). One youth minister was summoned before his church council on charges of having led a Bible study through the Apostle Paul's Epistle to the Romans. "Our church doesn't teach *that* book anymore," sniffed one board member.

Matthew records Christ's instructions about how to deal with a situation where self-discipline has broken down. To show how a case would progress through the later stages of discipline, Jesus considers the instance of a private offense between brothers:

> If your brother sins against you, go and tell him his fault between you and him alone. If he hears you, you have gained your brother. But if he will not hear you, take with you one or two more, that "by the mouth of two or three witnesses every word may be established" [Deuteronomy 19:15]. And if he refuses to hear them, tell it to the church. But if he refuses even to hear the church, let him be to you like a heathen and a tax collector. (Matthew 18:15-17)

To render a person judicially "like a heathen and a publican" is to treat him as an unbeliever. By *heathens* Jesus meant those who were already outside the church; *tax collectors* as a class had been excommunicated from temple and synagogue for their notorious dishonesty and collaboration with the Romans. It should be noted that Jesus is not commanding the Church to judge the state of anyone's *heart*; rather, He commands the Church to judge the *conduct* of the unrepentant sinner, and to treat him *as* an unbeliever.

Needless to say, a firm stand on discipline takes courage. That is why Jesus promises His special power, presence, and blessing in the faithful exercise of His commands. The passage in Matthew continues:

Assuredly, I say to you, whatever you bind on earth will be bound in heaven, and whatever you loose on earth will be loosed in heaven. Again I say to you that if two of you agree concerning anything that they ask, it will be done for them by My Father in heaven. For where two or three are gathered together in My name, I am there in the midst of them. (Matthew 18:18-20)

Of course, most offenses between brothers and sisters should simply be dismissed and forgotten, wherever possible. This is true of the overwhelming majority of cases. "Love will cover a *multitude* of sins," Peter reminds us (1 Peter 4:8). We should love our neighbor as we love ourselves — giving him the benefit of the doubt, placing the very best construction on his words and actions, believing in his honorable intentions, as we already do for our own (Matthew 22:39). There is no authority in Scripture for bringing official action against those who disagree, even with the elders, over policy issues. Even disagreements about inspired prophecies did not lead the early Christians into ecclesiastical court. In a very helpful study of this issue, Jerram Barrs writes:

When Paul and Barnabas disagreed over John Mark (Acts 15:36-39) they parted company, Paul taking Silas and Barnabas taking John Mark; but Paul did not discipline. In fact, we find Paul later referring positively to Barnabas's ministry (1 Corinthians 9:6) and recognizing the value of the ministry of John Mark also (Colossians 4:10; 2 Timothy 4:11; Philemon 24).

Consider also the different interpretation put by Paul on the prophecies given by Agabus and others concerning Paul's coming imprisonment (Acts 21:10-14). The fact that Paul disagrees with Luke and many others over whether to go to Jerusalem or not does not cause any kind of breaking of fellowship, and certainly no charges of rejection of God's authority or the prophet's authority.

All the examples of discipline given in the New Testament arise either from disobedience to God's Word in the area of doctrine or from disobedience to God's moral commandments. No authority is given to elders to discipline beyond these two areas. There is no suggestion that elders should make the personal decisions of church members for them, or that they have the

right to make rules for the details of others' lives. Rather an
elder's responsibility is to teach, exemplify and apply the Word
of God. He is to be hospitable, to pray for and care for people,
to serve, to counsel, encourage, reprove and rebuke, to rule
and prophesy (Acts 20:28-31; 1 Timothy 4:11-16; 2 Timothy
4:2; Titus 1:8-9; 2:1, 15; 1 Peter 5:1-3). In short, they are to be
shepherds, shepherds whose authority is defined under the
Word of Christ. . . .

Whenever human authority oversteps these boundaries it will
produce bondage. It will bear down with a crushing weight and
cripple the spirituality of the believers. It will result in imma-
turity in the church, growing inability of the members to make
decisions and increasing dependence on authority.[2]

Nevertheless, there is a mechanism ordained by Christ for
dealing with serious doctrinal and moral error: the process of
church government (cf. Galatians 1:8-9; 1 Timothy 1:19-20;
1 John 4:1-3; Revelation 2:2, 14-16, 20). That the Church was
constituted as a government by her Lord will be for many an entirely novel concept: our age, obsessed with what are called "relationships," has long insisted that the Church is nothing more
than a loose aggregate of voluntary associations with a rather
fluid membership policy. The Church is an organism, it is often
said, not an organization; a fellowship, not an institution. How,
then, could it be a *government*?

Bring Back the Institutional Church

Contrary to this recent view, the Church from the very beginning has been an institution — an institution with delegated
power and authority. Jesus declared to His disciple Simon, to
whom He had given the name *Peter* (meaning *rock*), "And I also
say to you that you are Peter, and on this rock I will build My
church, and the gates of Hades shall not prevail against it. And I
will give you the keys of the Kingdom of Heaven, and whatever
you bind on earth will be bound in heaven, and whatever you
loose on earth will be loosed in heaven" (Matthew 16:18, 19).
Teachers throughout Church history have recognized that this
authority was not granted to the Apostle Peter alone, but to him
as the representative of all the apostles, the first rulers of the
Church; Jesus explicitly granted the same authority to them all

in Matthew 18:18 and John 20:21-23. The early Church Father Cyprian (200-258) commented that "although to all the apostles, after His resurrection, He gives an equal power [cf. John 20:21-23], . . . yet, in the person of one man the Lord gave the keys to all, to signify the unity of all. Assuredly the rest of the apostles were the same as Peter was, endowed with an equal share both of honor and power; but the beginning arose from one man that the Church of Christ may be shown to be one."[3]

What did Jesus mean by giving His apostles the authority to "bind" and "loose"? In part, these terms are explained by another promise to these officers of the early Church: "If you *forgive* the sins of any, they are forgiven them; if you *retain* the sins of any, they are retained" (John 20:23). How does this work? What is the difference between the power of Church officers to forgive and retain sins and that of the individual believer?

The answer brings us directly to the issue of excommunication. Excommunication is, literally, *the exclusion of an offender from partaking in the Lord's Supper,* the sacramental meal of the Christian community. Such a serious step is, in the nature of the case, an official act of the Church. It is not the prerogative of the individual believer. Fred may not like Barney, but he has no right, as a private individual, to keep him from Holy Communion. Nor does he have the right, on the other hand, to grant Barney sacramental privileges if the Church has pronounced judgment against him. Only the pastors of the Church, acting in their official capacity, have the power of forgiving or retaining sins in this sense.

Certainly, as our Lord shows in Matthew 18, barring someone from participation in the Sacrament is not to be done lightly. It takes place only after other means (direct confrontation of the sinner with the sinfulness of his sin) have been exhausted. But that is no excuse for postponing judgment indefinitely. In his first canonical letter to the church at Corinth, the Apostle Paul deals with the case of a church member who was committing incest. His command for church policy is absolute and uncompromising:

In the name of our Lord Jesus Christ, when you are gathered together, along with my spirit, with the power of our Lord

Jesus Christ, deliver such a one to Satan for the destruction of the flesh, that his spirit may be saved in the day of the Lord Jesus. (1 Corinthians 5:4, 5)

One reason for such strictness in discipline is that the purity of the Church must be maintained before God and the world:

> I wrote you in my letter not to associate with immoral people; I did not at all mean with the immoral people of this world, or with the covetous and swindlers, or with idolaters; for then you would have to go out of the world. But actually, I wrote to you not to associate with any so-called brother if he should be an immoral person, or covetous, or an idolater, or a reviler, or a drunkard, or a swindler — not even to eat with such a one. For what have I to do with judging outsiders? Do you not judge those who are within the church? But those who are outside, God judges. Remove the wicked man from among yourselves. (1 Corinthians 5:9-13, NASB)

The Apostle Paul commands the Church "not even to eat" with the unrepentant sinner. Elsewhere, he says to "withdraw" from the disorderly brother (2 Thessalonians 3:6): "Note that person [i.e., *identify him publicly* — as Jesus said, 'tell it to the church'] and do not keep company with him, that he may be ashamed" (2 Thessalonians 3:14). All of this means two things: first, *all normal fellowship with him must be cut off* — although we must still "admonish him as a brother" (2 Thessalonians 3:15). The whole church is informed, not in order to humiliate the erring brother, but so that the church may minister to him. Such personal ministry is the responsibility of the church members, not only the leaders: "Now we exhort you, brethren, warn those who are unruly, comfort the fainthearted, uphold the weak, be patient with all" (1 Thessalonians 5:14). The second aspect of this stage of discipline is that *the unrepentant sinner must be excluded from the special fellowship of Holy Communion*, the covenant meal of the Church. Finally, if these measures fail to bring him to repentance, he must be "removed" from the community of the faithful: in Jesus' words, he is then to be treated "as a heathen and a publican."

It is at this point that the moral blindness of supposedly "compassionate" evangelicals becomes obvious. The Apostle

Paul, following the Lord Jesus Christ, has set forth the divine mandate; if the Church is truly the faithful Bride of Christ, we have no option but to obey. True compassion will first be honest before God and His holy law. Yet Richard Foster, in a book that does have some helpful insights on various subjects, offers the following counsel regarding the Church's treatment of "Christian homosexuals":

> The Christian fellowship cannot give permission to practice homosexuality to those who feel unable to change their orientation or to embrace celibacy. But if such a tragic moral choice is made, the most moral context possible should be maintained.
>
> An analogy may be helpful. If a war is entered into when it should have been avoided, there are still moral constraints upon the combatants. Just because the ideal has been violated does not mean that anything goes. A person continues to have moral responsibilities even when driven to engage in an activity that is less than the best. If we cannot condone the choice of homosexual practice, neither can we cut off the person who has made the choice. No, we stand with the person always ready to help, always ready to pick up the pieces if things fall apart, always ready to bring God's acceptance and forgiveness.[4]

Foster is certainly correct on one point. The Church should always stand prepared to minister forgiveness to those who repent. But the problem with his overall analysis is this: "cutting off" is precisely what Jesus and the Apostle Paul command the Christian community to do with the "so-called brother" who will not forsake his immoral behavior. *Remove the wicked man from among yourselves*, the Apostle Paul says, quoting the Old Testament. In fact, that phrase occurs several times in Biblical law to describe the death penalty, of which excommunication and removal form the ecclesiastical equivalent (Deuteronomy 13:5; 17:7, 12; 19:19; 21:21; 22:21).

Contrary to Foster's mistaken suggestion, the practice of homosexuality is not analogous to the undesirable but sometimes necessary practice of warfare. Under certain specific conditions, God authorizes people to engage in warfare and self-defense (Exodus 22:2; Deuteronomy 7:1-26; 13:12-18; 20:1-20; Jud. 3:1-4, 10, 15-31; 2 Samuel 22:35; Luke 3:14; 22:36-38;

Romans 13:4).⁵ But the Bible never, under any circumstances, allows the validity of homosexuality. It is always condemned whenever it is mentioned. The Church of Jesus Christ, if she is to be obedient to her Lord, has no option in the matter: unrepentant homosexuals must be excommunicated. Regardless of their profession, they are, *in practice*, unbelievers. They have no lawful place in the Christian community.

> Now by this we know that we know Him, if we keep His commandments. He who says, "I know Him," and does not keep His commandments, is a liar, and the truth is not in him. (1 John 2:3, 4)

> Do not be unequally yoked together with unbelievers. For what fellowship has righteousness with lawlessness? And what communion has light with darkness? And what accord has Christ with Belial? Or what part has a believer with an unbeliever? And what agreement has the temple of God with idols? For you are the temple of the living God. (2 Corinthians 6:14-16)

Restoring the Repentant

Excommunication and removal have an important judicial function in placing unbelievers outside of the covenant and the visible Church. But we must also recognize that a remedial function is operating as well. Removal from the protection of the covenant has the fearful effect, the Apostle Paul says, of "delivering one to Satan for the destruction of the flesh, *that his spirit may be saved* in the day of Christ Jesus" (1 Corinthians 5:5). The final, drastic step of removal may provide the pressure God will use to bring him to repentance.

If he does repent and return, what then? The Bible gives clear direction here too. The Apostle Paul wrote, in his second canonical epistle to the Corinthians, about how to restore a repentant offender who had been disciplined and removed:

> This punishment which was inflicted by the majority is sufficient for such a man, so that, on the contrary, you ought rather to forgive and comfort him, lest perhaps such a one be swallowed up with too much sorrow. Therefore I urge you to reaffirm your love for him. (2 Corinthians 2:6-8)

Three steps in restoration are commanded: First, he is to be *forgiven*. Forgiveness means *a promise that the offense will never again be held against him*. It will not be repeated to him or to others. It will not be stored away as the basis for a grudge. The case is closed, period. It is like God's forgiveness, in which He promises: "I will forgive their iniquity, and their sin I will remember no more" (Jeremiah 31:34). Just as He does not bring up against us our past sins, so we must forgive those who repent, receiving them as God for Christ's sake has received us.

Second, the repentant person must be *comforted*. The Greek word is *parakaleo*, which means to help, assist, counsel, and persuade, as well as comfort. True restoration will require various kinds of help, depending on particular needs of the person involved. In his very helpful *Handbook of Church Discipline* Jay Adams lists several forms such assistance may take:

> Counseling about the problems and the sins that led to their ouster in the first place. Help in becoming reassimilated into the body. Help in making new social contacts and reinstating old ones. Help in reconciling themselves with others to whom they spoke hard words or toward whom they did despicable things. They will need guidance in finding their place in the body so that they can once again begin to use their gifts (none of this business of making them wait six months to rejoin the choir!). They may need medical assistance; Satan can be rough, and if they have been in his hands for any length of time, they will probably bear the marks that show it. They may need financial help.[6]

Third, he must be *formally reinstated* to fellowship: "Reaffirm your love," says the Apostle Paul, using a term that speaks of official reinstatement. All the rights and privileges of membership should be restored to the repentant. This does not mean, of course, that he can simply leap into the saddle of leadership: office-bearing is not an automatic right of membership. But it must be made clear, to both the congregation and the repentant person, that he is being joyfully received back into full fellowship within the covenant family, once again in complete communion with Christ and His people.

What's So Important about Communion?

The disciplinary power of the Church ultimately boils down to its authority of excommunication—exclusion from communion. To some, this might not seem like much authority at all. Who cares if we are denied communion? Does it make a difference? Does such a power mean that the Church is infallible and can't make a mistake? Does excommunication "take effect" if the Church does make a mistake and excommunicates the wrong person? If not, then why is it important anyway?

The major reason why such questions are even asked is that many of us have forgotten (or have not been taught) the importance of the Lord's Supper. The early Christians were very different. They understood, with the Apostle Paul, that the Cup is truly, really, and substantially "the communion of [the *sharing* or *participation in*] the blood of Christ," that the Bread is "the communion of the body of Christ" (1 Corinthians 10:16). Their Lord had taught them to regard Holy Communion with utmost seriousness:

> Most assuredly, I say to you, unless you eat the flesh of the Son of Man and drink His blood, you have no life in you. Whoever eats My flesh and drinks My blood has eternal life, and I will raise him up at the last day. For My flesh is food indeed, and My blood is drink indeed. He who eats My flesh and drinks My blood abides in Me, and I in him. As the living Father sent Me, and I live because of the Father, so he who feeds on Me will live because of Me. (John 6:53-57)

Because Jesus Christ is central to the Christian faith, the participation in His body and blood through the celebration of the Eucharist (meaning *Thanksgiving*) is central to Christian worship. Luke's description of the first Christian congregations speaks of communion as an integral aspect of their activity (Acts 2:42, 46)—so much so that "to break bread" is the summary of what Christians *do* on the first day of the week (Acts 20:7). The *Didache*, an early Christian handbook of instructions, says the same thing:

> On the Lord's Day assemble together and break bread and give

thanks, first making public confession of your faults, that your sacrifice may be pure. (Chapter 14)

Universally throughout the history of the Church—until the corruption of the late medieval period—Christian worship on the Lord's Day was seen in terms of communion with the Lord at His Table. Somehow, through the action of the Holy Spirit, Christians really partake of the true body and blood of Christ in Holy Communion. We are mysteriously fed with His flesh, "a rich and inexhaustible fountain that pours into us the life springing forth from the Godhead into itself."[7]

When the churches begin to take the Eucharist seriously, as the basis for continuing covenant life (and not just an occasional or infrequent observance), its importance for discipline will become evident. Obviously, it seems like no big deal for an offender to be excluded from participation in a relatively rare event—one that is not even seen by the leadership as central to the church's life. But if the Eucharist *is* what the Church gathers to do on Sundays, that changes the whole picture. If it is as Ignatius said the "medicine of immortality,"[8] or, as Theodoret said, the "meal of eternal health,"[9] or, as Calumanus said, the "salve for every wound,"[10] then things are quite different. Suddenly excommunication means something very significant indeed, in terms of the offender's practical relationship to Christ and His people. It becomes clear to him that he is being excluded from Life.

Restoring Inter-Church Order

Of course, the person under discipline can always go to another church. That is part of the tragedy of the contemporary religious world: people can run away from discipline simply by joining some other group. But there is something we can do about it. If someone under discipline flees to another church, his pastors should immediately inform the leadership of that church about the offender's status, encouraging them to send him back to repent. Church governing boards should refuse to accept anyone as a member without finding out where he has come from. Is he a refugee from discipline? Force him to go back and straighten out the mess he has left behind before he makes another one in *your* church. This is where the Church can demonstrate the visible unity Jesus prayed for:

> . . . that they all may be one, as You, Father, are in Me, and I
> in You; that they also may be one in Us, that the world may be-
> lieve that You sent Me. (John 17:21)

None of this implies that the Church's judgment is infallible.
Churches and church councils sin and make mistakes, just as all
rulers do. Yet, in a way that is analogous to a child's submission
to his parents, it is important for us to have a submissive attitude
toward church discipline, even when we disagree with the court's
decision. Certainly, a church court does not have absolute or
universal authority. That is why, as the Bible indicates, a larger
structure of authority should surround the individual congregation, so that there is accountability for the church's decisions.
Members need a higher court to which they may appeal, and
through which they can bring about change. This was the pattern
of government set up by Moses in his system of elders in Israel:
an arrangement of higher and higher courts (Exodus 18:13-26;
Deuteronomy 1:9-18). There is every reason to believe that when
the early Church appointed "elders" under the Apostles, they
simply adopted the Mosaic system of presbyterial courts, a
structure we can see operating in Acts 15:2-6, 22-23; 20:17, 28.

It is also true, however, that the larger Church does function
as a check and balance on the individual church and denomination. A person who has been wrongfully disciplined can find
refuge in another court within the body of Christ. And a church
or denomination should always be ready and willing to call its
own judgments into question when it has been overruled by
another branch of the Church. Pastors must have the humility to
receive correction from their brethren. Diversity is a Spirit-
ordained means of maintaining genuine order rather than
goose-step uniformity. Wrongful excommunication works
against the order and unity Christ desires for His people. Just as
the individual has the responsibility to heed the wisdom of the
church, so the individual church or denomination has the responsibility to heed the wisdom of the rest of the Body.

God wants order in the Church. Our lives, individually and
corporately, are to be characterized by form as well as freedom.
Listen again to the Apostle Paul:

> For God is not the author of disorder but of peace, as in all the

churches of the saints. . . . Let all things be done decently and in order. (1 Corinthians 14:33, 40)

For though I am absent in the flesh, yet I am with you in spirit, rejoicing to see your good order and the steadfastness of your faith in Christ. (Colossians 2:5)

Therefore, brethren, stand fast and hold the traditions which you were taught, whether by word or epistle. (2 Thessalonians 2:15)

But we command you, brethren, in the name of our Lord Jesus Christ, that you withdraw from every brother who walks disorderly and not according to the tradition which he received from us. For you yourselves know how you ought to follow us, for we were not disorderly among you. . . . For we hear that there are some who walk among you in a disorderly manner. . . . (2 Thessalonians 3:6, 7)

Clearly, order is a priority in Scripture. Good order in our personal lives and in the Church honors God; the absence of order dishonors Him. Church discipline, properly administered, and centered on our common, covenant life in Holy Communion with Christ, works to restore and transform us into the very image of Christ.

The restoration of true order through the ministry and sacraments of the Church is not an optional matter. It is a command from the Lord. The welfare and the very future of the Church are at stake. Christ's final words to His churches, recorded in Revelation 2-3, warn us that when the Church fails to maintain order and exercise discipline, Christ Himself comes against the Church in judgment.

We must remember that the Church, as an institution, enters the disciplinary process only after it has gone beyond the first three stages mentioned in Scripture: self-discipline, confrontation between two brothers, and a confrontation with witness-counselors (Matthew 18:15-17); therefore, most problems never reach an official, formal stage of discipline. The goal of all other forms of discipline is to bring about self-discipline—the characteristic of all mature disciples. Because Church discipline is based on the authoritative command of Christ, its faithful exercise is a reflection of God's court; and, according to Christ's promise, the Church's maintenance of order manifests the very judgment of heaven.

If we are serious about the Reformation doctrine—an idea found in Scripture—that the Church reformed is always reforming, we must make room for growth in practices like divine healing in the modern Church. Divine healing was undeniably a part of Christ's ministry and something that he expected the Church to experience. So although we may never fully understand divine healing, nevertheless we must actually pray for the sick.

John Wimber, *Power Healing*
(San Francisco: Harper & Row, Publishers,
1987), p. 236

HEALING IN
THE CHURCH

Bless the LORD, O my soul,
And forget not all His benefits;
Who forgives all your iniquities,
Who heals all your diseases. (Psalm 103:2, 3)

The AIDS crisis poses a monumental challenge to the Church of the twentieth century: Can the Church be the Church? Is the Church able to minister the Spirit to those suffering from this terrible and frightening disease? Historically, Christians have proclaimed that through the work of Christ the Kingdom has come and continues to come in this world, in human history, as well as at the end of history in the world to come. One way this proclamation of the reality of the Kingdom has been tangibly expressed is through the healing ministry of the Church. No other agency on earth has been able to match the Church's record of success in caring for the afflicted. Yet at the very moment that Western culture most desperately needs the Christian ministry of healing, the Church is absent and invisible. Health care has become one of the most thoroughly secularized fields in the modern world.

But that isn't the way God intended it to be. From the Biblical perspective, health care is supposed to be a strictly Christian enterprise. Why? Because of one single fact that makes all the difference: the Lord Jesus Christ is enthroned in heaven.

Pentecost and the Gift of the Spirit

The resurrection and ascension of Christ made a radical break in history. The whole world works differently now. Originally, there was only one place on earth where people could fully worship God: the Temple in Jerusalem. This was because, in a very real sense, the only place where one can come before God is in heaven, where He holds His royal court. We cannot have an audience with the King unless we come to His throne. And that is why the Temple was created. Like its predecessor, the Tabernacle, the Temple was carefully constructed according to heavenly blueprints, designed as a symbolic replica of a pattern in heaven (Exodus 25:8, 9; 26:30; 2 Chronicles 28:11-19; Hebrews 8:1-5; 9:11, 12, 23, 24). The Temple on Mount Zion was supposed to be, in the most literal sense possible, "heaven on earth." It was the only place in the whole world where people could officially approach their Creator, for God Himself dwelled in it. Revealing Himself in rushing wind and flaming fire (Exodus 19:16-19; 40:34-38; 1 Chronicles 7:1-3), He entered the Temple and made it His covenantal house, His earthly heaven where He could ceremonially receive His worshipers.

In conversation with a Samaritan woman whose religious tradition held that Mount Gerizim in Samaria (rather than Zion in Jerusalem) was the proper site of worship, Jesus foretold the change that He would bring about: "Woman, believe Me, the hour is coming when you will neither on this mountain, nor in Jerusalem, worship the Father. You worship what you do not know; we know what we worship, for salvation is of the Jews. But the hour is coming, and now is, when the true worshipers will worship the Father in Spirit and truth; for the Father is seeking such to worship Him. God is Spirit, and those who worship Him must worship in Spirit and truth" (John 4:21-24). Jesus was bringing in a new era in history, in which the environment for worship—the heavenly "court" on earth—would not be tied to one locale, but rather would be created by the Holy Spirit.

That is what happened on the Day of Pentecost, ten days after Jesus ascended into heaven to obtain the promise of the Spirit for the Church (Acts 1:4-8). The Christians were gathered together for worship, when "suddenly there came a sound from heaven, as of a rushing mighty wind, and it filled the whole house where they were sitting. Then there appeared to them divided tongues, as of fire, and one sat upon each of them. And they were all filled with the Holy Spirit and began to speak with other tongues, as the Spirit gave them utterance" (Acts 2:2-4). The early Christians realized the significance of this event: the Church had taken the place of the Temple. God's presence would no longer be with the Old Covenant sanctuary; from now on, God's Temple would be the Church, the corporate Body of Christ. The supernatural noise, wind, and fire demonstrated that the Spirit had entered the Church, as He had entered the Tabernacle and the Temple hundreds of years before.

The Temple is no longer localized in one area. There is no longer one single, special "sacred space" where we must worship God — rather, the whole world has become sacred, cleansed by Christ's sacrifice. Worship is not centralized anymore, but *multi*centralized. Jesus assured His disciples that "where two or three are gathered together in My name, I am there in the midst of them" (Matthew 18:20). Wherever there is a congregation of God's people, there is the gate of heaven, the entryway into the very presence of God. When Christians break bread and share the Cup in the name of Christ, He is there, present with them, for they have been lifted up to heaven to feast with Him (Hebrews 12:22, 23).

The "Dynamis" of the Spirit:
Old Covenant vs. New Covenant

"You shall receive power [*dynamis*] when the Holy Spirit has come upon you," the risen Lord announced just before His ascension; "and you shall be witnesses to Me . . . to the end of the earth" (Acts 1:8). This text, and passages like it, have tended to get caught up in debates between charismatics and non-charismatics. What is lost is the fact that this is not a statement simply to individuals as such, but also to the official representatives of the Church. There is nothing in the New Testament to suggest that individuals are granted the Spirit apart from their relationship to Christ through His organized Body.

In his pathbreaking study of the Apostle Paul's missionary methods, Roland Allen wrote: "To the heathen crowd the Apostle Paul addressed himself as to a mass of souls from amongst which he was to gather the elect children of God. But he did not approach them as an isolated prophet: he came as an Apostle of the Church of God, and he did not simply seek to gather out individual souls from amongst the heathen, he gathered them into the society of which he was a member. He did not teach them that they would find salvation by themselves alone, but that they would find it in the perfecting of the Body of Christ. Souls were not invited to enter into an isolated solitary religious life of communion with Christ: they were invited to enter the society in which the Spirit manifested Himself and in which they would share in the communication of His life. It was inconceivable that a Christian taught by the Apostle Paul could think of himself as obtaining a personal salvation by himself. He became one of the brethren. He shared in the common sacraments. The Church was not an invisible body of unknown 'believers.' Men were admitted by their baptism into a very visible society, liable to be attacked by very visible foes. The Apostle who preached to them was a member of it, and he preached as a member of it, and as a member of it he invited them to enter it, to share its privileges and its burdens, its glory and its shame. Entrance into it was guarded by a very visible and unmistakable sacrament."[1]

The Church as the Temple is a Body, a known and organized group. The stress in the New Testament is not so much on every individual's possession of the Spirit (although that element is certainly there), but on the Church's possession of Him. While it is possible, according to one interpretation of the Apostle Paul's statement in 1 Corinthians 6:19, that the individual Christian is regarded by Scripture as a temple of the Holy Spirit, it is beyond question that the New Testament emphasis falls squarely on the Church, the collective Body of Christ, as the Temple. This is the point of most, if not all, the New Testament texts on the subject (see 1 Corinthians 3:16, 17; 2 Corinthians 6:16; Ephesians 2:20-22; 1 Peter 2:4, 5; Revelation 3:12). It is a striking symptom of a perversely individualistic reading of Scripture that this assertion will raise eyebrows among some groups; the notion that the individual's body is a "temple" is commonplace, while the thought of the Church as God's Temple *par excellence* is, too often, new and disturbing.

But it is as we are *the Church* that we have the Spirit, as the Apostle Paul affirms: we, the Temple, have been "built on the foundation of the apostles and prophets, Jesus Christ Himself being the chief cornerstone, in whom the whole building, being joined together, grows into a holy temple in the Lord, in whom you also are being built together for a habitation of God in the Spirit" (Ephesians 2:20-22). The Apostle Peter agrees: "You also, as living stones, are being built up a spiritual house" (1 Peter 2:5). The individual stones in the building are indwelt by the Spirit — not because of some other relationship they have with Him, but because He dwells in the "spiritual house" to which they belong!

Irenaeus (c. 130-200), one of the great Fathers of the early Church, warned his readers against slighting the divine institution of the Church: "For where the Church is, there is the Spirit of God; and where the Spirit of God is, there is the Church, and every kind of grace; but the Spirit is truth. Those, therefore, who do not partake of Him, are neither nourished into life from the mother's breasts, nor do they enjoy that most limpid fountain which issues from the body of Christ; but they dig for themselves broken cisterns out of earthly trenches, and drink putrid water out of the mire, fleeing from the faith of the Church lest they be convicted; and rejecting the Spirit, that they may not be instructed."[2]

As Cyprian (200-258) said, you can't have God for your Father if you don't have the Church for your Mother![3] All this is simply to point out that it is the Church that has the Spirit, and therefore it is the Church that possesses the world-transforming power, the *dynamis*, which Christ promised. As the Royal Priesthood the Church is the steward of the mysteries of God; to her care have been entrusted the oracles of God, the Gospel of Christ, the *dynamis* of God unto salvation. Equipped with this *dynamis*, she has been commissioned to disciple all nations to the obedience of Christ, and the very gates of hell are powerless to stop her course of empire. Our Lord has promised that His obedient Church will be invincible in its mission.

The difference made by the Spirit can be demonstrated by several powerful images used in the Bible. One of these is found in Haggai 2:10-14, where the prophet poses two technical theological questions to the priests. The questions are based on the teaching of Leviticus 6:27, that when "holy meat" (from a sacrificed offering) is being carried in a garment, that garment is thereby sanctified also. Therefore, Haggai asked, if the garment carrying the holy meat comes in contact with some other food, would that food in turn also become holy? "No," the priests said; the sanctifying virtue cannot carry that far. So Haggai asked his second question: What about the reverse? If someone or something ceremonially "unclean" (i.e., something that had contacted blood or death) happened to touch the garment carrying the holy meat, what would happen to the meat? Again the judgment was unanimous: the holy meat itself would be rendered unclean, defiled by contact with an unclean object or person. This was the essence of the Old Covenant: the unclean could defile the clean, but the clean could not change the unclean. Grace was, you might say, "static." Holy things were vulnerable, and had to be protected. Pollution was more powerful than cleanliness; evil's reach was longer and stronger than the force of good. Righteousness had to be essentially defensive, not offensive: the danger of corruption was everywhere.

Jesus came to change all that. He was, the Bible tells us, the pure Lamb of God, the sacrifice to which all other sacrifices pointed as their fulfillment (Isaiah 53; John 1:29; Hebrews 9:11-14, 23-28). He was, in the ultimate sense, the "holy meat." And all three Synoptic Gospels tell a striking story about this, one that seems to be deliberately related to Haggai's questions about holiness and pollution.

> And suddenly, a woman who had a flow of blood for twelve years came from behind and touched the hem of His garment; for she said to herself, "If only I may touch His garment, I shall be made well." But Jesus turned around, and when He saw her He said, "Be of good cheer, daughter; your faith has made you well." And the woman was made well from that hour. (Matthew 9:20-22; cf. Mark 5:25-34; Luke 8:43-48)

The Greek term translated here as *made well* is *sozo*, meaning *saved*: Salvation flows from Christ the Sacrifice, cleansing what was defiled. That is, in part, the point of the New Testament's observation that the evil spirits whom the Lord and the apostles drive out are *unclean*. In the New Covenant age brought in by Christ, the demons are disarmed, rendered powerless (Colossians 2:15); the Church has received *dynamis* through the baptism of the Holy Spirit.

Another image of the New Covenant *dynamis* is connected with the Laver in the Temple. The Laver was a huge basin, standing inside the southeast corner of the Temple (2 Chronicles 4:10), in which the priests washed as they performed their sacrificial duties. Only the priests had access to the Laver, and they could not be cleansed unless they came to it. Like the "static grace" of the Old Covenant, the Laver was stationary, its cleansing power accessible only to a few members of a chosen few.

After the Old Covenant Temple was destroyed by Babylon in 586 B.C., however, the prophet Ezekiel had a glorious vision of the future New Covenant Temple—the Spirit-filled Church of the Lord Jesus Christ. There were many aspects of this new Temple, Ezekiel saw, that would outshine the old. One especially striking feature was the position of the Laver—no longer standing still and inaccessible, but apparently *tipped over on its side*, spilling its contents out "from under the threshold of the temple toward the east, for the front of the temple faced east; the water was flowing from under the right side of the temple, south of the altar" (Ezekiel 47:1). Ezekiel began to follow the stream of water as it flowed out. At first, the water was ankle-deep. Farther out it came up to his knees, then to his waist. Finally it became "a river that I could not cross; for the water was too deep, water in which one must swim, a river that could not be crossed" (Ezekiel 47:2-5).

Then Ezekiel saw that this mighty torrent, originating from the Laver in the Temple, reached all the way to the Dead Sea, a lifeless area with no vegetation. But the river was bringing fresh water—and suddenly Ezekiel beheld groves of fruit trees lining the shore, and the waters teeming with fish. This was to be the promise of the New Covenant: instead of being locked up inside an unapproachable sanctuary, the Water of Life would flow out to transform the world!

Jesus borrowed from this prophecy in order to prepare His disciples for the *dynamis* of the Holy Spirit: "If anyone thirsts, let him come to Me and drink. He who believes in Me, as the Scripture has said, out of his heart will flow rivers of living water." After quoting this promise, The Apostle John explains its meaning: "But this He spoke concerning the Spirit, whom those believing in Him would receive; for the Holy Spirit was not yet given, because Jesus was not yet glorified" (John 7:37-39). In other words, the coming of the Holy Spirit on Pentecost, creating and filling the New Covenant Temple, would enable believers to fulfill Ezekiel's prophecy. Since Pentecost, rivers of living water have flowed from the hearts of believers to the "Dead Seas" of the world, bringing life and fruitfulness to the world. No longer is God's grace static and stationary. No longer is the water of life available only to a few. Eternal life, cleansing, and refreshment are flowing from the Church throughout the world. The world's pattern of influence has been reversed. Sin will no longer have the upper hand. Corruption cannot win the battle. The Spirit has been poured out from the glorified Lord, and all the *dynamis* is on the side of the Church!

It is an astonishing fact that the early Church won the population of the Roman Empire to Christ, at the rate of half a million converts every generation, while it was still a persecuted and illegal sect. This astounding achievement was accomplished without the help of organized missionary societies, parachurch ministries, or church growth conventions. How did the Christians do it? Theologian John Jefferson Davis tells us: "The high moral standards of the church and its demonstrated compassion for the less fortunate were important features of its life that attracted outsiders. Christianity set forth lofty ethical ideals and at the same time could demonstrate the power of those ideals to transform the lives of individuals. . . . Christians demonstrated love for their fellow men and women by caring for widows and orphans, helping the sick, infirm, and disabled, reaching out to slaves, prisoners, and those languishing in the mines, helping to find work for the unemployed, assisting in time of natural disasters, and showing hospitality to strangers and travelers. These acts of benevolence and compassion were in themselves powerful forms of evangelism."[4]

This is important. *The Church succeeds by being the Church* — by fulfilling her high calling to bring the water of life to a dead and hopeless world. The ministry of charity is indispensable to the work of extending Christ's Kingdom throughout the earth. But there is another important factor as well, Davis reminds us: "Less well known today is the fact that the demonstrated ability of early Christians to exorcise demons constituted a powerful weapon in their evangelistic arsenal."[5] In his recent study of the astounding growth of early Christianity Ramsay MacMullen observes that exorcism was crucial to the Church's success: "The manhandling of demons—humiliating them, making them howl, beg for mercy, tell their secrets, and depart in a hurry— served a purpose quite essential to the Christian definition of monotheism. It made physically (or dramatically) visible the superiority of the Christian's patron Power over all others."[6]

This cannot be just words. The Church either has the *dynamis* of the Spirit or she does not. The Lord Jesus says she does, as the direct result of His resurrection and ascension. The Lord was glorified in order to give His Church the power to get the job done. Obviously, some have misused and abused the gifts of the Spirit; that was true in the early Church as well. The problem lay mainly in the fact that some Christians were using the gifts for self-gratification and self-exaltation, instead of using them in a spirit of service, to minister to others, to bring the water of life to the world (see 1 Corinthians 12-14). The answer is not to forsake the Spirit. We must forsake the sin instead—and then use God's gifts for the progress of His Kingdom. This is not to suggest that we revive the hootenanny, three-ring-circus excesses that have characterized the backwaters of American fundamentalism. Nor is it an appeal for the frothy, lathered-up frenzies indulged in by religious quacks and medicine men. But we must insist that Biblical, orthodox Christianity includes exorcism and healing, in a proper balance with worship and the Church's ministries of teaching, evangelism, and charity. This is certainly the testimony of the New Testament. And it is witnessed by the historic Church as well.

St. Irenaeus wrote of this, more than a century after the Apostles had died: "Wherefore, also, those who are in truth His disciples, receiving grace from Him, do in His name perform miracles, so as to promote the welfare of other men, according to the gift which each one has received from Him. For some do certainly and truly drive out devils, so that those who have been thus cleansed from evil spirits frequently both believe in Christ, and join themselves to the Church. Others have foreknowledge of things to come: they see visions, and utter prophetic expressions. Others still, heal the sick by laying their hands upon them, and they are made whole."[7]

There is certainly no hint in Irenaeus that there is something strange or weird about these events. Rather, the gifts of the Spirit are regarded simply in terms of the ongoing life of the New Covenant Church, the Spirit-filled Temple overflowing with the water of life. "And what shall I more say? It is not possible to name the number of the gifts which the Church throughout the whole world has received from God, in the name of Jesus Christ, who was crucified under Pontius Pilate, and which she exerts day by day for the benefit of the Gentiles, neither practicing deception upon any, nor taking any reward from them. For as she has received freely from God, freely also does she minister to others.

"Nor does she perform anything by means of angelic invocations, or by incantations, or by any other wicked curious art; but, directing her prayers to the Lord, who made all things, in a pure, sincere, and straightforward spirit, and calling upon the name of our Lord Jesus Christ, she has been accustomed to work miracles for the advantage of mankind, and not to lead them into error."[8]

The Biblical Basis for Healing

The basis for healing is not really very complicated. It consists simply in the fact that the ascended, glorified Lord Jesus Christ has given gifts to His Church (Ephesians 4:7-16). The Apostle Paul sets forth "gifts of healings" as one aspect of the rich diversity of gifts showered on us through the Holy Spirit (1 Corinthians 12:4-14). Healing is supposed to be a normal part—not, to be sure, an overemphasized or exaggerated part, but a normal part—of the ongoing life of the Church. Among the "signs" which Jesus declared would characterize the believing community, we find that "they will lay hands on the sick, and they will recover" (Mark 16:17, 18).[9]

God can and does heal in answer to the prayers of the humblest believer. But there is a special place for healing as an official ministry of the Church. And this, the Bible says, is to be done in two ways. First, according to 1 Corinthians 12:9 and 28, God may provide individuals in the Church with "gifts of healings" (note the plural: not all healers are equal). It seems likely, from Biblical and historical evidence, that those who possess these

gifts are somewhat extraordinary. I doubt that the average congregation is supposed to have a healer on its staff. But the second
method of healing *is* intended to be normal and average, according to the direction of James:

> Is anyone among you sick? Let him call for the elders of the
> church, and let them pray over him, anointing him with oil in
> the name of the Lord. And the prayer of faith will save the sick,
> and the Lord will raise him up. And if he has committed sins, he
> will be forgiven. Confess your trespasses to one another, and
> pray for one another, that you may be healed. The effective, fer-
> vent prayer of a righteous man avails much. (James 5:14-16)

The Lord has appointed a special rite of healing, in connection with the sacred ministry, which He expects His people to
follow. In all normal circumstances, God has directed Christians
to be healed through the ordained government and ceremonies
of the Church. Ritual anointing for healing was appointed by
our Lord soon after He chose the apostles. He sent them out in
pairs to bring the message of His kingdom: "So they went out
and preached that people should repent. And they cast out many
demons, and anointed with oil many who were sick, and healed
them" (Mark 6:12, 13).

There are two important points to note about anointing.
First, contrary to a libertarian mythology that has become popular in Christian circles, God does not simply deal with His people as "individuals." God deals with His people in terms of His
ordained covenantal hierarchy over, under, and around them.
Can God heal in answer to the individual Christian's prayer?
Certainly—and a Christian should always pray that God will
meet his needs (Philippians 4:6-8; 1 Thessalonians 5:17). But this
important truth does not neutralize the fact that God saves His
people in the context of the Church, placing them under His appointed rulers. "Obey those who rule over you, and be submissive, for they watch out for your souls, as those who must give
account. Let them do so with joy and not with grief, for that
would be unprofitable for you" (Hebrews 13:17). So God does
answer prayer; and His usual way of healing is in terms of the
normal "chain of command" in the Body of Christ. God expects
us to honor His government. So the first point regarding anoint-

ing with oil is that it is part of the regular pastoral ministry of
Church officers.

Some ministers might balk at this. "What if I don't have the
gift of healing?" The issue is not whether you have been gifted
for this ministry: if a man has been ordained as a presbyter, we
know he has been divinely gifted to heal. The gift goes with the
office (cf. 1 Timothy 4:14). The Biblical teaching is straightforward on this point: *Pastors heal.*

Second, this ministry is performed in connection with confession of sins. It may be — although this is not always the case —
that the sick person is suffering illness because of sin. The Apostle Paul told the church at Corinth that because of their abuses of
the Eucharist "many are weak and sick among you, and many
sleep [have died]" (1 Corinthians 11:30). God does punish sin
with sickness, and this must be faced squarely and honestly in
any Biblical ministry of healing. Moreover, as Jay Adams's
studies have demonstrated, the effects of unconfessed and unfor-
given sin are pervasive throughout people's lives. Unresolved
guilt produces "psychosomatic" — but very real — illnesses of
every kind, including everything listed under the all-embracing
category of "mental illness."[10] People need to confess their sins:
to the ministering presbyters, to those whom they have wronged,
and (in some cases) publicly, before the church. In our church in
California, when healing is performed during the worship service, we provide a formal confession for the sick person to recite
as part of the ceremony.[11] In any case, whether the healing is
performed publicly or privately, confession of sin is absolutely
essential, not as a superstitious device to manipulate God into
answering our prayers, but as a sincere acknowledgement of our
trespasses against His holy law. This follows the example of our
Lord, who connected healing with forgiveness in His ministry
(Mark 2:1-12; John 5:14).

Both of these points — that healing is an aspect of the
Church's official ministry, and that it must be accompanied by
confession — tell us something significant about what I have
termed the "extraordinary" ministry of healing. God may grace
the Church with men who are especially gifted in praying for the
sick and healing them. But such a ministry must be carried on
within the structure of the institutional Church, never in opposi-

tion to it or in competition with it. Some of the greatest abuses in the history of the American Church have come through the "ministry" of "Lone Rangers," real or fraudulent healers who have conducted self-aggrandizing campaigns outside the covenantal boundaries ordained by God. There is not a shred of evidence, in either the New Testament or Church history, for the independent professional miracle-worker. It is especially notable that in the Apostle Paul's list of the various "charismatic" gifts in 1 Corinthians, the gifts are arranged in a specific hierarchical order, in terms of the divinely appointed government of the Church (1 Corinthians 12:28). The freelance healer is not even contemplated as an option.

In light of this, Jesus' stern warning in the Sermon on the Mount takes on even greater significance:

> Not everyone who says to Me, "Lord, Lord," shall enter the kingdom of heaven, but he who does the will of My Father in heaven. Many will say to Me on that day, "Lord, Lord, have we not prophesied in Your name, cast out demons in Your name, and done many wonders in Your name?" And then I will declare to them, "I never knew you; depart from Me, you who practice lawlessness!" (Matthew 7:21-23)

What About Medicine?

The issue of miraculous healing always raises the question of the legitimacy of medicine. Is it sinful to use "natural" or "human" means to restore health? Certainly not—so long as we do not fall into the same trap Asa did, who "did not seek the Lord, but the physicians" and so died (2 Chronicles 16:12). We must always recognize that health, in *every* case, is given through the work of the Holy Spirit. As we saw earlier, there is no such thing as an autonomous force of "Nature." "Every good gift and every perfect gift is from above, and comes down from the Father of lights, with whom there is no variation or shadow of turning" (James 1:17).

The pre-Christian work known as *Ecclesiasticus* was written by Joshua ben Sira of Jerusalem, a godly Jew who lived about two centuries before the birth of Christ. Informed by a solidly Biblical worldview, this book of practical wisdom was held in

high esteem by the early Church. In one important section
Joshua discusses the relationship of medicine and divine healing:

> Honor the doctor with the honor that is due in return for his
>   services;
>   for he too has been created by the Lord.
> Healing itself comes from the Most High,
>   like a gift from a king. . . .
> The Lord has brought medicines into existence from the
>   earth,
> And a sensible man will not despise them. . . .
> He has also given men learning
>   so that they may glory in his mighty works.
> He uses them to heal and to relieve pain,
>   the chemist makes up a mixture from them.
> Thus there is no end to his activities,
>   and through him health extends across the world.
> My son, when you are ill, do not be depressed,
>   but pray to the Lord and he will heal you.
> Renounce your faults, keep your hands unsoiled,
>   and cleanse your heart from all sin.
> Offer incense and a memorial of fine flour,
>   and make as rich an offering as you can afford.
> Then let the doctor take over—the Lord created him too—
>   and do not let him leave you, for you need him.
> Sometimes success is in their hands,
>   since they in turn will beseech the Lord
>   to grant them the grace to relieve
>   and to heal, that life may be saved.
> (Ecclesiasticus 38:1-14, *The Jerusalem Bible*)

From this balanced perspective the Apostle Paul was able to
take Dr. Luke along with him in his travels; the apostle called
him "the beloved physician" (Colossians 4:14). In addition, Paul
counseled Timothy to "use a little wine for your stomach's sake
and your frequent infirmities" (1 Timothy 5:23). There is no
hint here that Timothy was living in disobedience or lack of
faith. It is certain that Timothy himself, as a pastor, was regularly involved in the healing of others. Yet an inspired apostle
advises him to take medicine—because Paul knew that God uses
means. Like food, medicine will not work apart from the action

of God; so, as we do with food, we must *use* medicine *prayerfully.* If God's providence has led researchers to discover a cure or treatment for an illness, we are despising the Holy Spirit Himself if we neglect it!

Indeed, it is Christianity that brought the blessings of modern science and medicine into the world in the first place. Modern medicine, being creaturely and finite, has its limitations; but it's light-years ahead of anything produced by pagan witch doctors. And that is because it has developed in terms of a Christian worldview—the conviction that man is not at the mercy of "Nature," that man can and should fight to overcome evil and disease, that the universe is predictable because it operates in terms of God's Word, and therefore that true science is possible and desirable. On pagan, mystical presuppositions smallpox could never have been wiped out; on Biblical, Christian presuppositions it could be destroyed, and it was—along with numerous other threats to human life, health, and well-being. Medical science and technology are among the greatest continuing legacies of the Christianization of the West. As George Grant has argued:

> The advancement of modern medicine has a direct correspondence with the advancement of the Gospel. Christian nations are havens of medical mastery, guarding the sanctity of life. Where the Church of Jesus Christ is weak and faltering, however, medical technology degenerates to crude and barbaric superstition. When Asia Minor and Eastern Europe converted to the Faith throughout the first millennium after Christ, a revolution of compassionate and professional care blanketed those regions with a tenacious respect and protection of all life, from the womb to the tomb. But when successive waves of paganism, first the Ottomans and Tartars and then later the Fascists and Communists, snatched those realms from the fold of Christendom, medicine was reduced to a morbid and medieval malapropism of genocide, triage, atrocity, and perversion.[12]

Historically, Christians have led the way in health care. In fact, for over a thousand years Christian churches and monastic communities were the *only* agencies involved in ministry to the sick. Christians built hospitals and staffed them; Christians pioneered in the discovery and application of medical technologies and methods of care; Christians performed the messy, dirty, and often dangerous work of tending to the needs of the diseased and dying. And they did all of this in prayer. For the rationalist it poses a philosophical dilemma; for Christians through the ages, it is simply faithfulness to God's Word. The godly farmer plants, waters, fertilizes, prunes, fights off pests and predators—and prays for God to bring a harvest.

Does God Always Heal?

We must place the foregoing discussion in proper balance by pointing out that God does not always answer our prayers by healing the sick. Whatever we do, in any area of life, we must remember that God is always *God*: "He does whatever He pleases" (Psalm 115:3). He is not a cosmic short-order cook. He is not a genie who rushes to do our bidding at the drop of a dust rag. He is the Almighty Lord, the sovereign Creator and Planner, before whom the whole world is nothing more than fine dust on the scale of significance (Isaiah 40:15). We, as His redeemed creatures, with no "rights" to claim against Him, are to pray for His blessing; and while we should assume that in all normal cases He will grant our requests (Matthew 7:7-11), we must keep in mind that He is perfectly free to answer us in any way He chooses.

One of the most important lessons of the Book of Job is that the world does not revolve around man and his perceived needs. The world revolves around God and His plans; the universe exists for God's glory and pleasure. And God's purposes transcend our lives, our problems, our hopes and dreams. It can be a bitter pill to swallow, but we haven't gotten to first base yet if we fail to realize that people don't come first. God comes first. As He declared to Job, He brings rain "on a land where there is no one, a wilderness in which there is no man; to satisfy the desolate waste, and cause to spring forth the growth of tender grass" (Job 38:26, 27). Why does rain fall? For God's purposes, not for man's. God's ultimate answer to Job boils down to the simple fact that God is God, and Job is not (see Job 38-41).

The fact that I suffer is no argument against the justice or mercy of God. If He denies my request for healing, I must rest in the knowledge that I am suffering according to His will. The Apostle Paul, suffering from some unnamed affliction, asked God to remove it. When his request was denied, he understood that the sovereign purpose of God was being accomplished in his life: "Therefore most gladly I will rather boast in my infirmities, that the power of Christ may rest upon me. Therefore I take pleasure in infirmities, in reproaches, in needs, in persecutions, in distresses, for Christ's sake. For when I am weak, then I am strong" (2 Corinthians 12:9, 10). The modern evangelical heresy that godly people are free from suffering was unknown to the Apostle Paul. Suffering, an evil in itself, can have beneficial, sanctifying effects under the providence of God:

> Before I was afflicted, I went astray,
> But now I keep Your Word. . . .
> It is good for me that I have been afflicted,
> That I may learn your statutes. (Psalm 119:67, 71)

The Apostle Paul reveals no embarrassment about the fact that he was unable to heal his friend Trophimus (2 Timothy 4:20). He knew that prayer and anointing with oil are never ways of manipulating God. Prayer is neither mechanical nor magical; in an ultimate sense, there is no such thing as "the power of prayer." Prayer has no autonomous power. To think otherwise is pagan; it is to dream that man is greater than God. Prayer is nothing more than a request from children to their Father. The power belongs to the Father, not to the request itself. And God has never said that it is always His will to heal (although it is generally His will for His people to live healthy lives: 3 John 2). To the contrary: according to God's decree, "it is appointed for men to die" (Hebrews 9:27). Until the end of the world, there is no getting around this fact. Everyone will die, you and me included. At some point, prayers will be of no avail, and our spirit and body will be separated until the Resurrection at the Last Day. God's ultimate will is not to keep everyone reasonably healthy in this life; rather, it is to bring us, body and soul, into the fullness of the New Creation. And that blessed and eternal goal lies on the other side of death and resurrection. We cannot get there without following our Lord in the way He has gone before us.

Healing in the Context of the Priesthood

The Church's ministry of healing must not be separated from its proper context. Physical healing is just one part of the Church's ministry to the whole person. In closing this chapter, I would like to suggest the outlines of that larger environment.

The priestly context for healing can be summarized as *spiritual renewal and restoration through the pastoral ministry and the sacraments*. This means, for one thing, a revival of Christian theology and teaching from the pulpit. I was greatly saddened recently in dealing with a counseling situation that arose outside our church. The family was in desperate trouble, literally at each others' throats; the wife had repeatedly threatened to murder her husband, and she was the most religious member of the household! The churches they had attended over the last decade were touchy-feely emotional binges masquerading as worship, with almost zero doctrinal content. The result was predictable: without any theological moorings in Scripture and the historic Creeds of the Church, this family just drifted through life's problems, bouncing like pinballs against their circumstances, at the mercy of their momentary urges. Certainly, they must bear their own responsibility for the mess they have made of their lives. That should not be minimized. But they are also examples of the desolate result of today's Christian ministry. Their pastors failed them.

How can this be remedied? Pastors can begin by making a solemn vow not to bring their own peculiar hobbies into the pulpit, and renewing their commitment to "contend earnestly for the faith which was once for all delivered to the saints." This will mean rediscovering the orthodox teachings of the historic Church. Get Henry Bettenson's editions of *The Early Christian Fathers*, *The Later Christian Fathers*, and *Documents of the Christian Church*. Then pick up individual editions of *The Apostolic Fathers*, Athanasius's *On the Incarnation*, Gregory Nazianzen's *Orations*, Augustine's *Confessions* and *The City of God*, John Chrysostom's *On the Priesthood*, Gregory the Great's *Book of Pastoral Rule*, and

Henry R. Percival's edition of *The Seven Ecumenical Councils of the Undivided Church*. And then—*read* them. Find out what the Church has been concerned about through its history, and begin instructing your congregation in the Biblical and creedal Faith of our Fathers. Give your people a solid foundation for their thought and action. Now, any pastor who is doing his job will not have as much time to read as he would like. Even the basic list suggested here will take a few years to work through. But the result, for the pastor and his people, will be worth the effort.

Teaching alone is not enough. Instruction must be placed in the proper context of worship and sacrament, making Christ the Healer present to His people. He is the Great Physician, and sick people need His healing power at every point in their lives. Partaking of the Eucharist unworthily can bring on sickness and death; but to commune with Christ in truth gives life. "It is important to understand that *only* the Gospel gives men health. The labor of physicians is important, but only as a means of holding back the curse. *Physicians cannot give men true health.* Nor can eating 'health foods,' fasting, exercise, colonics, or any other feature of the Old Creation. The first creation is decaying. It is only the New Creation that can bring true health, through *transfiguration*. It is only in Christ, and in eating His Spiritual food, that healing can take place."[13]

This is simply to recognize the intimate Biblical connection between Word and Sign. The prophets, for instance, were always authenticated with special signs, miracles that confirmed their testimony (cf. Deuteronomy 18:21, 22). Isn't God's Word certain all by itself? Yes—but God characteristically confirms it nevertheless by adding an oath (Hebrews 6:17).

Consider how the Word was preached to Adam. God did not simply leave him with the message of redemption alone, but gave him a sign as well, clothing him with the skin of a sacrificed animal that had been slain in his place (Genesis 2:17; 3:21). Later, the Word was preached to Noah, in God's promise never to destroy the earth again by a flood. Again the Word was accompanied by a sign, the rainbow in the cloud (Genesis 9:12-17). When the proclamation of the Covenant was made to Abraham, God's Word was confirmed by the sign and seal of circumcision (Genesis 17:7-14).

This pattern of Word accompanied by Sign is followed throughout the Bible. The Old Testament is filled with special signs: sacrifices, miracles, memorial stones and pillars, washings, rituals, fulfilled prophecies, and so on. During Christ's ministry, He was constantly demonstrating the truth of His Word by His miraculous works. Moreover, He Himself was *the* Sign, God's greatest Miracle incarnate.

After Pentecost the *special* (not the only) continuing miracle in the Church is provided in the Sacraments. A weekly miracle is performed when the Church gathers before the Throne on the Lord's Day to partake of the Body and Blood of Christ. Naturally, this miracle has been superstitiously misunderstood and abused by some groups; but at least as dangerous has been the rationalistic tendency among other groups to deny or downplay the miraculous nature of Baptism and the Eucharist. The truth is that God not only gives us His Word, but provides us with witnesses to that Word, the sign-miracles of the Sacraments. These need to be restored, for the health of the Body of Christ. God's revelation is distorted when Word and Sign are separated. A further aspect of a holistic approach must be on the level of charitable activity, the establishment and maintenance of truly Christian hospital facilities. As the AIDS plague spreads, there will be an increasing need for Christians to recapture their rightful place in health care. We should be the leaders in this area, pioneers in the ministry of mercy. The Church must not miss this opportunity to bring the saving message of Christ's love to the needy. We are the only ones who can do the job. The Church alone possesses the *dynamis* of the Spirit.

The most of our brethren were unsparing in their exceeding love and brotherly kindness. They held fast to each other and visited the sick fearlessly, and ministered to them continually, serving them in Christ. And they died with them most joyfully, taking the affliction of others, and drawing the sickness from their neighbors to themselves and willingly receiving their pains. And many who cared for the sick and gave strength to others died themselves, having transferred to themselves their deaths. . . .

Truly the best of our brethren departed from life in this manner, including some presbyters and deacons and those of the people who had the highest reputation; so that this form of death, through the great piety and strong faith it exhibited, seemed to lack nothing of martyrdom. . . .

But with the heathen everything was quite otherwise. They deserted those who began to be sick, and fled from their dearest friends. And they cast them out into the streets when they were half dead, and left the dead like refuse, unburied. They shunned any participation or fellowship with death; which yet, with all their precautions, it was not easy for them to escape.

Dionysius of Alexandria, Easter Letter, A.D. 263;
in Eusebius, *Church History*, 7:22

TEN

PURE AND UNDEFILED RELIGION

He has shown you, O man, what is good;
And what does the LORD require of you
But to do justly, to love mercy,
And to walk humbly with your God? (Micah 6:8)

He was called the Apostate. Publicly renouncing the Christianity of his youth when he came to power at age 30 (A.D. 361), the Emperor Julian began a systematic attempt to revive Paganism and stamp out Christianity. He issued orders that all heathen temples were to be reopened; imperial revenues were to be lavished on the restoration of shrines that had fallen into ruin; banished demons were to be welcomed back from exile; Christians could be persecuted and even discreetly murdered without fear of punishment. Flushed with a convert's zeal, Julian went so far as to become high priest of the ancient cult. At dawn and dusk every day he offered sacrifices to the Sun-god; on high feast days, surrounded by whirling, frenzied attendants, he officiated in the temple of the god or goddess being honored: slaughtering the animal on the altar, plunging his hands into its shuddering body, pulling out its heart, liver, or intestines, and divining therein the messages of the gods. It soon became a popular joke that if this kept up cattle would become extinct. (The truth was much worse, however: on at least one occasion, a special crisis led him to disembowel a woman on the altar in order to examine her liver. Pagan logic was catching up with Julian.)

But he was aware that if his born-again Paganism was to reconquer the world it would have to offer more than bloody entrails. Christianity had gained too much ground to be overthrown so easily. Even the emperor's direct assaults, his open ridicule and harassment of Christians, were dismal failures—as was his attempt to discredit Christ's prophecy of the Jewish Temple's permanent destruction in A.D. 70 (Matthew 24) by having it rebuilt. The project ended in spectacular disaster: just after the ground had been cleared for laying the foundation, a massive earthquake toppled the surrounding houses, killing and maiming workers and onlookers alike; then, huge fireballs erupted from the bowels of the earth, devastating the site with explosions (historians have pronounced these to be gaseous deposits disturbed by the workmen). Julian knew that to supplant the Christian faith Paganism would have to make a lasting mark on the lives of the people, meeting their felt needs in practical ways. So he planned the construction and maintenance of hospitals and hospices, where the sick, the homeless, and travelers could find refuge and help in distress. Effective religion grapples with the real world.

The irony was that this was not "applied Paganism" at all—it was simply a bastard Christianity, and Julian knew it. In order to find a model for this kind of charity he was forced to go to the works of the Christians themselves, who for years had been active in establishing these very institutions. The best Paganism could accomplish would be a mere imitation of Christianity.

In the end, the plan miscarried. The very notion of charity to strangers was a Christian, not a Pagan, idea. Not only Julian's model, but the concept, the motivation, the inspiration for charity were wholly Christian. Julian's fellow Pagans—the real ones, not mere converts with ideals borrowed from Christianity—did not share his enthusiasm for a relevant, service-oriented faith. It was foreign to them, and Julian found himself caught between two religious worlds.(Once, deep in a cavern, he had attended the Pagan mysteries in which the priests ceremoniously invoked the presence of demons. When the spirits appeared, Julian panicked and instinctively made the sign of the cross; the spirits immediately fled, to the consternation and embarrassment of the priests.)

It soon became obvious to many that Christian ethics could not be supported by Pagan theology. But Julian had his supporters, who eagerly hoped for complete victory over Christianity and a restoration of the old order. Libanius, a popular heathen philosopher, was the one who had turned Julian away from the Christian faith. One day in 363, rejoicing in the rapid progress of his former pupil, he ridiculed a Christian schoolteacher's faith in an apparently defeated Christ. "What is the carpenter's son doing now?" he taunted. "Sophist," responded the Christian, "the Creator of all things, whom you in mockery call a carpenter's son, *is building a coffin*." It was true: within days, after a reign of only a year and eight months, Julian the Apostate lay dying on the field of battle, hurling his clotted blood toward heaven and crying in anguish: "You have conquered, Galilean!"

The "Galilean" had indeed conquered. Julian was instantly replaced by a Christian emperor, Paganism retreated into the shadows and caves for a thousand years, and the glory of ministering to the needy belonged to the Church alone. The institution that became the standard for centuries, in fact, was founded by a man who had been a fellow classmate of Julian's at the University of Athens—*and* a former student at Antioch under Julian's mentor, Libanius—Basil (330-379), who became Bishop of Caesarea. His vast establishment in a suburb of Caesarea was practically, as his friend Gregory of Nazianzus remarked, "a new city" in itself. The "Basiliad," as it came to be called, contained a church, homes, schools, workshops, a fully staffed hospital, and a hospice for poor travelers.

> Basil introduced a new dimension in monastic life for which he may claim originality. He established monasteries in cities as well as in the countryside—confirmation that religious life did not imply flight from the world but the overthrow of evil within it. To this end the monk worked with his hands. He lived in his Bible, as did Basil himself. He staffed schools, orphanages, and hospitals. If suited, he had scope for study as well as work. Basil's monasticism was a way of Christian life in which the monk was dedicated to the service of his fellows as well as to personal salvation. It came as near as any movement within the early church to a Christianity that aimed at changing society and transforming organized religion into a social as well as an individual creed.[1]

The Christian Health Care Tradition

St. Basil's example was multiplied repeatedly, as the Near East and Europe were gradually transformed into Christendom. Everywhere it went, the Church founded hospitals and other charitable institutions on a scale far beyond anything known or imagined in Pagan antiquity. Many monasteries ran hospitals as a standard ministry, and several Orders of monks — Hospitalers, Templars, Antonines, and Alexians — were formed for the specific purpose of serving the sick.[2] In Rome, a wealthy layman named Pammachius (340-410) joined the widow Fabiola (d. 399) and other Christians to create a famous hospital and hospice for the needy. Shortly after visiting Basil, Ephraim of Syria (306-373) went home and organized food relief for famine victims and set up numerous health care stations where the poor could be treated.

Another friend of Basil's was John Chrysostom (347-407), who early in life had been the star pupil of that unfortunate heathen philosopher Libanius. Shortly before his death, Libanius was asked whom he would choose as his successor. "*John,*" he replied instantly — adding with a sigh: "If only the Christians hadn't stolen him from us!" (One can almost feel sorry for old Libanius, doomed to a series of disappointments: the "carpenter's son" had triumphed over him again.) John was greatly concerned with the practical fruit of faith, a "hands-on" Gospel that would minister to the poor and needy according to Christ's example. One of his first acts upon becoming Bishop of Constantinople was to sell off the expensive plate and furniture of the episcopal palace, giving the proceeds to Christian charities, especially the hospitals for the poor. He encouraged his congregation to join him, not only in giving money to charitable causes but also engaging in hospitality and care themselves. The Christian hospital tradition was carried on by such men as Theodosius the Cenobiarch (423-529), who established communities throughout Palestine to care for the sick and the elderly; Benedict (480-550), who was vastly influential in the development of Christian ministries to the poor and the afflicted for centuries; Gregory the Great (540-604), whose concern for the poor and the sick was manifested in both his personal generosity and his administrative reform of Church revenues to provide relief for those suffering from war, pestilence, and famine. And these were not the last. For hundreds of years the Gospel advanced through the nations, transforming lives, cultures, and institutions. Clergymen and laymen alike worked to reconstruct all aspects of life in terms of God's Word, so that the Church became, among other things, "a continent-wide organization for charitable aid."[3] With all its problems — and, there is no doubt, the problems were many — this frontier era of Christianity has been rightly called the Age of Faith. (The pejorative terms "Middle Ages" and, worse, "Dark Ages" were both invented by the Neo-Pagans of the Renaissance, who looked on this great era of Christian missionary conquest as a dark period between the bright glories of pre-Christian Europe and its revival in the Renaissance — the "Rebirth" of Classical Paganism.)[4]

One of the most outstanding keepers of the Christian hospital tradition was John the Almsgiver (560-619), who became Bishop of Alexandria at a time when the church in that city was demoralized. Many had left to follow the Monophysite heresy (the false doctrine that Christ possessed only one nature, rather than His two distinct natures of divinity and humanity). John set about to bring the people back to the orthodox faith by an exemplary, godly life, and by ministering to them in practical ways. He founded and endowed hospitals, maternity clinics, homes for the aged, and hospices. He helped the poor of the city, not only by gifts, but by regulating weights and measures according to Biblical law (cf. Leviticus 19:35-37). He forced the clergy to become in deeds what they were in name: *ministers*. He provided aid for refugees and sent relief to victims of war and famine. In every area of life he sought to adorn the Gospel of grace with gracious works. The Last Will and Testament of John the Almsgiver says that he found the church's coffers full and left them empty: "I have done my best to render to God the things that are God's."

Many names of such saints, "heroes for Christ" during the Age of Faith, could be added. The following list[5] records just a handful of those who were active in relieving the afflictions of the sick, either through personal care or through establishing and maintaining monastic hospitals[6] for the poor.

- Waudru of Belgium (d. 688) devoted her life to caring for the poor and sick.

- Winnoc (d. 717) founded a monastery and a hospital near Dunkirk.

- Gregory II (d. 731), Bishop of Rome, established several new hospitals.

- Odilo (962-1049), Abbot of Cluny, provided both famine relief and care for the sick.

- Theodosius of Kiev (d. 1074) provided food and shelter for the sick and the poor.

- Hugh, Bishop of Grenoble (1053-1132), founded a hospital.

- Bernard of Clairvaux (1090-1153), helped establish the Order of Templars, a dedicated group of knights who would care for the sick. The influence of Bernard's life on Christians in ministry through the ages has been inestimable.

- Roger of Ellant (d. 1160) was famous for his ministry to the sick.

- Gilbert of Sempringham (1085-1189) established working monasteries with 1,500 personnel, as well as orphanages and hospitals for those suffering from leprosy.

- Uomobuono (d. 1197) was a successful businessman who gave much of his profits to relieve the sufferings of others, even taking people into his own home to care for them.

- Hugh, Bishop of Lincoln (1140-1200), defended the Jews from angry mobs, tended the sick, and worked for justice for the poor in the courts and against the depredations of wealthy and powerful oppressors.

- Hedwig (1174-1243) and her husband, Duke Henry of Silesia, gave generously to numerous charities; after his death she devoted herself to the welfare of the poor and the sick.

- Francis of Assisi (1181-1226) is one of the most well-known Christians of all time. The son of a wealthy merchant, Francis deliberately chose a life of poverty and hardship in order to care for the poor and the sick, including lepers, diseased outcasts whom no one would touch; he preached, healed, and created an Order that for centuries would be characterized by practical ministry to the needy.

- Elizabeth, Queen of Hungary (1207-1231), was Hedwig's niece. The queen spent huge sums of money to establish hospitals and orphanages; after her husband died she joined a lay order of Franciscans and devoted her life to caring for the sick and the elderly in a hospital.

- Louis IX (1214-1270), King of France, supported numerous charities — hospitals, asylums, monasteries, hospices, a home for redeemed prostitutes — and founded a hospital for the blind that housed 300 people. More than seven hundred years later, it is still an important medical center (in fact, half the hospitals in modern Europe were founded during the medieval period). Beyond all this, he personally brought the poor into his home to feed them and wash their feet; he fed lepers with his own hands; he daily gave alms to the poor and the sick. Under his blessed rule France experienced an unprecedented "Golden Age" of prosperity, security, and happiness.

- Margaret of Cortona (1247-1297), after living as a knight's mistress for nine years, repented and devoted her life to the care of the sick poor, first in her own house and then in a hospital she founded.

- Elizabeth, Queen of Portugal (1271-1336) was named after Elizabeth of Hungary, a distant relative; she founded hospitals, orphanages, and homes for fallen women.

- Bernardino of Siena (1380-1444) was a governor's son; when he was 20 years old he and his friends took over the operation of a hospital after most of the staff died of plague; he became a well-known Franciscan preacher, and through his ministry, as one biographer said, "the rule of Jesus made visible progress in society."

- Frances of Rome (1384-1440), wife and mother of six children, spent her life in serving the poor of the city, especially in the hospitals.

- Catherine of Genoa (1447-1510) converted her husband from a dissolute life, and together they devoted themselves to nursing the sick as volunteers in a hospital.

As I said, these are just a few out of many multitudes of Christian saints who gave of themselves to minister to the needs of others. It does not take too much imagination to understand that the accomplishments of even the few names listed here represent much struggle and toil, a divine and human drama of overcoming personal, economic, and social obstacles. If caring for diseased, poor, and helpless people can seem frustrating and hopeless now, think what it must have been like then, without the modern luxuries of wonder drugs, electricity, air conditioning, antiseptics, intravenous feeding, medical insurance, laboratories, ambulances, and thousands of other items that provide the infrastructure for modern hospitalization. And yet, health care in the Age of Faith provided something that too often is missing now.

Ministry to the Whole Person

In the summer of 1982 I was hospitalized for several days after a severe reaction to a pneumonia vaccine. The reaction was so unusual that at first the doctors suspected any number of exotic tropical diseases. My temperature skyrocketed, the blood analyses turned up conflicting data, I had difficulty breathing, my limbs swelled and ached, I was dizzy and weak—even after a few days the exhaustion of being propped up in bed was enough to put me back to sleep. I had to have help with *everything*.

I remember one young nurse who had both arms around me as she and another nurse struggled to get me across the room. Trying to make conversation, she asked cheerfully if the doctors had figured out what was wrong with me. I managed to whisper the latest intelligence. "They think . . . might be . . . malaria."

All the color drained from her face. Stark, naked terror stared out of her eyes. She made a strangled, squeaky noise and let go of me, staggered backwards toward the door and lurched into the hall. I never saw her again.

There was another nurse, an older woman named Jean who would come in and talk to me about her grandchildren, her travels, interesting books she'd read; she told jokes I was too weak to laugh at, asked questions I couldn't answer, and shared her faith in God, while she fed me, washed me, and tended to my needs. While I can't blame the younger nurse for being afraid of me, it still seems that the older one had a different concept of her task: she treated it as a divine calling, and she treated me, a stranger, as a person of real worth. She ministered to me, body and spirit, as a whole being.

As anyone who has served time in a hospital can attest, Jean was an exception. Certainly, there are many nurses and doctors who seek to treat patients as whole persons. But the modern hospital *system* itself, with few exceptions, militates against ministry. For one thing, most hospitals are secular, bureaucratic enterprises that are half business, half state agency in which the most important issue is whether the forms have been filled out properly. And this is true of the "religious" hospitals as well, which have fashioned themselves after the model of their secular counterparts so successfully that there is rarely any practical difference. The modern hospital exists, at best, to fix broken machine parts.

George Orwell, in one of his most memorable essays, told of the virtually inescapable indignities in hospital life — and death:

> I would be far from complaining about the treatment I have received in any English hospital, but I do know that it is a sound instinct that warns people to keep out of hospitals if possible, and especially out of the public wards. Whatever the legal position may be, it is unquestionable that you have far less control over your own treatment, far less certainty that frivolous experiments will not be tried on you, when it is a case of "accept the discipline or get out." And it is a great thing to die in your own bed, though it is better still to die in your boots. However great the kindness and efficiency, in every hospital death there will be some cruel, squalid detail, something perhaps too small to be told but leaving terribly painful memories behind, arising out of the haste, the crowding, the impersonality of a place where every day people are dying among strangers.[7]

What happened? How did the concept of health care become secularized? To answer that we must first remember what *Christian* health care is: a ministry to the whole person. The Bible does not compartmentalize man, as if he can be treated as *only* an intellect, *only* a soul, *only* a body. Man is a unity. Ministry, therefore, must address itself to the whole man. These early Christian charities transformed the character of Europe through a holistic approach, one which dealt with every aspect of man's being in terms of his most basic identity: the image of God. Their primary concern was with man in his relationship with

God, recognizing that all things in his life flow out of a *religious* center in man's heart (Proverbs 4:23). From this foundation the various ministries could offer health, food, clothing, counseling, shelter, occupation, a place of value for the person — not only in relation to the society, but with respect to the cosmos, to the whole order of things ordained by God. To go into a hospital was to be part of a community of faith. Soul and body were tied to each other, to the people of God of all ages in the communion of saints, to the Sacraments of the Church, to the Holy Trinity.

Then, in a number of different ways, Christendom began to break down. The change became evident early in the 1100s: people began receiving Holy Communion only once a year (if ever), on Easter Sunday; the Church began restricting the laity from drinking the Cup; children, who from the beginning had been admitted to Communion, were now barred from it; the rite of Confirmation was divorced from its historic connection with Baptism and postponed for years; the rite of Unction (anointing with oil) ceased to be regarded as a means of healing and became Last Rites, a preparation for death.

> The sense of great joy and inward freedom which the early Church derived from its possession of the Good News (which every one could read for himself), and its sense of union with the resurrected Lord, [became] overlaid by feelings of terror and estrangement. Men at their prayers no longer raised their arms and turned toward Christ, their rising sun, but folded their hands in the attitude of serfs, serfs of God and of their sin. Where formerly the priest had celebrated the Mass facing the people, in proof of his accessibility, now he turned his back on them and retreated into the vastness of the sanctuary, separated from the people's part of the church by a forbidding screen. Finally, the Mass was read in a language the people could not understand.[8]

It would be interesting to speculate on the precise reasons for such a radical change in the Church, but no matter what the cause was, the effect for health care was disastrous. Will Durant succinctly describes the tragedy:

> Until 1139 some members of the clergy practiced medicine, and what hospitalization could be had was usually to be found in

monastic or conventual infirmaries. The monks played an honorable role in preserving the medical heritage, and led the way in the cultivation of medicinal plants; and perhaps they knew what they were doing in mingling miracle with medicine. Even nuns might be skilled in healing. . . . As lay medicine developed, and the love of gain infected monastic healing, the Church (1130, 1339, 1663) progressively forbade the public practice of medicine by the clergy; and by 1200 the ancient art was almost completely secular.[9]

This doesn't mean that health care simply stopped, or that Christians ceased being active in hospitals. There were many attempts at reconstruction over the centuries, and some of the names listed above were active in such endeavors. Even Martin Luther, who was not given to unnecessary praise of Rome, spoke with effusive admiration of the hospitals and other charitable institutions he had observed during his travels in Italy.[10] Indeed, in the fifteenth century Florence alone had thirty-five hospitals. But, overall, an important focus had shifted. The central Christian base for health care had been ripped out from under the system. The process took time, and there were always exceptions—indeed, most of the people involved were Christians, so naturally they still acted in terms of Biblical ethics—but the definitive break had been made: the hospital was no longer defined as a specifically *Christian* ministry and mission. Its reason for existence became, virtually unnoticed, something very different from what it had been. Its goals changed. And slowly, almost imperceptibly, its practices were trimmed and altered to fit its new character.

To grasp the significance of the change, imagine your church coming under new management. The whole pastoral staff is replaced by an energetic team fresh out of business school, determined to transform the church into a successful institution. Many of the old services—preaching, sacraments, counseling, prayer meetings—will still be provided, but *efficiently*, and at a respectable profit. The church will no longer be at the mercy either of volunteers in its service groups or of contributions in its plates; *every* significant position will be filled by hired professionals, supported by paying customers (or Gold Cross Religion Insurance).

That's what happened to hospitals. From a fully integrated ministry of the Church, ministering Christ to the needy, they became a segregated, profit-seeking business concerned with treating body parts; completely prepared to turn away those who cannot pay. It is one of the greatest tragedies of all time.

Back to the Tradition

It seems to take a crisis to wake the Church out of its sleep. There is reason to hope that the AIDS plague is beginning to have that result. For the plain fact is that there is no real hope of fighting the disease if the Church does not pitch in.

Go back to Chapter 1 and look at those figures again. Within a few years, hundreds of thousands of people will be dying of AIDS in the U.S. alone, most of them with no place to go. Already, the single hospital in this country devoted to AIDS has had to close because of financial deficits. And, according to a recent study, ten percent of the nation's hospitals will be forced to close in the next ten years, for three reasons: "rising costs, fewer but sicker patients, and a harder time getting paid for care."[11] The numbers alone tell us that something different must be done. Mere technical advances in medicine, of themselves, will prove impotent to solve the problems facing the health care community. Hospitals will not survive unless they return to their religious base in the Christian Tradition. The terrible tragedy of AIDS is also a tremendous opportunity for the Church herself to "come out of the closet" and proclaim her redemptive and restorative mission to the world.

Roman Catholic Archbishop Philip Hannon of New Orleans has always been that city's most outspoken opponent of "gay rights." Even some Christian magazines would consider his stance hopelessly "homophobic." Yet he has also taken the leading role in establishing an AIDS hospice to minister to victims of the disease. Isn't there a contradiction there somewhere? Shouldn't it be impossible for someone committed to Biblical morality to help someone who is suffering as a result of violating that moral code?

"I don't see any contradictions," Archbishop Hannon says. "I believe the Church should be involved in the most difficult issues of society, and AIDS certainly is the most difficult issue facing us today. If there are people who are sick or hungry, the church wants to help."[12]

Archbishop Hannon's example is being imitated around the country, as more and more churches seek to find their place in ministry to the world around them. Protestants and Roman Catholics are joining together in Dallas, Houston, New York, and other cities to meet the need.

But much, much more remains to be done. The surface has barely been scratched. What we really need is for churches once again to establish "Basiliads," after the example of Basil the Great. We need Christian support groups in many areas of activity that will bring an evangelistic, healing, sacramental, ecclesiastical dimension to health care. We need Christian counselors to staff ministries, clinics, hotlines — counselors who will reach out in courage and compassion, speaking the truth in love. We need Christian institutions to give help to those suffering from drug abuse and alcohol abuse. Will we see a new Order of Hospitalers arise, one that wages a Crusade against the evils of our age? It should be recognized that such a ministry — especially to AIDS patients — involves serious risks. This is the front line of a battle in which the result could very well be death. Let us not kid ourselves about that; this is not a game. The Lord Jesus sternly warned us to look at the consequences of our actions, to count the cost of any enterprise. It is realism, not mere cowardice, that makes people with families to care for hesitant about exposing themselves to AIDS, especially at a time when even the most skilled researchers are in disagreement about the causes of the disease.

The Apostle Paul recognized this when he wrote to the church at Corinth about marital issues: "He who is unmarried cares for the things that belong to the Lord — how he may please the Lord. But he who is married cares about the things of the world — how he may please his wife. There is a difference between a wife and a virgin. The unmarried woman cares about the things of the Lord, that she may be holy both in body and in spirit. But she who is married cares about the things of the world — how she may please her husband. And this I say for your own profit, not that I may put a leash on you, but for what is proper, and that you may serve the Lord without distraction" (1 Corinthians 7:32-35).

The monastic ideal of celibacy for service in the Kingdom of God is not without its problems. Certainly, celibacy should not be mandatory for the pastoral ministry — indeed, the Bible indicates the very opposite (1 Timothy 3:2; Titus 1:6). But the Apostle Paul does have a category of special, undistracted service to God for both men and women that does involve a legitimate, voluntary celibacy. Protestants should not be afraid of calling for special Orders of men and women to serve God in unusually demanding and even dangerous situations. Past abuses should instruct us, but they must not deter us from doing what is right.

Obviously, there are many issues to be thought through. Different needs will call forth different solutions, and we as Christians, operating with varying skills in varying circumstances and from varying ecclesiastical traditions — we will need to be patient with each other. We should feel free to adapt to changing conditions, to compromise everywhere — *except* on the standards given to us by our Lord. He has set down His holy law for every area of life, including sexuality, marriage, and ministry to the needy. He has commanded us to speak and to serve in truth and in love.

As we come to the closing decade of this century, a great question confronts us: Can the Church be the Church? Who will provide Refuge for the lost?

Self-sacrifice brought Christ into the world. And self-sacrifice will lead us, His followers, not away from but into the midst of men. Wherever men suffer, there will we be to comfort. Wherever men strive, there will we be to help. Wherever men fail, there will we be to up-lift. Wherever men succeed, there will we be to rejoice. Self-sacrifice means not indifference to our times and our fellows: it means absorption in them. It means forgetfulness of self in others. It means entering into every man's hopes and fears, longings and despairs; it means manysidedness of spirit, multiform activity, multiplicity of sympathies. It means richness of development. It means not that we should live one life, but a thousand lives — binding ourselves to a thousand souls by the filaments of so loving a sympathy that their lives become ours. It means that all the experiences of men shall smite our souls and shall beat and batter these stubborn hearts of ours into fitness for their heavenly home.

Benjamin B. Warfield, "Imitating the Incarnation,"
in *The Person and Work of Christ*
(Philadelphia: The Presbyterian and Reformed
Publishing Co., 1950), pp. 574f.

ELEVEN

THE BALM OF GILEAD

Is there no Balm in Gilead?
Is there no physician there?
Why then is there no recovery
For the health of the daughter
of my people? (Jeremiah 8:22)

In practical terms, how can the Church *really* be the Church? How can we exercise our priestly duties in the midst of the horrific crisis that besets us on every side? How can we minister hope, healing, and wholeness to AIDS sufferers and their families? How can we take up the Gospel mantle of compassion and care in a fashion that will actually make a tangible difference in the lives of the afflicted?

Obviously, there are no easy answers. But the Bible assures us that there *are* answers. If we will simply buckle down and do the difficult work of being true disciples, healing *will* ultimately and finally blanket our land (2 Chronicles 7:14).

Getting Started With the Word

"Okay, okay," you say, "But now, where do we begin? The church I attend is very small. We're willing to do what we need to do to be faithful to God's call. But our resources are few and far between. Realistically, how can we help? What can we do?"

Well, we simply start at the start. We begin with the Word of God.

Not only must we nurture our own people with the rich truths of practical Biblical instruction, instilling in them a vision for service and sacrifice; we must get the Good News to the sick and suffering. Jesus made it clear that the Gospel was not privileged information to be preciously protected within the confines of a covenantal cabal. No, the Word of Hope and Truth is to be broadcast high and low, from the rooftops and in the hedgerows, along the highways and in the market square. We must always speak the truth in love, with gentleness and discretion (Ephesians 4:15; Colossians 4:5, 6). But first and foremost, we must speak it (Mark 16:15).

There are innumerable ways that we can effectively do this. Ways that any church—large or small, rich or poor—can undertake immediately.

One Presbyterian church in Houston recently began operating a twenty-four hour AIDS hotline. Volunteers from several Sunday School classes sign up for four hour shifts and simply share the Gospel with frightened or despondent callers from the large gay community in town. "We realized that the only information people were getting," the Pastor said, "was little more than propaganda. We felt obligated to provide *really* helpful medical information, *really* helpful spiritual and emotional counsel, and *really* helpful direction for the future." The volunteers go through an extensive six week training course where they learn not only how to share Christ and the Biblical hope, but also how to steer callers toward responsible medical, moral, and hygienic practices. "The response has been remarkable," said the Pastor. "Not only has the church been able to help the distressed and extend its evangelistic reach into the darkest corners of our community, but we've grown as a congregation, spiritually, emotionally, and even numerically. Folks can see by our commitment to this that we *really* mean business."

A Bible church in Philadelphia has used a different approach to getting the Word out to AIDS patients. Every Friday and Saturday night four teams of volunteers go visiting, room to room in four different hospitals, sharing the Gospel, lending a listening ear, and providing Bibles, Christian literature, and gifts. "Some of the people we've been able to minister to," the organizer of the program says, "are folks we *never* would have reached otherwise. Not by television. Not by radio. Not by evangelistic crusades. Not by any of the traditional approaches that our church has used for years. It took us going to *them*. It took us reaching into *their* world." Volunteers in the program have been amazed at the response they've gotten. "I met one young man," a volunteer related, "who had *never* before heard the Gospel. He was so completely overwhelmed by our willingness to visit him, to talk to him, to comfort him, and to just listen to him, that he broke down in tears, uncontrollably sobbing every time we came around. All his friends and loved ones had abandoned him. He was penniless and pathetic. He had given up all hope and was just waiting to die. One Saturday night he literally begged me to show him from the Bible how to become a Christian. He said that he *knew* that Christianity was real, that it was mankind's only hope, because he had *seen* it lived out. Well, you can just imagine what that did for *me*. I mean, suddenly *my* faith was being built up. I was seeing with my own eyes the power of service, the power of obedience, and the power of God for salvation! It has been an extraordinary experience for me. Now I know what Jesus meant when He said, 'It is more blessed to give than to receive.' Giving has been the greatest gift of all." Another volunteer concurred. "I wouldn't trade this experience for anything in the world. My faith is stronger. My commitment is surer. And my life is happier. It's amazing how a simple thing like visiting the sick can change such dire circumstances as the AIDS plague into an open window for the Kingdom."

A Nazarene church in San Diego has opened an AIDS Crisis counseling center three days a week where AIDS sufferers and their families can receive Biblical instruction and nurture for the difficult days ahead.

An Orthodox church in Detroit opens its doors once a month so that families facing the disruptive tragedy of AIDS can meet together to talk, to listen, to lend support to one another, and to learn God's perspective on sin, sickness, and sorrow.

A Baptist church in Denver recently established a day center for AIDS patients and their families near the downtown medical center. Bible studies and informal discussions are led by volunteers from the diaconate at least twice a day. Several ladies in the church provide refreshments and hospitality at mealtimes. And a quiet lounge with an adjacent library is made available throughout the rest of the day, as a kind of haven and refuge from the storms of affliction. A college group from a large charismatic church in Seattle has established a reading and information center in the gay section of town where Bibles, Christian books, tracts, magazines, and responsible medical information are distributed free of charge.

In a similar vein, an interdenominational college group at the University of Nebraska, inspired by the 19th-century London colportage societies of Charles Haddon Spurgeon, have begun a door-to-door distribution of Christian literature in the gay community, both on campus and off.

Each of these varied activities and programs, and dozens of others springing up daily all over the country, are united by their commitment to communicate the Word of God to every man. They are united in their knowledge that the Truth offers healing (Proverbs 12:18; 16:24), life (Proverbs 15:4), and liberty (John 8:32). Jesus has commissioned us to go forth with the Word to heal and reconcile any and all who will hear and heed (Matthew 10:1, 6-8). Now is no time to retreat. Now is no time to seek first our security, hiding the Word under a bushel basket of fear and trembling.

Word and Deed

The task of evangelism doesn't end with a proclamation of the Gospel. As important as that is, the Bible makes it plain that if we want to win the world for Christ we are going to have to match our words with deeds. We are going to have to authenticate the claims of the Gospel with *holy activity*. Faith without corresponding works is altogether worthless. It is in fact dead (James 2:14-26).

It is important that as our ministry to AIDS sufferers develops that we do more than preach and pass out tracts. We must *live out* our faith, and *flesh out* our compassion with *deeds* of kindness and charity.

One Reformed church in the Virginia suburbs of Washington, D.C. is attempting to wed Word and deed in their work among impoverished AIDS patients in the black community. "We recognized very quickly," one of the associate pastors said, "that the skyrocketing costs of AZT treatments and prolonged hospital stays were going to economically devastate the families of the patients. We began to develop a plan to try to help out as best we could." Early in 1982, at a time when most people were just beginning to hear about AIDS, the church was already buying up a block of small frame homes in the inner city, renovating them, and then renting them at rock bottom prices to families struck by the AIDS tragedy. "We wanted to make certain that the families would be able to stay together," said the minister, "but not *just* stay together. We wanted them to be able to stay together in a home environment." The church maintains an active ministry to each of the fourteen families it currently houses. Eight of the families have not joined the church, and six of them have been unable to pay the rent for several months in a row now. "Our intentions are not either proselytism or property management, so membership and rent checks are not big issues with us," said the minister. "Obeying Christ and meeting the needs of the helpless are what we care about." Of course, the charity dispensed by the church program is not without standards. "We try to make certain that our love is Scriptural and not simply sentimental. We don't want to be promiscuous in our care, so we require each family to meet certain requirements and to carry out particular responsibilities. We want to make certain that we *really* help these families. The worst thing we could do is to create for them a whole new environment of dependency."[1]

Another Reformed church in Dallas has a charity outreach to AIDS sufferers that is not less ambitious. A group of volunteers keeps track of hospital admission and then follows up through the chaplaincy offices to make certain that the patient's physical needs are met. They cover rent payments, buy groceries, pay utility bills, secure medical services, and provide job referrals. "Once the patients are diagnosed with full-blown AIDS," says the project coordinator, "they are all too typically abandoned by their friends, fired from their jobs, evicted from their apartments, and excluded from normal everyday life. Most of them have between two and three years to live, but already they are set out to die, cut off from virtually everything they've known and depended on. What are they supposed to do? Where are they supposed to go?" The Church has met with a good deal of resistance in their efforts to rehabilitate the patients and to meet their immediate needs, but they've also had a number of incredibly gratifying experiences. According to the coordinator, the purpose of the program is to "turn a terrible situation into a good one. Instead of turning the folks out into the howling wilderness we are attempting to drive them into the arms of the Church and into the heart of the Kingdom."

Two Baptist churches in Chicago have joined forces to provide part-time job referrals for AIDS sufferers who are unable to find any other work.

A coalition of several Minneapolis-St. Paul Methodist churches have put together a referral service for AIDS afflicted families so that they can provide free or nearly free medical care, counseling, day care, housing, and transportation.

An on-campus Presbyterian outreach has put together a foodbank for families of AIDS patients and sponsors a unique combination food drive and evangelistic thrust at the University of Alabama each year.

A large charismatic Episcopal church in Knoxville has opened a halfway house and hospice for impoverished AIDS patients who have nowhere else to go.

Each of these ministries has grown out of the peculiar circumstances and traditions of the sponsoring churches, but each of them shares a commitment to wedding Word and deed, faith and works. Each of them is committed to sharing the Gospel with uncompromising faithfulness, but in addition to that, they are each committed to fleshing out the Gospel in tangible acts of goodness and mercy. They know that it is only as the naked are clothed, the hungry fed, and the helpless cared for, will healing cover our land (Isaiah 58: 6-8).

Living Prayer

Preaching the Word and providing for needs is still not enough, though. There is something else that AIDS sufferers need. There is something else we can do that will minister to them significantly.

That something is prayer.

The abysmal lack of prayerfulness among the people of God is shocking. Despite the afflictions, the persecutions, the traumas, and the plagues of our day, the Church has been strangely, obscenely quiet. Where are our prayer warriors? Where are our seasons of intercession? Where are our days of fasting, our passionate petitioning, our solitary supplication?

One commonly neglected aspect of prayer is its *prophetic* character. We generally think of a prophet as someone who speaks to men on behalf of God. As far as it goes, that is accurate. But the Biblical concept of the prophet is much richer. According to Scripture, the prophet can speak to men because he has first spoken to God.

The prophet in the Old Testament was one who had been uniquely favored with the privilege of entering the very presence of God and the angels to witness the deliberations of the heavenly court, and even to take part in the discussions (see 1 Kings 22:19-22; Isaiah 6:1-8; Ezekiel 1-3, 10). God even declares that He does nothing without consulting His prophets (Amos 3:7), and it is on this basis that they could be heaven's authoritative spokesmen (Jeremiah 15:19; 23:16-22). This means something very important: *the characteristic activity of the prophet is intercession.* In fact, the very first occurrence of the word *prophet* in the Bible speaks not of "prophesying" in the usually accepted use of the term, but of Abraham's interceding for someone who is suffering under the judgment of God (Genesis 20:7). Another clear example of this is Abraham's intercession for Sodom (Genesis 18:16-33), in which he actually *argues* with God, seeking to change His mind. Isn't that presumption? Not at all; it is a spirited discussion between intimate friends (2 Chronicles 20:7; Isaiah 41:8; James 2:23). The Biblical prophet is on such close terms with God that he can argue with Him. This is why we so often find the prophets engaging God in debate, interceding and mediating for others (cf. Exodus 32:7-14; Amos 7:1-6). God and His prophets can speak freely and openly with each other (Genesis 18:17; Exodus 33:11).

But this prophetic privilege of intercession was limited to a select few in the Old Testament. No one could just decide to be a prophet. One could not speak unless he was spoken *to*. In order to be a prophet, one first had to be "raptured" by God's Spirit into the heavenly council chamber; one had to have God's Spirit placed upon him; one had to be filled with the Spirit. This did not happen to everyone. The prophets were an elite, exclusive group. Moses, the preeminent Prophet of the Old Covenant, acutely recognized this, and longed for a day when this blessing of intimate friendship with God would be extended to all: "Oh, that all the LORD's people were prophets and that the LORD would put His Spirit upon them!" (Numbers 11:29).

Moses' dream was fulfilled in Christ's institution of the New Covenant. That is why, in Jesus' parting instructions to His disciples, He gives them so much information about the Holy Spirit and about prayer (cf. John 14-16). Like the prophets of old, they had been raised to an intimate level of communication with Him:

> No longer do I call you servants, for a servant does not know what his master is doing; but I have called you friends, for all things that I heard from My Father I have made known to you. (John 15:15)

Soon the infant Church would be baptized with the Spirit, and they would be enabled to communicate with God in a new way. Because of Christ's ascension into the presence of God as the covenantal head of His people, and through the consequent outpouring of the Spirit, the Church has access to the throne of God in Jesus' name; we have complete freedom of speech and can draw near with boldness (John 7:37-39; Hebrews 10:19-22). That is the significance of the miracle at Pentecost (Acts 2:1-4): the believers were speaking with other tongues, Peter said, as the sign that the Spirit had been poured out upon the Church, and that all had become *prophets* (Acts 2:16-18). Moses' dream of "the prophethood of all believers" was now beginning to be fulfilled.

This has tremendous importance for our prayer life. Individually and corporately, *Christians are prophets*. Of course, this means that we are to speak God's Word to our culture; but the point I wish to stress here is that *we are privileged to pray*.

Please, hear me! Do not shift into "spiritual coma mode" at this point. Let's not turn this into sentimental gush. Look at the prayers of the great prophets in the Bible—Moses, and Jeremiah, and Daniel, and David in the Psalms. Look at the prayers of the great Prophet, our Lord Jesus. We find no sterile, trite, polite, cant phrases here. Instead, we are shocked to find storms, explosions, cries, outbursts, reasonings, supplications, arguments. Arguments! We find strong personalities who are so confident in their close friendship with God that they actually put on the gloves and duke it out with Him. They attempt to change His mind—and are often successful.

Prayer is not a game. It is not a religious exercise. It is an earnest discussion between the King and His closest friends. It is our opportunity, as those to whom God looks for counsel, to advise Him on matters of policy. We must remember, certainly, that God is always God, the Sovereign Lord of all creation, and that we approach Him only by His grace in Christ; but that should make us bold, not timid. Naturally, He does not have to take our advice; but Jesus promised us that He often will (John 14:13, 14). Indeed, we should *expect* affirmative answers to our prayers (Matthew 7:7-11; Luke 11:9-13), and we should keep asking until we get the answers we want (Luke 11:5-8; 18:1-8). We do not have, because we do not ask (James 4:2). We are prophets.

We are also a *Church* of prophets. There is tremendous power in the collective liturgical prayers of God's people. The Church meets as the heavenly Council before God's throne, one great assembly united for prayer (Hebrews 10:19-25; 12:22-24). When God's advisers agree together, their "influence" upon His decisions is compounded (Matthew 18:19, 20). As we pray together, especially on the Lord's Day, the powers of Satan are cast down more and more. Next time you're in public worship, pay attention! You are taking part in an historic event: for the prayers of the Church shape the future of the world (cf. Revelation 8:3-5).

This is not the place to provide a complete theology of prayer, and so I will mention only one other point briefly. As those who have been made God's intimate friends, it is passing strange that so many Christians do not seek regular fellowship with Him in prayer. When I fell in love with my wife, I made a nuisance of myself. I hung around her house, I called her on the telephone, I sent flowers to her home and office, I made a special effort to get on good terms with her family and friends, and in numerous ways barged into every aspect of her life. This was not always received with the enthusiasm I desired, but I persisted. While it is not quite true to say that she married me just so I would stop bothering her, I am happy to admit that my perseverance paid off. Why did I invest so much time and effort?

Because I was in love. Love made me determined to spend as much time as possible in the presence of my beloved.

Do Christians love God? Do we desire His friendship? If so, should it be all that hard to spend an unhurried hour or so in prayer every day? Who wouldn't want to spend time in the presence of his Beloved? Admittedly, prayer involves warfare. One reason it is so hard is that evil spirits work hard trying to keep us from doing it. From time to time, at least, we need help in starting. I usually begin my prayers with a prayerbook, a collection of prayers that have been prayed by godly men and women through the ages. Those that have been the most helpful to me are the following: *The Book of Common Prayer* (various editions), the *Private Devotions* of Lancelot Andrewes,[2] *A Manual of Eastern Orthodox Prayers*,[3] *The Book of Common Worship*,[4] and *The Valley of Vision*.[5] There are many other good prayerbooks and devotional helps for those, like me, who need them. The important thing is to find what works for you, and use it. Commune with God.

There is no way around the fact that prayer is a discipline. It takes determination and effort to succeed. It is a myth, a snare and a delusion, to suppose that prayer should not become a routine. It *must* be a routine, a habit, or it will not get done. Like any other habit, it gets easier: if you're used to taking a shower every morning, you feel incomplete if something prevents you from doing it. The habit becomes a joy, a release; but it begins, and is maintained, as a discipline.[6]

Living Examples

Fortunately, while most of us are like the Apostles at Gethsemane, asleep, there are a few stalwart disciples who have brought the force of prayer to bear against the devastating circumstances of AIDS. It would behoove us to imitate their example.

A small nondenominational church in Kansas City has undertaken a massive prayer campaign in their town. Whenever patients are diagnosed with AIDS in the city's dozen or so major hospitals, they are immediately assigned to a prayer partner by the volunteers who run the ministry. The patients and their partners remain entirely anonymous to one another. In fact, most of the patients have no idea the program even exists. But even though direct contact is never made with the patients, the prayer partners exercise a daily ministry of intercession for them. Explains the pastor, "We pray for repentance, for conviction, for healing, for consolation, for emotional stability, for finances, and for strength. We pray that God would simply work in their lives in a mighty way." One AIDS patient who heard about the program contacted the church about two years ago. He asked to be put in touch with his prayer partner. To his dismay, his partner was a teenager afflicted with cerebral palsy. He was so moved by this teen's selflessness and sacrificial service in the midst of great and grave personal travail that he began to seriously investigate the claims of the Gospel. Two months later he was converted and baptized. A month after that, his AIDS symptoms went into a sudden and unprecedented remission. That was two years ago. Today he is actively involved in the ministry himself. He has abandoned his homosexual lifestyle altogether and has dedicated the rest of his life, however long God grants him, to imitating the selfless service of his palsied teenaged mentor.

In Cleveland an evangelical Episcopal church has a service of healing every Thursday evening for AIDS sufferers. An entire liturgy, especially written for the AIDS crisis, walks the penitents through the various elements of the Gospel: proclamation, confession, restoration, thanksgiving, and adoration. "When we began a year and a half ago," the pastor said, "virtually no one showed up. But we conducted the services anyway. We were convinced that we needed to commit ourselves to lives of prayer." It wasn't long before word began to spread in the gay community and the service was packed. Patients who were too ill to come to the services began to flood the church offices with requests for private prayer. Soon the pastor was devoting his full attentions to liturgical prayer three days a week. "It has been remarkable how the Lord has used this little step of faith and obedience in our lives and in our witness to the community." The church has seen more than two dozen conversions. Its discipleship classes have swelled to include more than one hundred gays, and it has attested to at least five miraculous remissions of the deadly AIDS virus. In one case, a repentant teenager no longer even tests positive to either the ELISA test or the Western Blot test.[7]

A Church of Christ congregation in Oklahoma City that has been sponsoring a chapter of Homosexuals Anonymous for more than two years has a twenty-four hour prayer chain in operation that includes more than three thousand participants. AIDS sufferers from all over the United States and Canada have called in, placing their names on the massive twelve thousand-name intercession list.

A New York City Baptist church has an outreach to the various hospital chapels on Manhattan, holding weekly prayer services, distributing literature, and assigning prayer partners to patients that request them.

Another church in New York, this time an Assembly of God congregation, has a ministry of instruction, equipping individual Christians to gain access to hospital intensive care units to care for and pray for the dying. They show folks how to get permission from hospital administrators, governing boards, and chaplaincy alliances to meet with family members, provide spiritual materials, and offer Biblical counsel.

A Presbyterian church in the Los Angeles suburbs recently built a prayer tower that is open twenty-four hours a day, manned by trained volunteers and AIDS counselors. A phone operator takes prayer requests day or night and then passes them on to the intercessors scattered throughout the tower's four chapels.

Again, each of these ministries comes from a unique and distinct set of traditions and presuppositions. But each of them is united in its commitment to obey God by exercising unceasing intercession for the sick and suffering (1 Thessalonians 5:17).

The Opportunity and the Challenge

Obviously, the opportunity for the Church is great. If only Christians would undertake their God-ordained tasks of tending the sick and reconciling the repentant through Word, deed, and intercession, not only would we be able to offer our land the Medicine of Hope in this day of panicky hopelessness, we would be able to live up to the high call of priesthood and discipleship that God has placed on us. We would at last be able to see the Church *really* being the Church.

The challenge is before us. So, what will it be? Life or death? Faithfulness or fear? Obedience or selfishness? Will we turn tail and run or will the Church *be* the Church?

The future of our civilization may depend upon how we respond to this, the ultimate challenge.

Unless the battle has preceded, there cannot be a victory: when there shall have been, in the onset of battle, the victory, then also the crown is given to the victors. For the helmsman is recognized in the tempest; in the warfare the soldier is proved. It is a wanton display when there is no danger. Struggle in adversity is the trial of the truth. The tree which is deeply founded in its root is not moved by the onset of winds, and the ship which is compacted of solid timbers is beaten by the waves and is not shattered; and when the threshing-floor brings out the corn, the strong and robust grains despise the winds, while the empty chaff is carried away by the blast that falls upon it.[8]

But the first extraordinary fact which marks this history is this: that Europe has been turned upside down over and over again; and that at the end of each of these revolutions the same religion has again been found on top. The Faith is always converting the age, not as an old religion but as a new religion. . . .

In our own case we can see this oft-repeated process close at hand; we know how completely a society can lose its fundamental religion without abolishing its official religion; we know how men can all become agnostics long before they abolish bishops. And we know that also in this last ending, which really did look to us like the final ending, the incredible thing has happened again; the Faith has a better following among the young men than among the old. When Ibsen spoke of the new generation knocking at the door, he certainly never expected that it would be the church-door.

At least five times, therefore, with the Arian and the Albigensian, with the Humanist sceptic, after Voltaire and after Darwin, the Faith has to all appearance gone to the dogs. In each of these five cases it was the dog that died.

G. K. Chesterton, *The Everlasting Man*
(Garden City, NY: Image Books,
1955), pp. 255, 260f.

TWELVE

THE REFUGE

And He showed me a pure river of water of life, clear as crystal, pro-
ceeding from the throne of God and of the Lamb. In the middle of its
street, and on either side of the river, was the tree of life, which bore
twelve fruits, each tree yielding its fruit every month. And the leaves of
the tree were for the healing of the nations. (Revelation 22:1, 2)

Everyone has a worldview, a basic philosophy about life and
the meaning of events. Part of that worldview is a philosophy of
history, an explanation for how and why the world develops as it
does. Is the world headed anywhere in particular? Is there such
a thing as progress? Is there a Plan? If so, how does each event
fit into that Plan?

The consistent, Biblically informed Christian has an answer
for these questions. We have a worldview, an interpretation of all
reality and history, tailor-made to fit the real world by its
Creator and Planner Himself. That philosophy is summed up
by the Apostle Paul in his letter to the Roman Christians:

> For of Him and through Him and to Him are all things, to
> whom be glory forever. Amen. (Romans 11:36)

This means that all events fit into God's Plan. Everything ultimately serves the cause of His Kingdom and works for His
eternal glory. All facts are *created* facts, coming into existence
with an already built-in, definitive, authoritative interpretation.
Indeed, as the Apostle Paul says elsewhere, God works all things
together not only for His own glory but for the good of His people, the Church (Romans 8:28; cf. Ephesians 1:22). Benjamin
Warfield summed it up beautifully:

In the infinite wisdom of the Lord of all the earth, each event falls with exact precision into its proper place in the unfolding of His eternal plan; nothing, however small, however strange, occurs without His ordering, or without its peculiar fitness for its place in the working out of His purpose; and the end of all shall be the manifestation of His glory, and the accumulation of His praise.[1]

Now, saying that much is not to say everything. It certainly is not to say that we can see clearly *how* "each event falls with exact precision into its proper place." The Christian doctrine of knowledge insists that only God has comprehensive knowledge of all things; He alone has exhaustive understanding. But, as the One who knows, and knows because He is the Planner and Controller, the ultimate, infinite, and yet infinitely personal Environment for all things, He has assured us that He works all things according to His purpose and for His own glory. So we can *believe* and *know* it to be true without *comprehending* it.[2]

Warfield tells us something else about God's Plan for the world: not only that it exists but where it is headed. Again, it would be difficult to improve upon his almost poetic prose:

You must not fancy, then, that God sits helplessly by while the world, which He has created for Himself, hurtles hopelessly to destruction, and He is able only to snatch with difficulty here and there a brand from the universal burning. The world does not govern Him in a single one of its acts: He governs it and leads it steadily onward to the end which, from the beginning, or ever a beam of it had been laid, He had determined for it. . . . Through all the years one increasing purpose runs, one *increasing* purpose: the kingdoms of the earth become ever more and more the Kingdom of our God and His Christ. The process may be slow; the progress may appear to our impatient eyes to lag. But it is God who is building: and under His hands the structure rises as steadily as it does slowly, and in due time the capstone shall be set into its place, and to our astonished eyes shall be revealed nothing less than a saved world.[3]

What does this Biblical philosophy of history tell us about AIDS? It tells us several important things — perspectives that we must keep sight of amid all the confusion, fear, and frustration that have become associated with the disease.

First, the coming of AIDS tells us that we have reached a new era in human history. History is constantly moving toward the glory of God and the complete manifestation of His justice. The blessings and cursings of Deuteronomy 28 can never reach complete and perfect fulfillment in a world of sin. To say that there is unpunished sin anywhere is to acknowledge that God's justice, His reward and retribution, have not been meted out in fullness. Nevertheless, the Bible does point to a time, before the end of history and toward which history is racing, in which God's justice will overflow the earth, when the whole world will be filled with the knowledge of the glory of God, as the waters cover the sea (cf. Psalm 72; Isaiah 2:2-4; 11:1-10; 60; 65:13-25; Micah 4:1-5).

We must not miss the *eschatology* of AIDS. When a new disease appears in history, a disease that is both selective in terms of abominable actions *and* has the demonstrated capacity to flow out into the population at large, it is a manifest signal that Someone is knocking on the cosmic door. The world is becoming more differentiated; the world is looking more and more like an illustration of Deuteronomy 28. God is evidently punishing certain sins more strictly and directly than in past ages. As men are becoming more self-conscious in their rebellion against God, the public demonstration of His justice becomes more evident as well. We are watching an eschatological development take place in our midst: as history progresses, blessing and cursing becomes more pronounced, and less "common." Lest we think this somehow lets us off the hook, however, let us remember that it is the Church that allowed the abominations and perversions that are now polluting the land. God is *God*, the All-Controller: He can easily turn a specific judgment into a general judgment on the whole social order. If He wishes, all it will take is a sneeze, a glass of water, an arthropod with a deadly appetite.

Second, the coming of AIDS tells us where God wants His Church to move "in demonstration of the Spirit and of power" (1 Corinthians 2:4). Wherever there is a crisis, that is where the Church should be. Obviously, not everyone is called to an AIDS-related ministry. But the fact is this: Since every problem in the world is placed there by God (cf. Psalm 46:8), and since He has designed and destined His Church to rule on the earth (cf. Genesis 1:26-28; Ephesians 1:20-22; Revelation 2:26, 27; 3:21), *the fact that there is a problem in the world means that God wants the Church to solve it*, for His glory and the advance of His Kingdom into all the earth. We must not—we dare not—throw up our hands in helplessness at the sight of such a devastating tragedy. Jesus Christ is Lord, He is the One who heals and saves and rules, and He has committed His ministry and His power into our hands. We have the solution, because we have Christ to offer to the world. Every disaster is an opportunity. There are no accidents.

Ministry is a necessity for the Church Militant. We are in a warfare for the souls and bodies of all men, for the life of the world. The Church must respond as she has at other times in history, in conviction, in courage, in compassion. We are the Refuge. We are the Ark. There is no salvation for the world outside the Church of Jesus Christ. That is *why* we exist.

Are we willing to take on the awesome responsibility of ministry to a dying world? As the late Francis Schaeffer lamented again and again, too often the bourgeois church has chosen the route of "personal peace and affluence" in the face of God's demands. But there is little time left for that anymore. The disaster looming before us is too vast for that. The Church of this generation will either go down in history as the Church that turned around in its tracks and overcame by the blood of the Lamb, by the Word of its testimony, and loving not its own life, even to the point of death (Revelation 12:11)—or it will just go *down* in history.

We are afraid; but perfect love casts out fear. Some of us will die in this battle; but every battle costs lives, especially when there is something worth fighting for. Besides, we will all die someday anyway. Knowing that, how should we then live?

The Failure Generation

It's an embarrassing story. Here was the new nation of Israel, camped on the border of Canaan, the land God had promised to give them. The spies they sent in had returned after more than a month of reconnaissance, laden with astonishing examples of the country's abundant fruit: a single cluster of grapes had to be carried on a pole between two men. But they also told stories of fortified cities, of powerful nations, and of mighty men who looked like giants. Their concluding statement about these "giants" is psychologically revealing, telling us next to nothing about the actual size of the Canaanites, but volumes about the attitude of the Israelites—a cowardice that stemmed from disobedience to God's Word: "We were like grasshoppers in our own sight, and so we were in their sight" (Numbers 13:33). (Moral: If you feel like a bug, you probably will look like one!)

The majority of Israel listened to the fearful report of the great obstacles before them. Immediately they began to cry in terror. "I wish we were dead! If we go into the land, our children will be killed! Let's go back to Egypt!" Two of the spies, Joshua and Caleb, tried to reason with them. "The land is good," said Caleb. "If God is pleased with us, He'll bless us and give it to us. Don't be afraid of the Canaanites; God is with us." But it was to no avail. God's people refused to listen.

And so judgment fell upon the failure generation. God punished them by forcing them to wander like nomads in the desert for 40 years, until the whole older generation died out—all except for Joshua and Caleb, who led the younger generation to victory over all the enemies their parents had feared. Ironically, one of the main fears of those parents had been for their children's safety (Numbers 14:31, 32). Yet it was the disobedient parents who perished; and their obedient children defeated the "giants"!

But there is an even more ironic twist to the story: When the younger generation prepared to invade Canaan, they too sent spies into the land. The spies encountered a harlot named Rahab, who befriended and protected them—and gave them an astounding piece of information. Forty years before, she said, the Canaanites were waiting for the invasion. They knew that the Israelites were heading for Canaan, and were in a state of utter panic! Why? Rahab explained: "I know that the LORD has given you the land. The terror of you has fallen on us, and all the inhabitants of the land are fainthearted because of you. For we have heard how the LORD dried up the water of the Red Sea for you when you came out of Egypt. . . . And as soon as we heard these things, our hearts melted; neither did there remain any more courage in anyone because of you, for the LORD your

God, He is God in heaven above and in the earth beneath"
(Joshua 2:9-11).

Rahab was quite a theologian. That's an amazing confession of faith for a Canaanite harlot to make. But there's something even more significant. Rahab revealed the fact that at the very moment that the terrified Israelites were backing away from their promised inheritance, *their enemies were even more frightened than they were*. The "giants" were shaking in their seven-league boots!

It's important to note the reason for the Canaanites' fear — a fear which, unlike that of the Israelites, was completely rational and sensible. They had heard of the victories which God had given Israel over Egypt. The ancient Near Eastern news agencies had reported how, without firing a shot, the Israelites had left Egypt completely devastated, economically, politically, and militarily. The greatest power of the age had been brought to its knees by these slaves and their God. And now this invincible army was headed for Canaan, claiming that it belonged to them! The Canaanites knew that their defeat was inevitable, and they were petrified with fright. It sounds crazy, but it turns out that these heathen Canaanites had more faith in God's promises than the Israelites did! (And, as they waited in dread for forty years, they must have wondered: What's keeping them?)

The failure of the first generation is instructive for us as we face obstacles of our own. First, *unbelief is irrational*. Of course, Israel claimed to be just "looking at the facts" — the dangers facing them. But they were ignoring the greatest fact of all: that *all facts are created facts*, completely under God's control. As Rahab put it, God is "Lord of heaven and earth." Nothing is too great for His power. There is no enemy that He can't conquer, no obstacle that He can't overcome. We cannot understand "the facts" at all unless we see them in terms of God's Lordship.

Second, *unbelief is doomed to failure*. The entire first generation — the generation that had seen the plagues God sent on the Egyptians, that had experienced the Red Sea crossing, that had been led by the Cloud and fed miraculously by manna from heaven and water from the rock, that had every reason in the world to expect overwhelming triumph over all opposition — *that* generation was swallowed up by the sands of the desert. The victory that should have been theirs was enjoyed by their children instead.

Like the people of Israel, we have been given a territorial commission. The Lord Jesus Christ has commanded His people to capture not just a slice of geography in the Near East, but the whole world. And our commission is as deep as it is vast: We are expected not just to *witness* to the nations, but to *disciple* all nations as well (Matthew 28:18-20). And what is our response? "Well, Lord, there are these giants out there. . . ." *Of course* there are obstacles. They're supposed to be there. God has placed them there, not so that we will be defeated, but so He can demonstrate His great power in overcoming them through our weakness. Too often we're like the fearful, irrational Israelites who looked at the giants and said, "They're too *big* to hit!" We need to be like faithful Caleb and Joshua, who said, "Are you kidding? They're too big to *miss!*"

THE MINISTRATION
OF HEALING[1]

When the Ministration of Healing takes place at a service of public worship, it is desirable that it precede the distribution of Holy Communion. Appropriate passages of Scripture may be read, such as Psalm 23, 91, 103, 145; Matthew 9:2-8; Mark 16:15-20; Luke 17:11-19; John 6:47-57.

Instruction

The Officiant shall then begin the service of Healing, saying

Dearly beloved, The Apostle James instructs us that if anyone is sick, "let him call for the elders of the church, and let them pray over him, anointing him with oil in the name of the Lord. And the prayer of faith will save the sick, and the Lord will raise him up. And if he has committed sins, he will be forgiven. Confess your trespasses to one another, and pray for one another, that you may be healed. The effective, fervent prayer of a righteous man avails much."

Also, we read of our Lord Jesus Christ, in the Gospel of Mark, that He sent out His disciples to preach the Gospel, giving them power over unclean spirits: "And they cast out many demons, and anointed with oil many who were sick, and healed them."

In Scripture, the laying on of hands with the anointing of oil is a sign of the gracious work of the Holy Spirit, the Lord and Giver of Life. This rite finds expression in the New Covenant as an act of confession: a confession that only the power of the Holy Spirit can heal us of illness, and a confession that God's ordained government in the Church is, ordinarily, the place at which an appeal for special healing should be made.

The person seeking special healing, therefore, should confess sin, be anointed with oil, and then be prayed over by the elders.

Here may follow, if appropriate, a brief explanation of the circumstances of the present ministration.

Confession of Sin

The officiant then shall address the sick person, or the parents of the sick child, saying

Do you [on behalf of this child] confess that you have sinned against God, not only in outward transgressions, but also in secret thoughts and desires which you cannot fully understand, but which are all known to Him? If so, answer: I confess my sin.

Penitent: I confess my sin.

Officiant: Do you [on behalf of this child] confess that you are deserving of all misery and wrath for your sins, in this world and the next? If so, answer: I confess it.

Penitent: I confess it.

Officiant: Do you [on behalf of this child] flee for refuge to God's infinite mercy, seeking and imploring His grace and healing, for the sake of our Lord Jesus Christ? If so, answer: I do.

Penitent: I do.

Officiant: Almighty God have mercy on you, forgive all your sins through our Lord Jesus Christ, strengthen you in all goodness, and by the power of the Holy Spirit keep you in eternal life.

Let us pray.

O Lord, holy Father, giver of health and salvation: Send your Holy Spirit to sanctify this oil; that, as your holy apostles anointed many that were sick and healed them, so may those who in faith and repentance receive this holy unction be made whole; through Jesus Christ our Lord, who lives and reigns with You and the Holy Spirit, one God, forever and ever. Amen.

Anointing with Oil

The officiant then shall dip a thumb into the holy oil, and make the Sign of the Cross on the penitent's forehead, saying

(Name), I anoint you with oil in the Name of the Father, and of the Son, and of the Holy Spirit. Amen.

As you are outwardly anointed with this holy oil, so may our heavenly Father grant you the inward anointing of the Holy

Spirit. Of His great mercy, may He forgive your sins, release you from suffering, and restore you to wholeness and strength. May He deliver you from all evil, preserve you in goodness, and bring you to everlasting life; through Jesus Christ our Lord. Amen.

Then the elders shall place their hands upon the penitent, and the officiant shall continue, saying

(Name), we lay our hands upon you in the Name of the Father, and of the Son, and of the Holy Spirit, beseeching our Lord Jesus Christ to sustain you with His presence, to banish every unclean spirit, to drive away all your sickness, and to give you that victory of life and peace which will enable you to serve Him both now and evermore. Amen.

Then one or more of the following prayers shall be said:

General Prayers

Almighty God, the Father of our Lord Jesus Christ, whom You raised from the dead by the power of the Holy Spirit: Now pour out upon Your servant *(Name)* that same Spirit, the Lord and Giver of Life, whom You have promised to give to those who ask. Sanctify and cleanse *him* in body and soul, utterly banish from *him* all infection and disease, and drive away from *him* all unclean spirits, by the authority of the risen Christ, who has ascended to Your right hand, far above all principality and power and might and dominion, and every name that is named; under whose feet You have placed all things; whom You have given as head over all things to the Church; at whose Name every knee shall bow, of those in heaven, and of those on earth, and of those under the earth; whose Lordship every tongue is bound to confess; who now lives and reigns with You in the unity of the Holy Spirit, one God, now and forever. Amen.

O Father of mercies and God of all comfort, our only help in time of need: We humbly beseech You to behold, visit, and relieve Your sick servant *(Name)* for whom our prayers are desired. Look upon *him* with the eyes of Your mercy; comfort *him* with a sense of Your goodness; preserve *him* from the temptations of the enemy; and give *him* patience under *his* affliction. Restore *him* to health, and enable *him* to lead the residue of *his* life in Your fear, and to Your glory; and grant that finally *he* may dwell with You in life everlasting; through Jesus Christ our Lord. Amen.

O God, the strength of the weak and the comfort of sufferers: Mercifully accept our prayers, and grant to Your servant *(Name)* the help of Your power, that *his* sickness may be turned into health, and our sorrow into joy; through Jesus Christ our Lord. Amen.

O God of the heavenly powers, by the might of your command you drive away from our bodies all sickness and all infirmity: Be present in Your goodness with Your servant *(Name)*, that *his* weakness may be banished and *his* strength restored; and that, *his* health being renewed, *he* may bless Your holy Name; through Jesus Christ our Lord. Amen.

Prayers for a Sick Child

Heavenly Father, watch with us over Your child *(Name)*, and grant that *he* may be restored to that perfect health which it is Yours alone to give; through Jesus Christ our Lord. Amen.

Lord Jesus Christ, Good Shepherd of the sheep, You gather the lambs in Your arms and carry them in Your bosom; we commend to Your loving care this child *(Name)*. Relieve *his* pain, guard *him* from all danger, restore to *him* Your gifts of gladness and strength, and raise *him* up to a life of service to You. Hear us, we pray, for Your dear Name's sake. Amen.

Prayers Before an Operation or Medical Treatment

Almighty God, our heavenly Father, graciously comfort Your servant *(Name)* in *his* suffering, and bless the means made use of for *his* cure. Fill *his* heart with confidence that, though at times *he* may be afraid, *he* yet may put *his* trust in You; through Jesus Christ our Lord. Amen.

Strengthen Your servant *(Name)*, O God, to do what *he* has to do and bear what *he* has to bear; that, accepting Your healing gifts through the skill of surgeons and nurses, *he* may be restored to usefulness in Your Kingdom with a thankful heart; through Jesus Christ our Lord. Amen.

Heavenly Father, Giver of life and health: Comfort and relieve Your sick servant *(Name)*, and grant Your power of healing to those who minister to *his* needs, that *he* may be strengthened in *his* weakness and have confidence in Your loving care; through Jesus Christ our Lord. Amen.

Benediction and Dismissal

At the close of the prayers, if Holy Communion is not to follow, the Lord's Prayer shall be said by all, and then the officiant shall conclude, saying

The Almighty Lord, who is a strong tower to all who put their trust in Him, to whom all things in heaven, on earth, and under the earth bow and obey: Be now and evermore your defense, and make you know and feel that the only Name under heaven given for health and salvation is the Name of our Lord Jesus Christ. Amen.

END NOTES

Chapter 1 — The Plague

1. Robert Bazell in *The New Republic*, June 1, 1987, p. 14.
2. "The Meaning of AIDS," *National Review*, December 19, 1986, p. 19.
3. Cited in James I. Slaff, M.D., and John K. Brubaker, *The AIDS Epidemic: How You Can Protect Yourself and Your Family — Why You Must* (New York: Warner Press, 1985), pp. 3-4.
4. Ibid.
5. This information was obtained by telephone from the Centers for Disease Control (CDC) in Atlanta, Georgia.
6. Cited in Gene Antonio, *The AIDS Cover-Up? The Real and Alarming Facts about AIDS* (San Francisco: Ignatius Press, 1986), p. 12. This excellent book has been the basic resource for much of the medical information in this chapter.
7. Centers for Disease Control.
8. Gene Antonio, *The AIDS Cover-Up? The Real and Alarming Facts about AIDS* (San Francisco: Ignatius Press, 1986), p. 67.
9. Bazell, Sacramento *Union*, January 20, 1987, p. 14.
10. Antonio, p. 133.
11. Cited in William F. Buckley, *National Review*, April 25, 1986, p. 63.
12. Ibid.
13. For further insight into this complex but facinating field of study see Peter Jaret, "Our Immune System: The Wars Within," *National Geographic*, June 1986, pp. 702-34.
14. Katie Leishman, "AIDS and Insects," *The Atlantic Monthly*, September 1987, p. 71.
15. Cited in Antonio, p. 11.
16. Ibid, pp. 13f.
17. *Lancet*, January 25, 1986, p. 193; cited in Antonio, p. 19.
18. *Time*, February 16, 1987.
19. John Seale, "AIDS Virus Infection: Prognosis and Transmission," *Journal of the Royal Society of Medicine*, 1985, No. 78, p. 613; cited in Antonio, p. 24.
20. Antonio, p. 26.
21. Ibid., p. 28.
22. Ibid., pp. 118ff.
23. J. F. Grutsch Jr. and A. D. J. Robertson, "The Coming of AIDS," *The American Spectator*, March 1986, p. 13.
24. Ibid., p. 12.
25. *Time*, February 16, 1987, p. 51.
26. Ibid., p. 52.

27. Antonio, pp. 29f.
28. This information was obtained by telephone from the Sacramento AIDS Foundation.
29. Ibid.
30. *Time*, June 8, 1987, p. 21.
31. Charles Paul Freund, *The New Republic*, July 6, 1987, p. 8, reporting on articles in the New York *Native* and other gay publications.
32. *Time*, June 8, 1987.
33. Bazell, p. 15.
34. Ibid.
35. *Discover*, December 1985, p. 52.
36. Robert O. Hawkins Jr., "Women Who Prefer Gay Men," *Medical Aspects of Human Sexuality*, July 1985, p. 192; A. P. Bell and M. S. Weinberg, *Homosexualities: A Study of Diversity among Men and Women* (New York: Simon and Schuster, 1978) pp. 162, 286; cited in Antonio, p. 91.
37. David A. Noebel, *The Homosexual Revolution* (Manitou Springs, CO: Summit Press, 1985), p. 85; Antonio, p. 3.
38. Quoted in Antonio, p. 91.
39. "AIDS Victim Charged After Blood Sales," Sacramento *Union*, June 30, 1987.
40. "Study Says AIDS Antibodies Take As Long As a Year to Form," Orange County *Register*, October 3, 1987.
41. *Time*, March 30, 1987, p. 25.
42. *U.S. News & World Report*, June 1, 1987, p. 59.
43. *Dallas Gay News*, May 20, 1983; cited in Antonio, p. 77.
44. Antonio, p. 77.
45. "Suspected Hooker's Arrest Stirs AIDS Ethics Dilemma," Sacramento *Bee*, June 21, 1987.
46. Samuel Willard, *A Compleat Body of Divinity*, 1726 (New York: Johnson Reprint Co., 1960), p. 751. See David Chilton, *Productive Christians In an Age of Guilt-Manipulators: A Biblical Response to Ronald J. Sider* (Tyler, TX: Institute for Christian Economics, third ed., 1985), pp. 139-50. The best study of envy of any substantial length in this century is Helmut Schoeck's *Envy: A Theory of Social Behaviour* (New York: Harcourt, Brace & World, 1966).
47. Antonio, pp. 89ff.
48. William F. Buckley, *National Review*, October 18, 1985, p. 63.
49. Antonio, p. 108.
50. T. Tervo et al., "Recovery of HTLV-III from Contact Lenses," *Lancet*, February 15, 1986, pp. 379f.; cited in Antonio, p. 109.
51. F. Barre-Sinoussi et al., "Resistance of AIDS Virus at Room Temperature," *Lancet*, September 28, 1985, pp. 721f.; cf. the *Journal of the American Medical Association*, November 22-29, 1985, p. 2866; Antonio, pp. 110f.
52. L. Resnick et al., "Stability and Inactivation of HTLV-III/LAV under Clinical and Laboratory Experiments," *Journal of the American Medical Association* 1985, Vol. 225, pp. 1887-1981; cited in Antonio, pp. 111f.
53. Katie Leishman, "AIDS and Insects," *The Atlantic Monthly*, September 1987, pp. 56-72.
54. Ibid., p. 72. See also *First AIDS Report*, July 15, 1987 (P.O. Box 2396, Vancouver, WA 98668, $69 per year).
55. *Time*, June 15, 1987, p. 58.
56. Antonio, p. 134.
57. Ibid., p. 137.
58. Ibid., p. 136.

59. *U.S. News & World Report*, June 15, 1987, p. 18.
60. Ibid., p. 16.
61. The number of cases doubles every twenty months.
62. Cf. Antonio, pp. 137f.
63. Ibid., p. 138.
64. Slaff and Brubaker, p. 124.
65. Quoted in Otto Friedrich, *The End of the World: A History* (New York: Coward, McCann & Geoghegan, 1982), p. 113ff.
66. Ibid., p. 113.
67. Ibid., p. 117.
68. Ibid., pp. 124f.
69. Ibid., pp. 129-133.
70. An interview by Dr. James Dobson, broadcast on the March 17, 1987 radio program *Focus on the Family*. The number of blacks who are suffering from AIDS is thirteen times that of whites; for Hispanics, the number is eleven times that of whites. Part of the explanation for this, Koop said, is that in some sections of black and Hispanic culture male bisexuality is quite common, but is not recognized as homosexuality; instead, the bisexual regards himself as "macho," possessed with a large amount of sexual energy.
71. Albert Camus, *The Plague*, trans. Stuart Gilbert (New York: Penguin Books, [1948] 1960), p. 47.
72. Ralph Venning, *The Plague of Plagues* (London: The Banner of Truth Trust, [1669] 1965).

Chapter 2 — Deathstyle: AIDS and Divine Judgment

1. *Time*, June 29, 1987, p. 8.
2. J. Goedert et al., "Determinants of Retrovirus (HTLV-III) Antibody and Immunodeficiency Conditions in Homosexual Men," *Lancet*, 29 September 1984, pp. 711-15.
3. D. J. Anderson and E. J. Yunis, "'Trojan Horse' Leukocytes in AIDS," *New England Journal of Medicine*, 1983, No. 309, pp. 984f.; cited in Antonio, pp. 38f.
4. Gene Antonio, *The AIDS Coverup? The Real and Alarming Facts about AIDS* (San Francisco: Ignatius Press, 1986), p. 39.
5. Jeffrey Hart, "'Safe Sex' and the Presence of the Absence," *National Review*, May 8, 1987, p. 43.
6. Institute for the Scientific Investigation of Sexuality, *What Homosexuals Do* (Lincoln, NE: 1984); cited in Dick Hafer, *Homosexuality: Legitimate, Alternate Deathstyle* (Boise, ID: The Paradigm Co., 1986), pp. 54, 57.
7. Ibid.
8. Antonio, p. 51.
9. Cited in Hart, p. 43.
10. Antonio, p. 58; citing A. P. Bell and M. S. Weinberg, *Homosexualities: A Study of Diversity among Men and Women* (New York: Simon & Schuster, 1978), p. 312.
11. Bell and Weinberg, p. 239; cited in Antonio, p. 59.
12. Cited in "AIDS, Nature, and the Nature of AIDS," *National Review*, November 1, 1985, p. 18.
13. James I. Slaff, M.D., and John K. Brubaker, *The AIDS Epidemic: How You Can Protect Yourself and Your Family — Why You Must* (New York: Warner Press, 1985), p. 26.
14. Antonio, pp. 42f.

15. Rousas John Rushdoony, *The Institutes of Biblical Law* (Phillipsburg, NJ: The Presbyterian and Reformed Publishing Co., 1973), p. 423.
16. Rushdoony, pp. 326f.
17. Ibid., p. 425.
18. An editor at *The New York Native*, a homosexually oriented publication, provided me with this statistic. The factor that makes homosexuals more susceptible to AIDS, he says, is the prevalence of syphilis among them.
19. Stephen Jay Gould in *The New York Times Magazine*, April 19, 1987, p. 33.
20. Ibid.

Chapter 3 — All the King's Horses

1. A. E. Lambert, ed., *A Report on the Interscience Conference on Antimicrobiol Agents*, (New York: St. Regis Reports, 1987), p. 32.
2. Ibid., p. 67.
3. Ibid., p. 69.
4. *The Tennessean*, October 6, 1987.
5. Slaff and Brubaker, *The AIDS Epidemic* (New York: Warner Books, 1985), p. 185.
6. J. C. Terrel, *Critical Evaluations of the AIDS Contagion*, (Dallas, TX: Baptist Free Press, 1987), p. 7.
7. Slaff and Brubaker, p. 185.
8. Ibid., p. 186.
9. Ibid.
10. Terrel, p. 12.
11. *Surgeon General's Report on AIDS*, October, 1986, p. 31.
12. George Grant, *The Big Lie: The Scandal of Planned Parenthood*, (Brentwood, TN: Wolgemuth and Hyatt, Publishers, 1987).
13. Ibid.
14. Ibid.
15. *The Tennessean*, October 6, 1987.
16. See David Chilton, *Paradise Restored: A Biblical Theology of Dominion* (Fort Worth, TX: Dominion Press, 1985), p. 216.
17. Robert Ruff, *Aborting Planned Parenthood* (Houston, TX: Life Advocates, 1987).
18. Ibid.
19. C. S. Lewis, *Mere Christianity* (New York: Macmillan Publishing Co., revised edition [1952] 1960), pp. 64f.

Chapter 4 — How the World Works

1. See John C. Whitcomb and Henry Morris, *The Genesis Flood: The Biblical Record and Its Scientific Implications* (Phillipsburg, NJ: The Presbyterian and Reformed Publishing Co., 1961), p. 241; Joseph C. Dillow, *The Waters Above: Earth's Pre-Flood Vapor Canopy* (Chicago: Moody Press, 1982), pp. 93-98.
2. Auguste Lecerf, *An Introduction to Reformed Dogmatics*, trans. André Schlemmer (Grand Rapids: Baker Book House, [1949] 1981), p. 147.
3. Ibid., pp. 147f.
4. Herman Bavinck, *Our Reasonable Faith: A Survey of Christian Doctrine*, trans. Henry Zylstra (Grand Rapids: Baker Book House, 1956), p. 178.
5. John Calvin, *Commentaries on the Four Last Books of Moses*, trans. Charles William Bingham (Grand Rapids: Baker Book House, 1979 reprint), Vol. 1, p. 386. See

also Calvin's comments on Christ's use of this text against the Tempter, in his *Commentary on a Harmony of the Evangelists*, trans. William Pringle (Grand Rapids: Baker Book House, 1979 reprint), Vol. 1, p. 215: "The whole world is preserved, and every part of it keeps its place, by the will and decree of Him, whose power, above and below, is everywhere diffused. Though we live on bread, we must not ascribe the support of life to the power of bread, but to the secret kindness by which God imparts to bread the quality of nourishing our bodies."

6. James B. Jordan writes: "Scripture teaches that God sustains life directly, not indirectly. There is no such thing as Nature. God has not given any inherent power of development to the universe as such. God created the universe and all life by immediate *actions*, not by mediate *processes*. When God withdraws His Breath (which is the Holy Spirit, the Lord and Giver of life), death follows immediately (Genesis 7:22). The idea that God wound up the universe and then let it run its course, so that there is such a thing as Nature which has an intrinsic power, is Deism, not Christianity." (*Judges: God's War Against Humanism* [Tyler, TX: Geneva Ministries, 1985], pp. 37f.)

7. Jordan continues: "We tend to place too little confidence in the eternally active, loving, Fatherly God. Our modern philosophy of process makes us hesitant about taking matters of our daily life to God in prayer. It is as easy for God to keep my car running as it is for Him to let it run down. When we see that God is active in everything, our dependence on Him should greatly increase. . . . We should be looking all the time for the eternally active God to bring things to pass. There is much that we should be asking for, except that our Baalistic philosophy of process causes us to think that it is no use asking for it. We should take everything to God in prayer.

   "There are things in our lives that we have gotten used to, and we think, 'Well, that's just the way things are.' In reality, however, these things we have gotten used to are the way God is doing things, and God can do things differently if He wants to. There would probably be a lot less chronic sickness among us if we would stop treating sickness as a process and start treating it as the action of God, correctable by Him. In 2 Chronicles 16:12 Asa is condemned for looking solely to the physicians rather than to God for healing. James 5:14, 15 tells us the primary thing we should do in the case of sickness (without despising the ministries of Luke the physician)." (Ibid., p. 130f.)

8. Calvin, *Institutes* 1:16:7, p. 206.

9. John Calvin, *Commentaries on the First Twenty Chapters of the Book of the Prophet Ezekiel*, trans. Thomas Myers (Grand Rapids: Baker Book House, 1979 reprint), Vol. 1, pp. 339f.

10. Martin Luther, *Table Talk*, ed. and trans. Theodore G. Tappert (Philadelphia: Fortress Press, 1967), p. 82. It is obvious from his works that Luther had a strong sense of angelic activity in the world (cf. his hymn "A Mighty Fortress"). In another *Table Talk* discussion he observed: "The angels are very close to us and protect us and other creatures of God at his command. To be able to protect us they have long arms, and so they can easily chase Satan away when he tries to harm us. They stand before the face of the Father, next to the sun, but without effort they swiftly come to our aid. The devils, too, are very near to us. Every moment they are plotting against our life and welfare, but the angels prevent them from harming us. Hence it is that they don't always harm us although they always want to harm us.

   "There are many demons in the woods, water, swamps, and deserted places who may not injure people. Others are in dense clouds and cause storms, light-

ning, thunder, and hail, and poison the air. Philosophers and physicians attribute these things to nature and I don't know what other causes. . . ."
(p. 172).

11. "How may we attribute this same work [the Chaldeans' theft of Job's flocks] to
God, to Satan, and to man as author, without either excusing Satan as associated with God, or making God the author of evil? Easily, if we consider first the
end, and then the manner, of acting. The Lord's purpose is to exercise the patience of His servant by calamity; Satan endeavors to drive him to desperation;
the Chaldeans strive to acquire gain from another's property contrary to law
and right. So great is the diversity of purpose that already strongly marks the
deed. There is no less difference in the manner. The Lord permits Satan to
afflict His servant; He hands the Chaldeans over to be impelled by Satan, having chosen them as His ministers for this task. Satan with his poison darts
arouses the wicked minds of the Chaldeans to execute that evil deed. They dash
madly into injustice, and they render all their members guilty and befoul them
by the crime. Satan is properly said, therefore, to act in the reprobate over
whom he exercises his reign, that is, the reign of wickedness. God is also said to
act in His own manner, in that Satan himself, since he is the instrument of
God's wrath, bends himself hither and thither at His beck and command to execute His just judgments. I pass over here the universal activity of God whereby
all creatures, as they are sustained, thus derive the energy to do anything at all.
I am speaking only of that special action which appears in every particular
deed. Therefore we see no inconsistency in assigning the same deed to God,
Satan, and man; but the distinction in purpose and manner causes God's righteousness to shine forth blameless there, while the wickedness of Satan and of
Man betrays itself by its own disgrace." John Calvin, *The Institutes of the Christian
Religion,* trans. Ford Lewis Battles (Philadelphia: The Westminster Press, 1960)
2.4.2 (pp. 310f.).

12. This is not the place to develop this thesis in detail. Those who wish to pursue it
further should consult the following works: Rousas John Rushdoony, *The Insti-
tutes of Biblical Law* (Nutley, NJ: The Craig Press, 1973); Greg L. Bahnsen,
Theonomy in Christian Ethics (Phillipsburg, NJ: The Presbyterian and Reformed
Publishing Co., 2nd ed., 1984); James B. Jordan, *The Law of the Covenant: An
Exposition of Exodus 21-23* (Tyler, TX: Institute for Christian Economics, 1984).

Chapter 5 — The Failed Priesthood

1. For a detailed examination of this, see Meredith G. Kline, *Images of the Spirit*
(Grand Rapids: Baker Book House, 1980); see also Gordon J. Wenham, *Commentary on the Book of Genesis* (Waco: Word Publishers, 1987).

2. For an in-depth examination of this and related issues, see James B. Jordan,
The Sociology of the Church: Essays in Reconstruction (Tyler, TX: Geneva Ministries,
1986), chap. 3, pp. 83-123.

3. Philip Schaff, *History of the Christian Church,* Vol. 1: *Apostolic Christianity, A.D.
1-100* (Grand Rapids: William B. Eerdmans Publishing Co., [1910] 1971), p. 3.

4. See St. Irenaeus, *Against Heresies* I.xxiv.5 and I.xxvii.3.

5. Brief but very helpful accounts of the true nature of monasticism may be found
in Alexander Schmemann, *The Historical Road of Eastern Orthodoxy* (Crestwood,
NY: St. Vladimir's Seminary Press, [1963] 1977), pp. 103ff., and Louis Bouyer,
The Spirituality of the New Testament and the Fathers (Minneapolis: The Seabury
Press, 1963), pp. 303ff.

6. Herbert Schlossberg, *Idols for Destruction: Christian Faith and Its Confrontation with American Society* (Nashville: Thomas Nelson Publishers, 1983), p. 6.

7. Ann Douglas, *The Feminization of American Culture* (New York: Alfred A. Knopf, 1977), p. 24. Three other important books that deal with this subject are: Patricia Cayo Sexton, *The Feminized Male: Classrooms, White Collars and the Decline of Manliness* (New York: Random House, 1969) — unfortunately, this extremely helpful work is out of print; George Gilder, *Men and Marriage* (Gretna, LA: Pelican Publishing Co., 1986); and Weldon M. Hardenbrook, *Missing From Action: Vanishing Manhood in America* (Nashville: Thomas Nelson Publishers, 1987).

8. James B. Jordan writes: "Scofieldian dispensationalism accepts only Acts through Revelation 3 [as relevant for the life of the Church today], thus putting aside 87 percent. Bullingerites accept only Paul's prison epistles, thus putting aside 98.2 percent. Modified Bullingerites (Grace Movement) accept all of Paul, putting aside the remaining 94 percent of Scripture. The popular notion that the Old Testament is gone and only the New Testament is canonical sets aside 69 percent of Scripture." *The Sociology of the Church: Essays in Reconstruction* (Tyler, TX: Geneva Ministries, 1986), p. 7.

9. Among the best recent documentations of this trend are Francis A. Schaeffer, *The Great Evangelical Disaster* (Westchester, IL: Crossway Books, 1984), and Franky Schaeffer, *Bad News for Modern Man: An Agenda for Christian Activism* (Westchester, IL: Crossway Books, 1984).

10. George Gilder, *Men and Marriage* (Gretna, LA: Pelican Publishing House, 1986), pp. 75f. Italics added.

Chapter 6 — Gospel Ethics: Holiness and Love

1. Dr. J. L. Fletcher, cited in Gene Antonio, *The Aids Cover-Up? The Real and Alarming Facts about AIDS* (San Francisco: Ignatius Press, 1986), p. 200.

2. Francis A. Schaeffer and C. Everett Koop, M.D., *Whatever Happened to the Human Race?* (Old Tappan, NJ: Fleming H. Revell Co., 1979), p. 191.

3. Ibid., p. 191.

4. Ibid., p. 194.

5. Ibid., pp. 195ff.

6. *Surgeon General: Report on AIDS*, 1986.

7. Antonio, p. 199.

8. John Owen, *Of Communion with God*, William H. Goold, ed. *The Works of John Owen*, 16 vols. (Edinburgh: The Banner of Truth Trust, 1965-68), Vol. 2, p. 145.

9. Albert Camus, *The Plague*, trans. Stuart Gilbert (New York: Penguin Books, [1948] 1960), p. 184.

10. Ibid., p. 187.

11. See Alexander Schmemann, *For the Life of the World: Sacraments and Orthodoxy* (Crestwood, NY: St. Vladimir's Seminary Press, revised ed., 1979).

12. Benjamin B. Warfield, "The Emotional Life of Our Lord," *The Person and Work of Christ* (Philadelphia, PA: The Presbyterian and Reformed Publishing Co., 1950), pp. 116f.

13. Francis A. Schaeffer, *The God Who Is There*, in *The Complete Works of Francis Schaeffer*, five vols. (Westchester, IL: Crossway Books, second ed., 1985), Vol. 1: *A Christian View of Philosophy and Culture*, p. 117.

14. Francis A. Schaeffer, *The Church Before the Watching World*, in *Works*, Vol. 5: *A Christian View of the Church*, p. 173.

Chapter 7 — Is Change Possible?

1. John Calvin, *Commentary upon the Acts of the Apostles*, ed. Henry Beveridge, 2 vols. (Grand Rapids: Baker Book House, 1979 reprint), Vol. 2, p. 244.

2. See Greg L. Bahnsen, *Homosexuality: A Biblical View* (Grand Rapids: Baker, 1978) and Leanne Payne, *The Healing of the Homosexual* (Westchester, IL: Crossway Books, 1984).

3. Jay E. Adams, *The Christian Counselor's Manual* (Philadelphia: The Presbyterian and Reformed Publishing Co., 1973), p. 406. I regard this volume, and Adams's earlier work *Competent to Counsel* (Nutley, NJ: Presbyterian and Reformed Publishing Co., 1970), as virtually indispensable resources for counseling in any area. See below for references to other useful works by Adams.

4. See John Murray, "Definitive Sanctification" and "The Agency in Definitive Sanctification," in *The Collected Works of John Murray*, four vols. (Edinburgh: The Banner of Truth Trust, 1976-82), Vol. 2, pp. 277-93.

5. John Murray, *The Epistle to the Romans*, Vol. 1 (Grand Rapids: William B. Eerdmans Publishing Co., 1959), p. 229. Cf. the more extended development of this line of thought in his essay on "Law and Grace" in *Principles of Conduct: Aspects of Biblical Ethics* (Grand Rapids: William B. Eerdmans Publishing Co., 1957), pp. 181-201.

6. *The H Solution* (Reading, PA: Quest Learning Center).

7. Cornelius Van Til, *Apologetics* (Phillipsburg, NJ: Presbyterian and Reformed Publishing Co., 1976), p. 2.

8. I am indebted to Jay E. Adams for his exposition of these points, especially in his books *A Theology of Christian Counseling: More than Redemption* (Grand Rapids: Zondervan Publishing House, [1979] 1986), and *How to Help People Change: The Four-Step Biblical Process* (Grand Rapids: Zondervan Publishing House, 1986).

9. Ann Douglas, *The Feminization of American Culture*, published in hardcover by Alfred A. Knopf, and in mass-market paperback by Avon.

10. Weldon M. Hardenbrook, *Missing from Action: Vanishing Manhood in America* (Nashville: Thomas Nelson Publishers, 1987).

11. Ibid., p. 30.

12. Douglas, p. 6.

13. Perry Miller, *The New England Mind: The Seventeenth Century* (Boston: Beacon Press, [1939] 1961), p. 68.

14. Ibid., pp. 86f.

15. Hardenbrook, p. 30.

16. Ibid., pp. 143f.

17. Adams, *How to Help People Change*, pp. 145f.

18. Jerry Bridges, *The Practice of Godliness* (Colorado Springs: NavPress, 1983), p. 46.

19. See Cornelius Van Til, *Christian Theistic Ethics* (Nutley, NJ: Presbyterian and Reformed Publishing Co., 1977), pp. 45f.

Chapter 8 — Ministry and Sacraments: Restoration to True Order

1. "Tragic Confusion," *National Review*, March 13, 1987, p. 21. Unfortunately, the best the conservative editorialists of *National Review* could come up with in response was this anemic blather: "These befuddled ministers, priests, and bishops had better be extremely careful. In this and other matters they are talk-

ing arrogant nonsense and offending against the *consensus gentium*, the agreement of the human race."

2. Jerram Barrs, *Freedom and Discipleship: Your Church and Your Personal Decisions* (Leicester, England: InterVarsity Press, 1983), pp. 64ff.

3. St. Cyprian, *On the Unity of the Church*, ch. 4; see Alexander Roberts and James Donaldson, eds., *The Ante-Nicene Fathers*, 10 vols. (Grand Rapids: William B. Eerdmans Publishing Co., 1970), Vol. 5, p. 422; cf. John Calvin, *Institutes of the Christian Religion*, 4:6:4 (ed. John T. McNeill, trans. Ford Lewis Battles; Philadelphia: The Westminster Press, 1960), p. 1106.

4. Richard J. Foster, *Money, Sex, and Power: The Challenge of the Disciplined Life* (San Francisco: Harper & Row, Publishers, 1985), p. 112.

5. For a discussion of the Biblical and historic Christian tradition of the just war, see Keith B. Payne and Karl I. Payne, *A Just Defense: The Use of Force, Nuclear Weapons, and Our Conscience* (Portland: Multnomah Press, 1987).

6. Jay E. Adams, *Handbook of Church Discipline* (Grand Rapids: Zondervan Publishing House, 1986), p. 95.

7. John Calvin, *Institutes of the Christian Religion*, 4:17:9.

8. Ignatius, *To the Ephesians*, 20.

9. Jon Bulliard, *The Patristics and the Eucharist* (New York: St. Latimer Bindry, 1967), p. 14.

10. Ibid.

Chapter 9 — Healing in the Church

1. Roland Allen, *Missionary Methods: The Apostle Paul's or Ours?* (Grand Rapids: William B. Eerdmans Publishing Co., 1962), p. 76.

2. St. Irenaeus, *Against Heresies*, iii. xxiv. 1.

3. St. Cyprian, *On the Unity of the Church*, 6.

4. John Jefferson Davis, *God's Victorious Kingdom: Postmillennialism Reconsidered* (Grand Rapids: Baker Book House, 1986), p. 71.

5. Ibid.

6. Ramsay MacMullen, *Christianizing the Roman Empire: A.D. 100-400* (New Haven: Yale University Press, 1984), p. 28; quoted in Davis, pp. 71f.

7. Irenaeus, *Against Heresies*, ii. xxxii. 4.

8. Ibid., ii. xxxii. 4, 5.

9. Unfortunately, these verses have been, in effect, edited out of some modern Bible translations, due to the influence of B. F. Westcott and F. J. A. Hort's peculiar theory of textual criticism. Recently, however, scholars have begun to realize what most Christians have known all along — that the last twelve verses of Mark's Gospel are inspired Scripture. For a discussion of these verses, see John W. Burgon, *The Last Twelve Verses of the Gospel According to Mark*, in David Otis Fuller, ed., *Counterfeit or Genuine? Mark 16? John 8?* For a critique of the Westcott-Hort theory, see Wilbur N. Pickering, *The Identity of the New Testament Text* (Nashville: Thomas Nelson Publishers, 1977); Jakob van Bruggen, *The Ancient Text of the New Testament* (Winnipeg: Premier Printing Ltd., 1976).

10. Jay Adams, *Competent to Counsel* (Nutley, NJ: The Presbyterian and Reformed Publishing Co., 1970).

11. See Appendix as well as James B. Jordan's essay "A Liturgy of Healing" in his *Sociology of the Church: Essays in Reconstruction* (Tyler, TX: Geneva Ministries, 1986), pp. 283-93.

12. George Grant, *The Big Lie: The Scandal of Planned Parenthood* (Brentwood, TN: Wolgemuth & Hyatt, Publishers, 1988).

13. Jordan, p. 288.

Chapter 10 — Pure and Undefiled Religion

1. W. H. C. Frend, *The Rise of Christianity* (Philadelphia: Fortress Press, 1984), p. 631.

2. See Will Durant, *The Age of Faith* (New York: Simon and Schuster, 1950), pp. 78, 531, 636, 652, 785, 807, 831, 998, 1001f.

3. Ibid., p. 831.

4. One of the best brief discussions of this period is in William Carroll Bark, *Origins of the Medieval World* (Stanford: Stanford University Press, 1958).

5. Brief accounts of these men and women can be found in Donald Attwater, *The Penguin Dictionary of Saints* (New York: Penguin Books, 1965, 1983), and David Hugh Farmer, *The Oxford Dictionary of Saints* (New York: Oxford University Press, 1978, 1983).

6. It is important to recognize that the monasteries were not retreat centers for irrelevant academics and mystics, but rather missionary outposts for Christianity, fortresses on the frontier where the monks lived and worked among the barbarians of pagan and hostile lands. The monks were, by and large, courageous men who went out, without financial support, to teach, build, plant, heal, and preach the Gospel. More than a thousand years ago, they converted *your* ancestors to the Christian faith.

7. George Orwell, "How the Poor Die," in *The Orwell Reader* (New York: Harcourt, Brace and Co., 1956), p. 94.

8. Friedrich Heer, *The Medieval World: Europe 1100-1350*, trans. Janet Sondheimer (New York: New American Library, 1962), p. 199.

9. Durant, p. 998.

10. "They are splendidly built, the best food and drink are at hand, the attendants are very diligent, the physicians are learned, the beds and coverings are very clean, and the bedsteads are painted. As soon as a sick man is brought in, all his clothes are taken off in the presence of a notary and are faithfully kept for him. He is then dressed in a white smock and laid in a handsomely painted bed with clean sheets. Two physicians are fetched at once. Attendants come with food and drink, served in immaculate glass vessels; these are not touched with so much as a finger but are brought on a tray. Honorable matrons, who are completely veiled, come in, minister to the poor for several days without identifying themselves, and then go back to their homes." Martin Luther, *Table Talk*, trans. Theodore G. Tappert (Philadelphia: Fortress Press, 1967), p. 296.

11. Charles Petit, "High Costs to Shut Hospitals, Survey Says," *San Francisco Chronicle*, July 30, 1987. The survey was conducted by Arthur Anderson & Co., of Chicago.

12. Randy Shilts, "In New Orleans, the Church Pitches In," *San Francisco Chronicle*, July 29, 1987.

Chapter 11 — The Balm of Gilead

1. See George Grant's books on Biblical charity for more on this subject, especially *The Dispossessed: Homelessness in America* (Westchester, IL: Crossway Books, 1986).

2. This has been published in two helpful editions: *The Private Devotions of Lancelot Andrewes*, translated by F. E. Brightman (Gloucester, MA: Peter Smith, 1978); and the less expensive *Lancelot Andrewes and His Private Devotions*, translated by Alexander Whyte (Grand Rapids: Baker Book House, 1981).
3. Crestwood, NY: St. Vladimir's Seminary Press, 1983.
4. Published by the Board of Christian Education of the Presbyterian Church in the United States of America, 1946.
5. Arthur Bennett, ed., *The Valley of Vision: A Collection of Puritan Prayers and Devotions* (Edinburgh: The Banner of Truth Trust, 1975).
6. See Richard J. Foster, *Celebration of Discipline: The Path to Spiritual Growth* (San Francisco: Harper and Row, 1978).
7. For more on these tests see Paul Douglas and Laura Pinsky, *The Essential AIDS Fact Book* (New York: Pocket Books, 1987).
8. Cyprian, *On the Mortality*, 12.

Chapter 12 — The Refuge

1. Benjamin B. Warfield, "Predestination," in *Biblical and Theological Studies* (Nutley, NJ: The Presbyterian and Reformed Publishing Co., 1968), p. 285.
2. See John M. Frame, *The Doctrine of the Knowledge of God* (Phillipsburg, NJ: The Presbyterian and Reformed Publishing Co., 1987).
3. Benjamin B. Warfield, from a sermon on John 3:16 entitled "God's Immeasurable Love," in *Biblical and Theological Studies*, pp. 518f.

Appendix — The Ministration of Healing

1. Some of the prayers in this service have been adapted from *The Book of Common Prayer* of the Protestant Episcopal Church (1977 edition), pp. 453-460.

SELECT BIBLIOGRAPHY

Healing

MacNutt, Francis. *Healing*. Notre Dame: Ave Maria Press, 1984.

_____. *The Power to Heal*. Notre Dame: Ave Maria Press, 1977.

_____. *The Prayer that Heals*. Notre Dame: Ave Maria Press, 1981.

Wimber, John. *Power Evangelism*. San Francisco: Harper and Row, Publishers, 1986.

_____. *Power Healing*. San Francisco: Harper and Row, Publishers, 1987.

History of Medicine

Barnett, James M. *The Diaconate: a Full and Equal Order*. Minneapolis: The Seabury Press, 1979.

Cartwright, F. F. *A Social History of Medicine*. London: Longman House, 1977.

McNeill, William H. *Plagues and Peoples*. Middlesex: Penguin Books Ltd., 1976.

Numbers, Ronald L. and Amundsen, Darrel W. *Caring and Curing: Health and Medicine in the Western Religious Traditions*. London: Collier Macmillan Publishers, 1986.

Church and Sacraments

Adams, Jay E. *Handbook of Church Discipline*. Grand Rapids: Zondervan Publishing House, 1986.

Barrs, Jerram. *Freedom and Discipleship: Your Church and Your Personal Decisions* (Leicester, England: InterVarsity Press, 1983).

Bouyer, Louis. *Eucharist: Theology and Spirituality of the Eucharistic Prayer.* Notre Dame: University of Notre Dame Press, 1968.

Calvin, John. *The Institutes of the Christian Religion.* Translated by Ford Lewis Battles. 2 vols. Philadelphia: The Westminster Press, 1960.

Howard, Thomas. *Evangelical Is Not Enough.* Nashville: Thomas Nelson Publishers, 1984.

Jordan, James B. *The Sociology of the Church.* Tyler, TX: Geneva Ministries, 1986.

Schaeffer, Francis A. *The Church at the End of the Twentieth Century.* Downers Grove, IL: InterVarsity Press, 1970.

Schaff, Philip. *The Principle of Protestantism.* Translated by John W. Nevin. Philadelphia: United Church Press, 1964.

Schmemann, Alexander. *For the Life of the World: Sacraments and Orthodoxy.* Crestwood, NY: St. Vladimir's Seminary Press, revised ed., 1979.

Stevens, R. Paul. *Liberating the Laity: Equipping All the Saints for Ministry.* Downers Grove, IL: InterVarsity Press, 1985.

Thurian, Max. *The Mystery of the Eucharist: An Ecumenical Approach.* Grand Rapids: William B. Eerdmans Publishing Co., 1984.

Tillapaugh, Frank R. *Unleashing the Church: Getting Out of the Fortress and Into the Ministry.* Ventura, CA: Regal Books, 1982.

Webber, Robert E. *Worship: Old and New.* Grand Rapids: Zondervan Publishing House, 1982.

Counseling

Adams, Jay. *The Christian Counselor's Manual.* Nutley, NJ: The Presbyterian and Reformed Publishing Co., 1973.

——————. *Competent to Counsel.* Nutley, NJ: The Presbyterian and Reformed Publishing Co., 1970.

——————. *How to Help People Change: The Four-Step Biblical Process.* Grand Rapids: Zondervan Publishing House, 1986.

——————. *A Theology of Christian Counseling: More Than Redemption.* Grand Rapids: Zondervan Publishing House, 1986.

——————. *The Use of the Scriptures in Counseling.* Grand Rapids: Baker Book House, 1975.

Crabb, Lawrence J. Jr. *Effective Biblical Counseling: A Model for Helping Caring Christians Become Capable Counselors.* Grand Rapids: Zondervan Publishing House, 1977.

Payne, Leanne. *The Broken Image.* Westchester, IL: Crossway Books, 1981.

Care for the Dying

Hamilton, Michael P., and Reid, Helen F., eds. *A Hospice Handbook.* Grand Rapids: William B. Eerdmans Publishing Co., 1980.

Richards, Larry, and Johnson, Paul. *Death and the Caring Community.* Portland, OR: Multnomah Press, 1980.

Stoddard, Sandol. *The Hospice Movement: A Better Way of Caring for the Dying.* New York: Vintage Books, 1978.

Biblical Law

Bahnsen, Greg L. *Theonomy in Christian Ethics.* Phillipsburg, NJ: The Presbyterian and Reformed Publishing Co., 1977.

Jordan, James B. *The Law of the Covenant: An Exposition of Exodus 21-23.* Tyler, TX: Institute for Christian Economics, 1984.

Kaiser, Walter C. Jr. *Toward Old Testament Ethics.* Grand Rapids: Zondervan Publishing House, 1983.

Rushdoony, Rousas John. *The Institutes of Biblical Law.* Nutley, NJ: The Craig Press, 1973.

Sexuality, Homosexuality, and AIDS

Antonio, Gene. *The AIDS Cover-Up? The Real and Alarming Facts about AIDS.* San Francisco: Ignatius Press, 1986.

Bahnsen, Greg L. *Homosexuality: A Biblical View.* Grand Rapids: Baker Book House, 1978.

Bell, A. P., and Weinberg, M. S. *Homosexualities: A Study of Diversity among Men and Women.* New York: Simon and Schuster, 1978.

Davis, John Jefferson. *Evangelical Ethics: Issues Facing the Church Today.* Phillipsburg, NJ: The Presbyterian and Reformed Publishing Co., 1985.

Douglas, Ann. *The Feminization of American Culture.* New York: Alfred A. Knopf, 1977.

Gilder, George. *Men and Marriage.* Gretna, LA: Pelican Publishing House, 1986.

Grant, George. *The Big Lie: The Scandal of Planned Parenthood.* Brentwood, TN: Wolgemuth and Hyatt, Publishers, 1988.

Hafer, Dick. *Homosexuality: Legitimate, Alternate Deathstyle*. Boise, ID: The Paradigm Co., 1986.

Hardenbrook, Weldon M. *Missing from Action: Vanishing Manhood in America*. Nashville: Thomas Nelson Publishers, 1987.

Institute for the Scientific Investigation of Homosexuality. *What Homosexuals Do*. Lincoln, NE: ISIS, 1984.

Magnuson, Roger J. *Are Gay Rights Right? Homosexuality and the Law*. Minneapolis: Straitgate Press, 1985.

McKeever, James. *The AIDS Plague*. Medford, OR: Omega Publications, 1986.

Rueda, Enrique T. *The Homosexual Network*. Old Greenwich, CT: The Devin-Adair Co., 1982.

Siegal, F. P., and Siegal, M. *AIDS: The Medical Mystery*. New York: Grove Press, 1983.

Slaff, J. I., and Brubaker, J. K. *The AIDS Epidemic: How You Can Protect Yourself and Your Family — Why You Must*. New York: Warner Books, 1987.

Terrel, J. C. *Critical Evaluations of the AIDS Contagion*. Dallas: Baptist Free Press, 1987.

COLOPHON

The typeface for the text of this book is *Baskerville*. Its creator, John Baskerville (1706-1775), broke with tradition to reflect in his type the rounder, yet more sharply cut lettering of eighteenth-century stone inscriptions and copy books. The type foreshadows modern design in such novel characteristics as the increase in contrast between thick and thin strokes and the shifting of stress from the diagonal to the vertical strokes. Realizing that this new style of letter would be most effective if cleanly printed on smooth paper with genuinely black ink, he built his own presses, developed a method of hot-pressing the printed sheet to a smooth, glossy finish, and experimented with special inks. However, Baskerville did not enter into general commercial use in England until 1923.

Substantive editing by George Grant
Cover design by Kent Puckett Associates, Atlanta, Georgia
Typography by Thoburn Press, Tyler, Texas
Printed and bound by Maple-Vail Book Publishing Group
Manchester, Pennsylvania
Cover Printing by Strine Printing, York, Pennsylvania